# THE BATTLE OF
# FLODDEN
# 1513

JOHN SADLER & ROSIE SERDIVILLE

The History Press

*This one is for all those involved in the*
*Remembering Flodden and Flodden 500 Projects*

*Front cover images:* The field where the battle took place. *Authors'*
*collection;* Two Medieval swords. *iStockphoto*
*Back cover image:* Norham Castle, through the west gate looking towards
the great Norman keep. *Authors' collection*

First published 2013

The History Press
The Mill, Brimscombe Port
Stroud, Gloucestershire, GL5 2QG
www.thehistorypress.co.uk

British Library Cataloguing in Publication Data.
A catalogue record for this book is available from the British Library.

ISBN 978 0 7524 6537 1

Typesetting and origination by The History Press
Printed in Great Britain

# CONTENTS

# ACKNOWLEDGEMENTS

This fresh story of one of Britain's bloodiest battles comes as a consequence of several convergent elements. Both writers have an ongoing obsession with the landscape of Northumberland and the Borderland, matched by an endless fascination with three long centuries of endemic strife which so shaped the souls of all who can claim descent from those hardy and resilient marchers.

The authors would like to express their thanks to the following for their assistance and courtesy: Chris Burgess, Manager of Northumberland Conservation and County Archaeologist; Chris Bowles, archaeological officer at Scottish Borders Council, Dr David Caldwell of National Museums of Scotland, Dr Paul Younger of Newcastle University, Nicky Clarke at the Society of Antiquaries of Newcastle-upon-Tyne Library, the staff at the Literary and Philosophical Society, Newcastle; the Northumberland County Archives at Woodhorn, the National Archives, Adam Goldwater and colleagues at Tyne and Wear Museums, Tony Ball and staff at Newcastle Keep, colleagues from the North East Centre for Lifelong Learning, Sunderland University; Barbara Spearman of English Heritage, Ailsa MacTaggart at Historic Scotland, Shona Corner at National Galleries of Scotland, Stuart Ivinson of Royal Armouries, Clive Hallam-Baker, Jenny Vaughn, John Nolan, Ann and John Ferguson, Frank Robinson and all those involved in the Remembering Flodden Project; Coldstream and District Local History Society, Berwick-upon-Tweed records Office, Andrew Cochrane and Catherine Neil at Alnwick Castle, Paul Thompson of Ford Castle, Peter Blenkinsopp of TillVAS, Glendale Local History Society, Chris and Barry Butterworth of Coquetdale Archaeology Group, Dr Jo Bath for sharing her research, John and George Common for information on Harbottle Castle, Terry Kowal of the Scottish Assembly, Robert Brooks of Hotspur School of Defence, Captain Sam Meadows, Lieutenant Rebecca Sadler, Trevor Sheehan and Graham Trueman for the soldier's view, Adam Barr for the photography and Chloe Rodham for maps, another successful joint collaboration. Also to Sue Ward for putting up with so much thinking aloud and to Gerry Tomlinson for endless patience and cups of tea.

As ever, the authors remain responsible for all errors and omissions.

*Rosie Serdiville & John Sadler,*
*2013*

# A NOTE ON SOURCES

My promise was, and I record it so,
To write in verse (God wot though little worth)
That war seems sweet to such as little know
What comes thereby, what fruits it bringeth forth:
Who knows none evil his mind no bad abhors,
But such as once have felt the scorching fire,
Will seldom efte to play with fire desire.

George Gascoigne

Contemporary accounts of the Battle of Flodden are scarce and patchy. We are obliged, in no small part, to rely upon the work of later Tudor chronicles. One version which appeared shortly after is 'the trewe encountre or batayle lately between Englande and Scotland'. This was penned by Richard Faques [Fawkes], 'dwelling in Poulys Churche Yerde'. It tells of 'the manner of the advancelynge of my lord of Surrey the Courier and Marshall of Englande ande leuetenute generall of the north pties of the same with xxvi M. men to wardes the kynge of Scott and his armye belived and nombred to an hundred thousande men at the lest'. That this is contemporary or very near is attested by an observation that two knights on the English side remain unaccounted for at the time of writing.

Interestingly, the editor notes *some provincialisms* which suggest to him that the author was Northumbrian. He also observes, quite rightly that 'the trewe encountre' is closely followed by Hall and, in terms of detail it is the most comprehensive account. There appear to be no doubts regarding its authenticity. In the course of this narrative we will review Gerard F.T. Leather's interesting account of the battle, *New Light on Flodden*, which alleges the Scots were attempting to withdraw on 9 September. It could be suggested that the 'trewe encountre' lends weight to this as the author infers the Scottish army was withdrawing towards Scotland.

This source would appear to bear out the dispositions of the two armies as later witnessed by Hall. Tantalisingly the description does not, by any means, exclude the possibility that the Scots were in the act of withdrawing and that the fight developed as a series of encounters. Colonel Leather's 'take' is arresting but cannot ultimately be proven on the basis of chronicle evidence.

'The Articles of the Bataill bitwix the Kinge of Scottes and therle of Surrey in Brankstone the 9 day of September' has been attributed to Thomas Howard as his official dispatch. This covers only the battle itself rather than the campaign and, whilst clearly contemporary, may be said to be partisan in that it is not calculated to diminish the role of the Howard family. Thomas was too canny not to appreciate that news of a great victory on the border might not read as well in France where tangible triumphs were scarce. After all, this was just supposed to be the sideshow to which his father had been relegated. The *Calendar of State Papers* contains other fragments including Bishop Ruthal's letter to Wolsey, written a mere eleven days after the fight. The Prince Bishop is keen to stress the providential talisman of St Cuthbert's banner which the Prior of Durham had entrusted to Surrey and whose magic had not failed what was perhaps its greatest test. Regrettably, the bishop is less fulsome about the events of the campaign itself.

Though Howard's account is pithily terse, as befits a general officer's dispatch, it would seem to suggest that this was not an encounter battle. His description of the Scots' deployment clearly implies divisions arrayed in line, 'every bataille an arrow shotte from the other', he confuses the deployment to a degree in that he brigades Huntly's men in with those of the three earls. In the circumstances this is perhaps not surprising. He also refers to the fight in this section of the field as being of short duration; 'shortly theire bakes were turned, and the most parte of them slayne'. He describes the fighting in the centre in one short paragraph and confirms that James fell 'within a spere length from the said Erle of Surrey'. The Lord Admiral is scathing on the conduct of the commons under his brother, many of whom it seems 'never abode stroke' [i.e. ran away]. Pinkerton's *History of Scotland* features a contemporary account, penned in French, the *Gazette*, which though brief offers a terse and pithy account of the fight.

Edward Hall's quite detailed narrative on which much of our understanding of the events is based – *The Triumphant Reigne of Kyng Henry the VIII* – first appeared in print in 1548 but had been compiled some years prior to that. That meant some of those who fought were still alive. Hall certainly appears to have had access to at least one contemporary source previously printed in 'Fletestrete [Fleet Street] at the sign of the George by Richard Pynson, printer unto the King's noble grace' – penned by one who may have actually participated in the campaign. It was this account along with the 'trewe encountre' which furnished Hall with details of the English muster and campaign. Holinshed was writing considerably later than Hall, in Elizabeth's reign, and did not publish till 1571.

Scottish accounts are even thinner on the ground and our best rendition comes from Robert Lindsay of Pitscottie (1500–65) who, though writing some decades later, gives a detailed account. Pitscottie's grandfather served during the campaign but the chronicler is concerned rather with advancing a moral argument that James' ruin was brought about by his addiction to the sins of the flesh and dalliance; brought low by 'his own sensual pleasures which was the cause of his ruin'. James VI's tutor, the accomplished George Buchanan (1506–82), has also left us an account. The ballad *Scotish Feilde*, composed by Leigh of Baggagley, is a paean to the achievement of the Stanleys as, to an extent, is *Flodden Field*.

There are other timely references to the battle. Sir Richard Assheton's memorial in his parish church of St Leonard's in Middleton. Sir Marmaduke Constable has his own memorial brass and other dalesmen from Littondale, Arncliffe and Hawswick are remembered in St Oswald's Church at Arncliffe in their native Yorkshire. As Niall Barr rightly points out, these are amongst the very earliest war memorials in Britain.

# CHRONOLOGY

**1488** – James IV of Scotland ascends the throne.

**1494** – French armies invade Italy.

**1496** – James supports the pretender Perkin Warbeck.

**1497** – Scots besiege Norham Castle.

**30 September 1497** – England and Scotland enter into a 30-year truce at Ayton.

**8 August 1503** – The truce, ratified as a Treaty of Perpetual Peace in 1502, is consolidated by the marriage between James IV and Margaret Tudor.

**1508** – The Scottish border warden Sir Robert Ker is killed on a truce day by the 'Bastard' Heron of Ford.

**22 April 1509** – Henry VIII succeeds to the throne of England.

**March 1510** – Treaty between England and France.

**May 1511** – English expedition to assist Ferdinand of Aragon.

**November 1511** – England enters into an accord with Pope Julius II and joins the 'Holy Cause'.

**1512** – James renews the 'Auld Alliance' with France.

**10 August 1512** – Anglo-French naval engagement off Brest, death of Sir Edward Howard.

**1513** – The Emperor Maximilian joins the Holy League.

**May 1513** – The French queen appeals to James to intervene.

**24 May 1513** – James writes to Henry requiring him to desist from hostilities against France.

**30 June 1513** – Henry VIII lands at Calais.

**12 July 1513** – Newcastle is appointed as the muster for the English army.

**21 July 1513** – the Earl of Surrey organises his personal staff.

**21 July 1513** – Henry leads the main body of the English army in France toward Therouanne.

**24 July 1513** – James orders a general muster on the Burgh Muir of Edinburgh.

**1 August 1513** – Surrey establishes a temporary HQ at Pontefract.

**13 August 1513** – The 'Ill Raid'.

**17 August 1513** – The Scots complete their muster on the Burgh Muir.

**21 August 1513** – The Scots army marches south to the advance muster at Ellam Kirk.

**22 August 1513** – The Scots cross the Tweed at Coldstream.

**24 August 1513** – James IV holds his final Parliament at Twizelhaugh.

**24 August 1513** – The Scots siege of Norham Castle begins.

**26 August 1513** – Surrey advances to York.

**29 August 1513** – The earl moves north to Durham, collects the sacred banner of St Cuthbert.

**29 August 1513** – Norham Castle capitulates.

**30 August 1513** – Surrey reaches Newcastle where the English army is mustering.

**1 September 1513** – Ford Castle surrenders, Scots establish HQ there.

**1 September 1513** – The English army marches out of Newcastle, north to Bolton near Alnwick.

**4 September 1513** – Surrey marshals the English army at Bolton where he is joined by his son the Lord Admiral. The English hold a council of war.

**5 September 1513** – Surrey formally unfurls his banners at Bolton.

**5 September 1513** – The Scots army digs in and deploys on Flodden Edge, the English herald Rouge Croix is sent with a challenge to James.

**6 September 1513** – The English advance from Bolton to Wooler.

**7 September 1513** – Rouge Croix is released and is sent back with a second message.

**8 September 1513** – The English flank march begins. The Scots remain at Flodden.

**9 September 1513 (a.m.)** – The English cross the Till and advance toward Branxton.

**9 September 1513 (p.m.)** – The Scots deploy in their second position on Branxton Edge.

**9 September 1513 (p.m.)** – The English cross the Pallinsburn and begin their deployment.

**9 September 1513 (p.m.)** – The Battle of Flodden.

**14 September 1513** – Surrey disbands his army.

**24 September 1513** – Tournai surrenders after an eight-day siege.

**25 September 1513** – News of the victory reaches Henry at Tournai.

**26 November 1513** – A general council in Scotland invites John, Duke of Albany, to assume the governorship/regency of Scotland.

**2 April 1514** – James IV's flagship *Michael* is sold to France for £18,000 Scots.

**March 1514** – The dissolution of the Holy League.

**March 1514** – An Anglo-French truce is negotiated.

**7 August 1514** – The truce is ratified as a peace treaty, the French cease all assistance to Scotland.

# DRAMATIS PERSONAE

## SCOTS

### James IV of Scotland (1473–1513)

The Scottish king has popularly had a rather poor press since his death in battle at Flodden in 1513. He came to the throne at an early age after the sudden and unlamented demise of his father, James III, following the rout at Sauchieburn. The Stewart dynasty, established on the Scottish throne for nearly a century and a half, could claim its descent from Anglicised Norman knights who came north to Scotland in the train of the Anglophile David I. The latter had spent his early life at the English Court.[1]

It was Robert II 'The Steward' who came to the throne in 1371 on the sudden death of his childless predecessor David II. His reign was followed by that of the melancholic Robert III, rendered at least partially disabled by a kick from his brother's horse, an experience which did not assist his depressive temperament. The three James who succeeded him all met violent deaths, the first to assassins' knives, the second when one of his great guns exploded at the siege of Roxburgh and the third, also murdered. Scotland, throughout the fifteenth century, had been burdened with a series of minority kingships. However, despite his difficult start, James IV achieved much. He finally abolished the largely moribund title of Lord of the Isles in 1493.[2] The MacDonald hegemony in the Highlands had been a near constant wellspring of fissiparous tendencies.[3] His administrative reforms were comprehensive and it is probably due to this solid foundation that the country was able to function after the disaster and the loss of such a high proportion of the nobility.

James was a truly Renaissance figure, active in the lists, addicted to finery and seduced by the lures of war (*Plate 1*). He had, like his unfortunate grandfather James II, a fascination with artillery.[4] By 1508 his master gunner, Robert Borthwick,[5] was casting guns in Edinburgh. Ordinances seeking to promote practice at the butts in preference to more popular pastimes such as golf or football were enacted, even if, subsequently, they were rarely heeded. By 1502 he was able to dispatch a contingent of 2,000 spears to fight in Denmark and he invested heavily in the creation of a Scottish navy. The most potent manifestation of which was the king's flagship, the *Great Michael*, launched in 1511, 240ft in length, with a beam of 56ft, mounting 36 great guns and 300 lesser pieces, and served by 120 gunners. With a crew of 300 mariners and carrying 1,000 marines, she was one of the most powerful man-o'-war afloat at the time.[6]

Shaky truce notwithstanding, James was prepared to connive at the piratical activities of some of his more flamboyant skippers, including Andrew Wood of Largo and the Barton clan. Of the latter, Andrew Barton remained one of James' favourites until his death from wounds following an epic sea fight with the English Lord Admiral Edward Howard. Had James not engaged in battle in September 1513 and lived to die in his bed, history may well have judged his reign as a successful one. But the weight of his achievements could never balance the loss at Flodden and his conduct both during the campaign and on the field has been branded as rash and quixotic. The English Tudor chronicler Edward Hall summed up the prevailing view when he wrote: 'O what a noble and triumphant courage was this, for a king to fight in a battle as a mean soldier. But howsoever it happened, God gave the stroke, and he was no more regarded than a poor soldier, for all went one way.'[7]

## Margaret Tudor, Queen of Scotland (1489–1541)

Margaret was Henry VIII older sister, whose great grandson James VI of Scotland was, in 1603, to unite the two realms as James I of England. When during September 1497, James IV's commissioner, Pedro de Ayala, was negotiating the terms of marriage and truce, some English advisers were fearful this might bring the Stewart kings of Scotland directly into the line of English succession, Henry cannily responded:

What then? Should anything of the kind happen (and God avert the omen), I foresee that our realm would suffer no harm, since England would not be absorbed by Scotland, but rather Scotland by England, being the noblest head of the entire island, since there is always less glory and honor in being joined to that which is far the greater, just as Normandy once came under the rule and power of our ancestors the English.[8]

This was a most perceptive analysis, presaging historical reality by a century.

The young queen's arrival in her new realm was celebrated by William Dunbar, who had been involved in the marriage negotiations, in several adulatory poems including 'The Thistle and the Rose', 'Gladethe, thoue Queyne of Scottis Regioun', the song 'Now Fayre, Fayrest of Every Fayre' and 'Blyth Aberdeane', written on Margaret's welcome to Aberdeen. In his 'Thistle and the Rose', the bard has forest birds serenading the conjoined York and Lancastrian roses, a symbol of Margaret's dual lineage:

The merle scho sang, 'Haill, Roiss of most delyt,
Haill, of all flouris quene and soverane,'
The lark scho song, 'Haill, Rois, both reid and quhyt,
Most plesand flour, of michty cullouris twane;'
The nychtingaill song, 'Haill, naturis suffragene,
In bewty, nurtour and every nobilness,
In riche array, renown, and gentilness.'[9]

Though born a Tudor (*Plate 2*) Margaret never deviated in her loyalty to Scotland. She, perhaps more than any of her court, understood the nature and character of her dangerous and mercurial brother. Margaret with Douglas and Bishop Elphinstone represented the voice of caution and compromise in the increasingly bellicose counsels of 1513.

### Alexander, 3rd Lord Home (d. 1516)

One of the king's principal divisional commanders in the coming struggle. Scion of an ancient borderline. Lord Alexander occupied the crucial post of Scottish East March warden, an office which many of his forbears had previously held. He also succeeded his father as Chamberlain from 1506.[10] The wardenship was no sinecure. In the rough and tumble of border politics diplomacy, open warfare and constant banditry were very much the norm. The Homes had frequently seen their lands (around Greenlaw in the Merse) wasted by the English. In the course of the riposte following James' championing of the pretender Perkin Warbeck in 1497, Home had seen his castle at Ayton slighted.

Over a century before, an ancestor, Sir Alexander Home, had been one of the many Scottish knights captured in the rout of Homildon (1402).[11] He had later died fighting for France against the English.[12] The family had benefited from lands confiscated from their powerful neighbours, the earls of Dunbar, by James I in 1436. By 1473 Sir Alexander Home had attained a peerage and acted as an overseas ambassador to James III. He had, however, subsequently quarrelled with that doomed, hedonistic monarch over the transfer of revenues from Coldingham Priory.

Home and his border lances had ridden against James III at Sauchieburn. The dead king's grateful son, who had, at least in name, led the revolt, quickly returned this lost source of income. Other rewards followed, the wardenship was restored and augmented with the offices of Grand Chamberlain and Keeper of Stirling Castle, both plum appointments. The 3rd Earl led a disastrous *chevauchee*[13] into Northumberland in the summer of 1513, the first overt move in the campaign. His riders had been ambushed and roundly thrashed by English archers under Sir William Bulmer.

There is an enduring question as to the nature of his relationship with James IV. The Homes were never easy subjects and thoroughly steeped in the impenetrable web of cross-border alliances and discreet understandings. Home has been criticised for apparent inactivity after the early success against Edmund Howard's wing of the English army and for failing to come to the aid of the king's division at the crisis point. For a borderer, expediency usually, almost invariably, prevailed over the more remote national interest. Defeat for Scotland inevitably meant that the vengeance of the English would fall heavily on the marches and a careful warden would do best to husband his resources. It has even been suggested that Home had an arrangement with Lord Dacre, the English East-March warden, that the borderers on both sides would look to themselves. Such an understanding would not have been without precedent.[14]

### Archibald Douglas, 5th Earl of Angus (1449–1513)

One of King James' senior magnates and a constant source of trouble, Douglas was aged 64 in 1513 and died of natural causes that November. He was one who, with the queen and Bishop Elphinstone, resolutely opposed the war. He spoke out to that effect in council, though Buchanan asserts he was reduced to tears by the king's violent outburst.[15] He did not fight in the battle though two of his sons did and failed to return. He was nominated to succeed Arran as admiral when the former exceeded his instructions (see Chapter 4).

He was dubbed the 'Great' Earl and more popularly as Archibald 'Bell-the-Cat'.[16] Famously, he had quarrelled with James III during the failed campaign of 1482, when Gloucester was before the walls of Berwick, his contribution being to lead the savage cull of the king's favourites at Lauder. He later commanded those forces which defeated James at Sauchieburn. Appointed as a guardian of young James IV, he lost his seniority to the rising star of the Hepburns. Never averse to a measure of duplicity he was, in the 1490s, offering his services as an effective fifth column to Henry VII. Grim Hermitage Castle, formidable sentinel and gateway to Liddesdale, was to be handed over in return for estates in England.

Throughout the whole of his tumultuous career Angus see-sawed between loyalty and dissent. In 1491 his ancestral hold of great Tantallon was forfeited but, back in favour, he served as chancellor for five years from 1494. Three years later, he was incarcerated for a period in the great rock fortress of Dumbarton. As difficult and contentious a subject as he was, the Douglas did give sage advice in 1513 but his moderating voice, along with that of Elphinstone, went unheeded in the feverish rush to war.

## *Alexander Gordon, 3rd Earl of Huntly (d. 1523/24)*

The Gordons were grand magnates of the north, Huntly's descendant the celebrated 'Cock of the North' would lead the Catholic reaction during Mary's reign, before being defeated by James Stuart, Earl of Moray at Corrichie.[17] They held vast estates in the north-east. Alexander succeeded on the death of his father the 2nd Earl, who had previously fought for James III at Sauchieburn. The Gordons had for centuries been active in the patriot cause and had suffered in consequence. Sir Adam Gordon had died a heroic if futile death at Homildon in 1402 when he led a doomed charge of Scottish chivalry into the arrow storm. An earlier scion had fallen at Otterburn thirteen years previously.

His conduct on the field at Flodden was not distinguished as he appears to have been led by his co-commander Home. He had, however, previously seen active service, being instrumental in breaking the Donald Dubh rebellion.[18] Having survived the battle, he became active in the affairs of the regency council and was apparently well regarded by his contemporaries. Holinshed confirms he was held: 'in the highest reputation of all the Scottish nobility for his valour joined with this wisdom and policy'.[19]

## *Matthew Stewart, 2nd Earl of Lennox (c. 1455–1513)*

The Stewarts were another fighting name who had more than 'done their bit' for the patriot cause. Sir Alan Stewart of Dreghorn fought for Edward Bruce during the latter's ill-judged intermeddling in Ireland. He survived the disaster there only to fall at Halidon Hill in 1333. Sir John Stewart of Darnley served in a senior capacity with Scottish forces fighting in France in the wake of Agincourt, taking part in the victory at Bauge. Matthew Stewart's father had enjoyed uncertain relations with both James IV and his father, leading to open rebellion and dishonour, albeit temporary.

Matthew succeeded his father on the latter's death in 1495 when the long sought after earldom had been attained. Sometime in the 1470s, he married his first wife, Margaret, daughter of Lord Lyle. In 1494, he married for a second time. Elizabeth was a daughter of the Earl of Arran and was to bear Matthew two sons and four daughters. On the field of Flodden he was joint commander of the Highland division with Argyll and did not display any trace of distinction before falling to Stanley's arrows. It is possible that Lennox may be the dead Scottish noble the English Clerk to the Signet refers to in his report of 2 September 1513 (this is discussed more fully in Chapter 9).

## *Gillespie Archibald Campbell, 2nd Earl of Argyll (d. 1513)*

The Campbells (Gaelic *Cam-beull* or 'wry-mouth') have not enjoyed a good press, frequently viewed as the venal aggressors in inter-clan strife. This is only partly true of a name which claims descent from none other than King Arthur! After the forfeiture of the Lordship of the Isles in 1493 the king had sought to exercise dominion over the fissiparous Highlands with local surrogates. The Campbells were one name which enthusiastically sought to fill the void. They were not wholly successful, ushering in an age of fearful internecine violence dubbed 'the Age of Forays'. Archibald was the son of Colin Campbell and his wife Isabella and married Elizabeth Stewart who bore him four sons and five daughters. From 1499 to 1502 he was, to all intents and purposes, a lessee of the former lordship and put down a series of disturbances two years later.

Archibald was Matthew Stewart's brother-in-law and had risen high in the king's service; securing a plum appointment as Lord High Chancellor. He had acted as James' Master of the Household and chief officer in the west where his predecessors were hereditary sheriffs of Lorne and Argyll. He may not have been entirely free of the taint of compromise, possibly being overly close to wilder spirits such as Torquil MacLeod, MacLean of Duart and that evergreen rebel Donald Dubh.[20] Clan Campbell was set to rise, even the anarchy of the Age of Forays would not deflect their progress. Perhaps only the Gordons, in the east, rivalled their growing status.

In 1511, he was one of those Scottish commissioners listed to meet with Lord Dacre and Sir Robert Drury to discuss the wild state of the borders – his is the first name listed, an indication of high status. Two years later Campbell was also one of those who treated with English ambassador Nicholas West, essentially a strategy of prevarication. West found Campbell rather trying as the latter refused to provide any assurances – 'no answer could be given till they knew what justice they should receive in England … how justices should be administered in the borders'. Infuriated by these perceived obfuscations, West spoke 'roundly and sharply' to Argyll. This does not seem to have assisted the diplomatic process.

## Adam Hepburn, 2nd Earl of Bothwell (1492–1513)

Yet another fighting line, coming originally from Northumberland, where their castle still stands, the Hepburns featured in many border skirmishes. Adam's father, Patrick, had earned his earldom after siding with James against his father at Sauchieburn. The rise of the Hepburns was very much linked to royal patronage. The 2nd Earl inherited in 1508 and married his wife Janet Stewart (born *c.* 1480), natural daughter of James Stewart, Earl of Buchan, three years later. She survived not only him but another three husbands, living till 1557. The marriage was something of a royal connivance as Janet already had an illegitimate child by the king. Adam surrendered some lands which James then passed to her as a dowry. Hepburn was something of a royal favourite, one who hunted and hawked with his monarch[21] and served in a diplomatic capacity, as ambassador to France in 1492. His uncle George Hepburn held high ecclesiastical office as Abbot of Arbroath (1504), Bishop of the Isles (1510) and also as Treasurer from 1508–10. He too fell at Flodden.

### John Lindsay, Earl of Crawford (c. 1460–1513)

Crawford may have had a hand (abetted by his brother-in-law) in the suspicious death of his elder brother in 1490. He certainly undertook a pilgrimage to Amiens in 1506, possibly a gesture of repentance? Thirteen years previously he had married Home's daughter Mariota and, though the marriage proved childless, he had at least one acknowledged bastard, also named John, whose mother is referred to as 'Maukyne' Deuchar.

# ENGLISH

### King Henry VIII of England (1491–1547)

The king's biographer describes his subject as a 'knight errant'. Henry was indeed addicted to romance and chivalric feats. Yet, like his brother-in-law, he was also held up by contemporaries, even those as eminent as Erasmus, as the model of the Renaissance prince. He loved finery, the tilt, vast excesses of gaming, gorging and bling. In his youth his physique and prowess at arms were impressive, a mirror of his grandfather Edward IV, the greatest knight of his age. He craved military glory and renown though, in reality, these eluded him. He never led an English army to victory on any field and his expeditions proved expensive fiascos. He was immensely sociable, his court a blaze of pageantry and excess but all this outward show hid a markedly dark side. He is described as being 'highly strung and unstable, hypochondriac, with a strong steak of cruelty'. The arm he draped around the neck of Thomas More as he walked with him in his garden would latterly be employed in signing his death warrant. Two of his six wives went to the block.

In terms of his relations with Scotland and his attitude to his brother-in-law, these were never cordial. He had spitefully withheld his sister's legacy from their father's estate for no better reason than he could. Henry had effectively winked at Bastard Heron's killing of Ker, the Scottish warden, a matter which rankled with James, and had ignored his protests over the death of Barton. Henry advised he did not care to be troubled over the fate of mere pirates. There was a great deal of truth in this; Barton was well aware of the risks he'd been running and the likely consequences. Henry's eyes were always fixed on the greater game in Europe. Scotland was an irritation, albeit a potent one which had to be guarded against. Surrey's great victory was in fact bitter gall to Henry. He hungered for renown and the idea that the honours from the campaign should be vested in a subordinate, particularly one who had been cast aside and relegated to managing a sideshow, was humiliating indeed.

In 1513 Henry left his queen, Katherine of Aragon, as regent and she proved highly capable. She wrote fulsomely to her husband in praise of his petty skirmish at the 'Battle' of the Spurs. But she could also send him the bloodied surcoat of his dead brother-in-law and announce a signal victory won during her regency. Henry's role in the events in North Northumberland was essentially peripheral though it was he who, by his conduct, set the whole dire process in train. James was not a warmonger and can be said to have exercised all reasonable endeavours to maintain the fragile peace. James has been damned for his perceived impetuosity yet his conduct appears more balanced and statesman like. Henry was a headstrong, spoilt and, at this early stage, rather a naïve young man, let loose with his father's substantial inheritance.

### Thomas Howard, Earl of Surrey, 2nd Duke of Norfolk (1443–1524)

Despite the weight of his 70 years and affliction with gout so severe that he was frequently obliged to travel by carriage, Thomas Howard remained a powerful figure. His career in arms had begun over forty years previously when he had fought for the Yorkist king Edward IV in his victory over Warwick the Kingmaker at Barnet in 1471. He had remained loyal to Edward's brother Richard III and had been present on the fateful field of Bosworth on 22 August 1485 when both Richard and Howard's own father, the 1st Duke, had perished. The penalty for supporting the loser had been three and a half years' incarceration in the Tower and the loss of his estates. When questioned, Howard had summed up his reasons for championing Richard succinctly: '[because] he was my crowned King and if parliamentary authority set the crown on a stock, I will fight for that stock. And as I fought for him, I will fight for you.'[22]

Having been offered and declined an opportunity to secure freedom by throwing in his lot with Lincoln's rebels in 1487, Howard began his rehabilitation. Released and partially re-instated in 1489 he quickly proved his worth, swiftly suppressing disturbances in the north. Henry VII now appointed him as lieutenant general of the border with further devolved responsibility for the Middle and East marches (young Prince Arthur was nominal warden).

With his titles if not yet all of his estates returned to him, Howard confirmed the king's sound judgement when he dealt speedily with fresh troubles in 1492. In his prime, he was now regarded as England's premier general and a close counsellor to Henry. It was Howard who brokered the truce and royal marriage in 1502 and, in the following year, accompanied Princess Margaret north to Scotland. There he met James and the two men may have formed an instant bond, to a degree which sparked a jealous complaint from the bride! Within five years all of his family's lands were back in his possession. The old Yorkist had come full circle. On the accession of Henry VIII in 1509, Howard might have expected to continue in the role of senior advisor but found his position challenged by the parvenu Thomas Wolsey. Although his talents were still useful (he headed the peace delegation to France in 1510), the earl found himself increasingly sidelined. Peevishly, he flounced out of the court two years later.

It was probably, certainly in Howard's eyes, Wolsey's pernicious influence with the king that denied him a command in the forces being mustered for France. Manning the border against possible Scottish incursion appeared a far drearier prospect with little chance for spoil or glory. Ironically, Wolsey had done his perceived rival a considerable favour for it was on the despised frontier that the only martial glory of 1513 was to be won. He was clearly the best qualified of the English magnates to hold the northern command. He knew the marches, he knew the borderers and he knew the man against whom he would have to fight. On 1 February 1514, in consideration of his great victory, he was created 2nd Duke of Norfolk.[23]

### Thomas Howard, latterly Earl of Surrey and 3rd Duke of Norfolk (1473–1554)

In 1513 Thomas Howard was forty, 'small and of spare stature', dark haired like his father. His early career had rather been overshadowed by the more swashbuckling persona of his brother Edward. Both were accomplished in the lists, Thomas the more so, but Edward had that swagger that Henry admired. As Lord Admiral, he defeated and killed Andrew Barton and went on to blockade the French fleet in Brest on the outbreak of hostilities. It was in the course of a typically buccaneering cutting out action that Edward was killed[24] and Thomas succeeded to his high office.

The campaign of Flodden was to be the first major test of his leadership skills and he would not be found wanting. In due course he succeeded to his father's dukedom and was active in putting down the Pilgrimage of Grace in 1536–37. A staunch recusant he remained a powerful figure at court though his plans to marry the ageing king off to his nubile niece, Katherine Howard, backfired horribly. On the night of Henry's death, Howard was in the Tower awaiting the executioner's attentions in the morning. Reprieved by fate, he went on to play his part in the reign of Mary Tudor.

### Lord Edmund Howard (1478–1539)

The younger and less distinguished son, he fought valiantly at Flodden but never enjoyed the favour and advancement of his older brothers though he did father a future if disastrous queen, Katherine Howard. He died before she married the king and seems to have been regarded as something of a wastrel by contemporaries, amassing large debts and spending much time avoiding his creditors.[25]

## Sir Edward Stanley, 1st Baron Monteagle (1463–1523/24)

The Stanleys were a martial family whose decisive intervention on behalf of Henry Tudor at Bosworth had changed the course of English history. Hitherto, they had been staunch Yorkists and Sir Edward was a worthy heir to this tradition, acting as a pallbearer at Edward IV's funeral. His ideas were, for the period in which he lived, unconventional; 'this most martial and heroic captain, soldier-like, lived for some time in the strange opinion that the soul of man was like the winding up of a watch, that when the spring was down, the man died and the soul determined.' He was appointed, in 1485, High Sheriff of Lancashire and also served as Commissioner of Array for Yorkshire and Westmorland.

He was of mature years at Flodden though his father, the Earl of Derby, was still actively campaigning in France. Sir Edward was in fact the earl's fifth son. Although his contingent was late in arriving on the field, mislaid temporarily in the fog of war or, in this case, the mist and rain of wet Northumberland, he and his affinity did good service, turning the probability of English victory into a certainty. It was Bishop Ruthal of Durham who recommended his elevation to the peerage.

## Thomas Dacre, 2nd Baron Dacre (1467–1525)

The Dacres were a famous Cumbrian name, active throughout the Border wars.[26] Randolph, Lord Dacre of Gilsland had died fighting for the House of Lancaster at Towton in 1461. Thomas fought for Richard III at Bosworth, though his backing of the wrong side didn't appear to spoil his prospects under Henry Tudor. The successful usurper recognised Dacre's talent and the importance of his name on the marches. In May 1486, Thomas was appointed deputy warden in the west and served as full warden from 1509. He was admitted as a Knight of the Bath in 1503 and latterly to the order of the Garter.

A canny borderer, there was always the suggestion that he and Home had colluded prior to Flodden. Such private arrangements would not be, by any means, unusual. Surrey, who admired the Cumbrian's ready courage, was less impressed by his organisational skills, 'a peerless knight but neglectful of order'.[27]

## Sir Marmaduke Constable (c. 1458–1518)

> Sir Marmaduke Constable stout
> Accompanied by his seemly sons
> Sir William Bulmer with his rout,
> Lord Clifford with his clapping guns

> Ballad: Battle of Flodden Field

Known as 'the little'; Sir Marmaduke was a Yorkshire knight whose seat was at Flamborough. Another who had fought for Richard III, nonetheless he enjoyed favour with both Henry VII and his son; serving from time to time as High Sheriff of both his native county and of Staffordshire. At Flodden, his affinity not only included three of his sons but also his son-in-law, William Percy, and a brother, Sir William Constable. Ironically one of his descendants, another William, became one of the regicides in 1649.

## John Heron, Bastard of Ford (d. 1524)

Black sheep of an English gentry family, Heron resided at Crawley Tower near Wooler. Perhaps the most notorious incident in a career of thuggery was the killing of Scottish Middle march warden, Sir Robert Ker of Cessford, at a Truce day in April 1508. Ker was the King's Butler, Master of Ordnance and royal favourite. Nonetheless, 'he seems to have drawn great odium from the borderers of both kingdoms by the severe and rigorous manner with which he exercised his jurisdiction'.[28] Both of Heron's seconds or accomplices, Lilburn and Starhead, paid for participation in this crime with their lives, though John apparently evaded all attempts at justice. Despite James' voluble protests, Heron's depredations appear to have been winked at by the English authorities.

Killing Sir Robert Ker, whether this was plain murder or the outcome of a duel, ranked as a clear and serious breach of the prevailing accord between both kingdoms. Sir William Heron of Ford, the Bastard's half-brother, was apparently handed over as a surety and found himself confined within the barren reaches of Fast Castle, perched dramatically above the North Berwickshire Coast. Legend (largely apocryphal) asserts John swiftly moved to enjoy the favours of his sister-in-law, Lady Heron at Ford. Edward Hall is adamant that it was Heron who rescued Edmund Howard at Flodden whilst Dacre's men stood idly by.[29]

## Sir John Stanley ('The Bastard') – dates uncertain

Though a mere stripling of seventeen, John led the contingent raised by his father, the Bishop of Ely, also Sir John Stanley. The younger John was knighted by Surrey for his services during the fight. He'd apparently vowed to endow a chapel if he survived the campaign and a memorial in Manchester cathedral attests to this fact. Shortly after his return he married the 12-year-old heiress of William Handforth who had been killed in the battle. In 1528 the couple parted by agreement in order that both could enter holy orders.[30]

## Lady Elizabeth Heron – dates uncertain

Our main source for all alleged intimacy between the King of Scots and Lady Heron is Pitscottie. She was married to William Heron, whose older brother

John had been English East and Middle march warden. John died at the age of 26 in 1498, leaving William as his heir and successor as Middle march warden. William may not have been as disreputable as his notorious half-brother but he may have been equally involved in border skulduggery. He was handed over as hostage after the killing of the Scottish warden and not released till after Flodden when he was exchanged for George Home.

Pitscottie avers that: 'the lady of Ford was a beautiful woman, and that the King meddled with her, and also his son, Alexander Stuart, bishop of St. Andrews with her daughter which was against God's commandment'. This is all rather soap opera and has no corroboration. Sir William himself died in 1535 leaving a widow Agnes, clearly a second wife. No daughter is mentioned and his son, another William, had predeceased him.[31]

NOTES

1. It was David I who began filtering Anglo-Norman barons into Scotland.
2. The Lordship of the Isles was the princely status enjoyed by chiefs of Clan Donald, inheritors of Somerled.
3. The Battle of Harlaw 1411 marked the major clash of arms between the Lordship and Crown forces under the Earl of Mar.
4. His grandfather James II had been killed at the siege of Roxburgh in 1461 when one of his own cannon exploded.
5. By 1512 he was described as 'master meltar' of royal ordnance; Caldwell, D.H., *Scottish weapons & fortifications 1100–1880* (Edinburgh, 1981), pp. 73–93.
6. Macdougall, N., *James IV* (Edinburgh, 1989), pp. 235–6.
7. Edward Hall, *King Henry the VIII*, vol. 1 (London, 1904), p. 109.
8. Polydore Vergil, Historia Anglia 26, chap 41.
9. Tasioulas, J.A. (ed.), *The Makers* (Edinburgh, 1999), p. 277 stanza 25.
10. Macdougall, p. 254.
11. The Battle of Homildon Hill 1402, a major defeat for the Scots near Wooler.
12. The Scottish contingent defeated the English at Bauge but were decimated at Verneuil in 1424.
13. A 'chevauchee' was a substantial raid aimed at inflicting economic damage; it derives from the time of the Hundred Years War.
14. Home died a traitor's death in 1516.
15. Buchanan, *History*, II, pp. 253–5.
16. This epithet is said to derive from Douglas' willingness to slaughter the king's favourite, Robert Cochrane and others.
17. The Earl of Moray, with Queen Mary's blessing, defeated Huntly's Catholic rising. 'The Cock of the North' died, probably from natural causes in the aftermath.
18. Macdougall, pp. 188–90.
19. Taylor, J., *The Great Historic Families of Scotland* (1889), vol. II, p. 298.
20. Macdougall, pp. 184–6.
21. *Ibid.*, p. 306.
22. Campbell, W., *Materials for a History of the Reign of Henry VII*, vol. II (1877), p. 480.
23. Scarisbrick, J.J. *Henry VIII* (London, 1968), p. 39.
24. *Ibid.*, p. 34.
25. See Bindoff, S.T., *The House of Commons 1509–1538* (London, 1982), p. 564.

26. Dacre's famous Red Bull banner would fly over many a border fight.

27. Gibbs, V. (ed.), *Complete Peerage* (1916), vol. IV, p. 20.

28. Wright T., *History of Scotland* (London), vol. I, p. 279.

29. Bates C.J., *History of Northumberland* (London, 1895), pp. 206–8.

30. See, Ferguson, J.A., *Lords to Labourers; the named English participants in the 1513 Flodden campaign* (Northumberland, 2011), p. 25.

31. Hedley, Percy W., *Northumberland Families* (Newcastle 1970), vol. 2, p. 43.

# I

# MUD, BLOOD AND MYTH:
## BEING INTRODUCTORY

GREEN Flodden! On thy blood-stain'd head
Descend no rain nor vernal dew;
But still, thou charnel of the dead,
Whitening bones they surface strew!
Soon as I tread thy rush-clad vale, wild fancy feels the clasping mail;
The rancour of a thousand years
Glows in my breast; again I burn
To see the banner'd pomp of war return,
And mark beneath the moon, the silver light of spears.

J. Leyden, 'Ode on Visiting Flodden'[1]

Few battles in British history have produced such a mantle of romantic gloss, perhaps most markedly on the Scottish side, where Flodden, understandably, still rates as a major calamity. James IV who, had he decided otherwise on the day, might well have been remembered as one of the nation's most successful, rather than rashly quixotic and foolhardy monarchs, has been blamed ever since. This is in fact unfair. James was an excellent ruler in many ways and his failure at Flodden did involve a fair measure of sheer bad luck. The Flodden tradition, ably abetted by Scott and other nineteenth-century romantics, has woven itself into the consciousness of a nation. As ever with history, the reality is more complex and multi-layered. The contemporary sources are patchy, so we are frequently thrown back upon heroic assumption. Both James IV and Henry VIII are fascinating characters and it is the underlying dynamic between these two aggressive and able monarchs that lies at the root of this conflict.

James was more mature and in many ways more astute. Henry VIII's campaign in France was a vainglorious puff that emptied his father's wonderfully hoarded treasury and achieved nothing in strategic terms. The only laurels won in 1513 were garnered in cold and distant Northumberland, not the universal cockpit of Flanders and Artois. Henry's vaunted victory – the 'Battle of the Spurs' – was an insignificant skirmish whilst Flodden proved the bloodiest fight in three centuries of savage and bitter cross-border strife. Less certain is the extent of the consequences. Some writers, notably Peter Reese, see the consequences as far reaching and damaging, weakening the northern kingdom for the remainder of the sixteenth century. Whilst the evils of minority kingships were frequent visitors to Scotland, other chroniclers see the battle, despite the level of loss, as having remarkably few long-term consequences. What is remarkable is the manner in which the Scottish polity bore the loss, steadied and continued, even fighting back later the same year.

## The Battle

> With fire and sword the country round
> Was wasted far and wide.
> And many a chiding mother then
> And new born baby died:
> But things like that, you know must be
> At every famous victory
>
>                              Robert Southey, 'After Blenheim'

It was on a wet, blustery afternoon in late summer that King James IV of Scotland committed his army to battle against an English force led by Thomas Howard, Earl of Surrey. Only the monument atop Piper's Hill by the pleasant, if unremarkable, north Northumbrian village of Branxton marks the site of the epic clash of arms which followed. So small a village that Remembering Flodden is constructing a visitor centre in a disued phone box, the smallest information point in Britain! This proved one of the bloodiest days in British history, the most prodigious slaughter in three centuries of border warfare between England and Scotland.[2] Despite the level of carnage, Flodden is barely remembered in England; some distant battle that no longer features on any school curriculum. In Scotland the situation is very different. Here echoes of that day still resonate, distorted by successive overlays of romance and myth. Perhaps more so now than ever, as the independance debate gathers increasing momentum.

Sir Walter Scott has much to answer for in this. He relates how, on the eve of battle, the young Earl of Caithness, with 300 of his affinity, presented himself before King James. The earl was under something of a cloud, having been outlawed for recent misdemeanours. The king, nonetheless, allowed expediency to triumph over form and admitted the Caithness contingent to his rank. Decent of him, unfortunate for them, as they fell to a man on the field. The earl's affinity wore green and the colour was, even at the time of the *Minstrelsy*, still considered unlucky in Caithness.[3] Such Flodden traditions have a romantic ring and yet many may be true; no less than eighty-seven Hays fell around the banner of their chief.

This new history, coming hard upon the heels of so many others is, in part, an attempt to rip away the fustian and enter into a fuller understanding of the actual protagonists, a risky undertaking at best, since they themselves remain obdurately silent down the centuries. It is also an attempt to present a current history fitted to the 500th anniversary and taking note of recent and exciting archaeological work that remains ongoing. Further, it will attempt, and this is risky territory, to assess what the battle means today to people in England and Scotland, where perceptions clearly differ and where the prospect of enhanced devolution adds a fresh and tantalising element.

The bare facts of the campaign and Battle of Flodden may be summarised quite succinctly. It was fought as a consequence of strategic decisions made by Henry VIII of England, principally his intention to invade the realm of France in 1513 in support of his ally, the Habsburg emperor. In so doing, he was fully aware this would antagonise his brother-in-law, James IV of Scotland, who might, in support of his French ally, launch an attack on Northern England. James, stung by Henry's contemptuous rebuttal of several ultimata, pushed ahead with his plans for an invasion of Northumberland, his efforts boosted by supplies of bullion, arms and a cadre of military advisers from France. James, under the influence of his French advisers, had resolved to drill his raw levies in advanced pike tactics, developed and practised with great élan and success by redoubtable Swiss mercenaries and Imperial *Landsknechts*.

Thomas Howard, Earl of Surrey, latterly 2nd Duke of Norfolk – England's venerable senior commander, who had started his long career in arms as a Yorkist, led the English host. His available forces were undoubtedly inferior in numbers to the Scots. Most contemporary commentators give the English between 16,000–26,000 effectives. These troops were made up mainly from retainers of the magnates and shire levies from those counties north of the Trent. Surrey's eldest surviving son, the Lord Admiral, brought a stiffening of 1,200 marines from the fleet whilst Lord Dacre furnished some 1,500 border horse. Surrey also had an artillery train (though his was made up of lighter field pieces). These English guns could not compare with the Scots train in terms of weight of shot but were faster firing and more manoeuvrable. On the field, English gunners did briskly murderous service and emerged victorious from the opening artillery duel. This virtually decided the outcome.

After the initial Scottish muster on Burgh Muir, the host moved south-ward to the border to commence the siege of Norham.[4] This was the Prince Bishop's great hold by the Tweed – *Queen of Border Fortresses*. The castellan had advised Surrey he could hold out until relieved, echoing the earlier siege of 1497. But this time the Scottish train was vastly more formidable. Following a mere five days of bombardment and infantry assault, the fortress surrendered on terms. Wark soon followed. James went on to take lesser holds at Etal and Ford, both of which were then slighted. There is no indication that James intended to seek battle. His objectives could, and indeed largely had been attained, without the hazard. He may, however, have wished to put his army to the test but the first position he chose, astride Flodden Edge and overlook-ing Millfield Plain, was entirely defensive. His guns were well dug in and the ground favoured the Scots.

There is magic in these otherwise unremarkable hills. Scottish camp fires above plundered Fishes Steads[5] were laid on top of Iron-Age cooking pits, older to them than they to us (*Plate 3*). The landscape remains essentially unchanged, though far more is now beneath the plough and generations of patient drainage have drawn the sting from fatal mosses. We can walk the same ground as the combatants of five centuries past, happily devoid of the irritat-ing accretions that besmirch so many of our over-regulated heritage sites. To do so is a remarkable experience; to attempt to visualise the great Scottish army bivouacked by the farm, aptly named Encampment, to clothe these regular fields with a swarm of crude bothies for the commons and proud pavilions of the gentry, the smoke of several thousand fires, pungent aroma of cooking, human and animal waste, wet wool, sweat and the acrid tang of spent powder as the great guns practised their killing reach (*Plate 4*).

Surrey's decision to attempt an outflanking manoeuvre and occupy Branxton Hill was a bold one which nearly came unstuck as a significant gap opened between his and Thomas Howard's division. James chose not to exploit the opportunity but to await his enemies' full deployment.[6] This was entirely consistent with Swiss doctrine. Combat began with a brisk artillery duel. The heavier Scottish ordnance, having been dragged over the intervening saddle, could not be properly dug in. Nor were the gunners necessarily Scotland's best as many of these were attached to the fleet. Very quickly the English gunners established fire supremacy, their Scottish counterparts fell or deserted, and round shot began to fall amongst the densely packed ranks of pikes.

For James this was intolerable: he unleashed Home and Huntly's powerful division on the Scottish left. At the outset, his choice of tactics appeared fully validated. At this point on the ground the lateral burn, running by the foot of Branxton Hill and which was to bring ruin to the king, was a far lesser obstacle and Edmund Howard's weak brigade on the English right almost instantly folded. Only Howard himself with a handful of knights stood his ground and fought on against hopeless odds. A timely intervention by Dacre's Horse restored the position, shoring up this crumbling flank. Home's unwillingness to continue the fight smacked to many of both treachery and collusion between the wardens; scarcely an unusual arrangement in border warfare!

Meanwhile, the division of Errol, Crawford and Montrose hurled themselves downhill, followed by the king's vast, bristling phalanx to smash the English centre. The ground, however, proved far more difficult than a view from the hilltop might suggest. The burn ran deeper and its banks proved more slippery than either appeared. Momentum, key to success with pikes, was lost and with it cohesion. The Scots struggled through wet and mire to find themselves slogging up a rise to meet an English line which surged forward to engage. Now crucial impetus was lost, their pikes proved no match for the formidable English bill. Most dropped staves to draw swords and Howard's men swiftly gained the upper hand. D'Aussi's reserve merely added to the scrum and many Scots began filtering away.

Only the Highland division under Lennox and Argyll remained uncommitted and the clansmen were scattered by Edwards Stanley's brigade. Though Stanley's men came late to the fight, an opportune, brilliant flank attack broke the Highlanders and killed their chiefs. Appeals to Home to bring his and Huntly's men into the ring fell on deaf ears. James had, in fact, battered a salient into the mass of the English centre, one which was in danger of being annihilated as the bills closed in. King and nobles, encased in fine harness, fought on doggedly whilst many of the commons decided upon discretion. In a final quixotic gesture, James and his household men flung themselves upon Surrey's banners. The King of Scotland died almost unseen in the ruin of his proud army.[7] As dusk fell, the English were left masters of the field, perhaps as many as 8,000 Scots fell, with English losses far less, maybe 1,000 in all.

Today there is a car park in Branxton and the church certainly repays a visit. The monument, erected in 1910, is in the form of a large granite cross set on Piper's Hill, roughly on ground held by the English right and is now well furnished with good-quality interpretation panels. This slight eminence gives an excellent view of the field. Directly ahead of you stands the ridge itself and one can see the commanding nature of the Scottish position. Although the burn has been diminished as an obstacle by subsequent field drainage, we can perceive just how difficult this would have proved at the time coupled with the unexpected extent of the slope leading up to the English position.

Stand at the top of the ridge, however, and these obstacles are far less apparent. We can see why James, with no scouting, could have been so dangerously misled. Flodden Edge, south of the Branxton position, over the undulating saddle which links the two, is also interesting as evidence of field fortifications remains and these are now being exposed by the spade. Standing here, looking over the plain below, one can easily discern why Surrey would shudder at the thought of a frontal assault. There are now a series of excellent footpaths over the ground which is mainly under the plough. Take the track beyond the cross towards Branxton Stead and then ascend Branxton Hill, turn left by the farm and pick up the road back down to Branxton. Marden Farm is to your right and a footpath links this to the settlement.

Nearby, at Etal Castle (*Plate 7*), English Heritage has mounted an excellent display and interpretation of the battle. The castle itself, of course, featured in the action of 1513 and the site is well worth a visit. Norham Castle should also be on anyone's itinerary (*Plate 5*). The castle still dominates the river crossing and the pleasant village below. The magnificent stone keep still offers note of the importance of the Prince Bishop's great fortress in border warfare.

# Legend

We'll here nae mair lilting at our ewe milking,
Women and bairns are heartless and wae,
Sighing and moaning on a ilka green loaning,
The flowers of the forest are a wede away.

'Flowers of the Forest' perhaps typifies the sentiment expressed towards the battle, more on the Scottish than English side where it is less remembered, yet another 'dim, weird battle' in the north, in the unending strife between Northern English and Scots. And perhaps that is the key – Flodden was a northern battle. Losses on the English side were overwhelmingly from the northern shires whilst Scottish dead came from every corner of the nation. What is equally remarkable is that the immediate political consequences of so significant a victory were, on the Entlish side (in the opinion of the present writers), relatively muted.

King James IV's fatal decision to fight has tarnished if not damned his memory ever since. He is viewed as reckless and grossly deficient in tactical judgement. Some of this derives from his earlier biographers such as Robert Lindsay of Pitscottie[8] who sends the doomed king to a fittingly Wagnerian final flourish led by the four horsemen who appear on the field: 'They raide the field and horsed the King and brocht him fourtht of the field on ane dune haiknay ... Quhat they did with him thair I can not tell'.[9] Other accounts insisted that James, like Harold after Hastings, somehow miraculously escaped the wrack of his army. Pitscottie had a further twist to the moral tale – the king had brought ruin upon himself through his addiction to women, particularly his supposed dalliance with Lady Heron, compounded by his wilful refusal to accept the good advice of his subordinates.

Even James' distinguished contemporary biographer Norman Macdougall takes the view that the king 'was determined to fight'.[10] We are not as readily persuaded, particularly when we strip away the mythology. Even Pitscottie himself is not entirely confident of the more apocryphal episodes. Until the afternoon of 9 September James had conducted a very successful campaign. He had brought into being a large national army, trained and equipped in the modern fashion. Strategic objectives, the taking of Norham and tying down large English forces, denying these to his brother-in-law, had been accomplished with minimal loss.

He had cannily heeded the advice of his French professionals and avoided battle thus far, refusing to budge from his near-impregnable position astride Flodden Edge. Humbugged by Surrey's flank march and surprised by the appearance of English forces in his rear, the fight was forced upon him. Perhaps he should have retreated beforehand as more cautious counsels suggested but his forces were large, well victualled and, till that crucial juncture, unchallenged. At least one distinguished author, Gerard F.T. Leather, writing in the pre-war period, is very much of the view James *was* attempting to retreat and the fight came about as a series of encounters (see below).

Clearly, he did not reject the idea of battle; his attempt to deploy massed phalanxes on the field was in precise imitation of Swiss masters. However, his inexperience failed to allow any realisation of the peril of unfavourable ground. His forces were neither trained nor motivated to the level of their continental contemporaries. That he should lead his division in person was far less reckless than commentators have suggested. This was precisely how Swiss captains conducted themselves, the cult of personal leadership being a paramount concern. James appreciated his army was far less cohesive than a professional mercenary company and the example of sharp-end leadership by the sovereign carried even greater import. Had James lagged back it is still unlikely he could have exercised any further degree of personal control.

Once committed, pikes were essentially a 'one shot weapon'. There was no possibility for recall and reforming. It was win through or die. James had grasped the theory but lacked sufficient capacity to translate this onto the field under battle conditions and on bad ground. It might be fair to argue that he was just damned unlucky. Swiss pike-men were trained relentlessly and ruthlessly for years. They were an elite professional force motivated by commercial incentive and long standing élan. Not only was discipline murderously enforced but the phalanx included additional specialists: halberdiers in the centre to act as shock troops if momentum faltered, clouds of marksmen on the flanks and, in front, fearsome swordsmen wielding hefty double-handers to scythe a passage into packed ranks of the foe.

For the Renaissance monarch renown was all important. Victory had to belong to the prince. It could not be the work of subordinates. In this, 1513 was to prove a rather bad year for both James IV and Henry VIII. The former lost his army and his life, the latter his cash inheritance, frittered away in a pointless, vastly expensive chevauchee which produced not a scrap of strategic gain for England. The Earl of Surrey, venerable old warhorse, put out to involuntary pasture as watchman, with his sons who accompanied him on the field, was the true winner. His dogged persistence, belligerence and tactical nerve won the day and inflicted a crushing defeat on the Scots. Whatever glory there was, was his. Henry and Wolsey were doubtless giving thanks through gritted teeth!

## The Three Hundred Years War

They were kneeling in a small box-shaped pit sunk into the stone floor, huddled together in fear, their arms and hands entwined in support. Normally the hole would have been used to store grain and covered with the wooden trapdoor that now lay upright on its hinges behind their backs. It would have been the ideal place to hide. Close the lid and the pit would be nearly invisible. There would have been just enough room for three people to hide beneath it. What gave them away? I wondered. A cough, a sob?

Two of the women were in their twenties; the third was an old lady. Someone had shot her in the mouth and her shattered dentures cascaded with her own teeth down her front like mashed melon pips. One girl had been shot repeatedly in the chest. It was difficult to tell if the other had had her throat cut or been shot; a great gash of blood crescented her neck. The expression on their faces had survived the damage. It was so clear: a time valve that opened directly onto those last moments. So you saw what they saw. I hope beyond hope that I never see it again.[11]

Those three centuries of cross-border and interstate conflict between the two realms bore no resemblance to Scott and Lochinvar. It was far more Ratko Mladic – the passage above derives from the Balkan wars of the 1990s. It was unendingly brutal, bloody, vicious, savage and endemic. The Flodden campaign and the Anglo-Scottish War of 1513, whilst very much part of this doleful cycle, also form part of a wider conflict that was engulfing Europe following the French invasion of Italy in 1494.[12] At the same time it is impossible to fully understand the combatants' motivation without considering the preceding history of Anglo-Scottish relations.

These were traditionally far from cordial. England had laid claim to overlordship since before the Norman Conquest, the Kings of Wessex had certainly numbered Scottish rulers amongst their vassals.[13] Malcolm III, the hero of Shakespeare's *Macbeth*, had bent his knee to William I in 1072.[14] Several of his successors had followed suit. When Alexander III died in 1286 and was followed shortly by his infant granddaughter, Scotland was without a king. Edward I of England, 'Longshanks' called upon to adjudicate, finally and after very considerable deliberation, decided in favour of John Balliol, 'Toom Tabard'[15] who did not hesitate to recognise the English king as his feudal superior. Edward's subsequent high handedness provoked a Scottish reaction and led to the outbreak of war in 1296.[16]

From the outset, a dire litany of bloody conflict was marked by a significant surfeit of brutality, *frightfulness* – terror as we might describe it. As Longshanks viewed the Scots as rebels, the niceties of chivalric convention could be easily disposed of. Fire, sword and rope became the order of the day. William Wallace and Andrew Murray raised the torch of freedom and struck back at Stirling Bridge and that flame, though it frequently faltered, was never totally extinguished:

[Malcolm] commanded them no longer to spare any of the English nation, but either to slay them all or to drive them away under the yoke of perpetual slavery ... Old men and women were either beheaded by swords or stuck with spears like pigs destined for the table ... babes were tossed high in the air and caught on the spikes of spears ... Malcolm watched all these things without pity, merely ordering his slave drivers to make haste.[17]

Bruce finally secured a significant victory at Bannockburn in 1314 though Scottish independence was not grudgingly conceded for another fourteen years thereafter.[18] On both sides, war was characterised by casual atrocities; murder, rapine, waste and blackmail flourished. Bruce elevated state-sponsored terrorism to a fine art. In due course the north of England, constantly attacked, became increasingly militarised. The northern barons, in October 1346, at Neville's Cross just outside Durham, saw off a major Scots invasion and captured David II.[19] By this time Edward III, Longshanks' grandson, had fixed his ambitions on the throne of France. His archers had decimated Scots' forces at Dupplin Moor[20] and Halidon Hill[21] but even these signal victories had failed to cow the Scots or secure English domination, other than in the very short term. 'Scotland was hammered into nationhood by the Wars of Independence, but the anvil of its forging was the border countryside. And the borders have never recovered from that historical curse.'[22]

David II had launched his ill-fated expedition in support of his ally France, hard pressed since the earlier and resounding English triumph at Crecy. This alliance between France and Scotland, born out of mutual fear of England and English expansionism, was essentially a marriage of convenience and one which the French were happy to manipulate according to expediency. In spite of this and due to continuing English aggression, the accord was regularly refreshed. Even an anglophile such as James III recognised the dangers posed by his powerful neighbour, notwithstanding the long and debilitating dissension of the Wars of the Roses. In 1482 Richard of Gloucester, the future Richard III, had wrested Berwick back from the Scots. Prior to this the town, now a frontier bastide, had changed hands some fourteen times!

James IV ascended the throne at a young age in 1488 after his father was conveniently murdered following a defeat by disaffected magnates at Sauchieburn.[23] The new king showed his teeth eight years later when, championing the cause of the Pretender Perkin Warbeck, he struck at Northumberland, looting and burning in time-honoured fashion. The following year he returned, laying siege to Norham before being seen off by Surrey, his future nemesis.

French intervention in Italy had been the catalyst for an extended conflict and these 'Great Wars' were to drag on for several decades. Despite having been a strong advocate for French interests, Pope Julius II was alarmed by such rampant aggression and altered his stance, providing an irreproachable figurehead for resistance to his former favourite's ambitions. In 1510 he instigated a 'Holy League' against Louis XII which drew in Henry's wily father-in-law Ferdinand of Aragon and the opportunistic Venetians. The French king riposted by setting up a contentious General Council of the church, an ill-judged move which allowed Pope Julius to preach his war as a crusade against schismatics.

## On the matter of ground

The stable burning with the black smoke ...
The open war with wounds all bleeding ...
The carrion in the bush, with throats cut;
A thousand slain ...
The tyrant, with prey seized by force;
The town destroyed, there was nothing left.

Chaucer, 'The Knight's Tale'

It has been said, flippantly perhaps, that the Anglo-Scottish borderland is the Flanders of Britain. In part this is true, here was the cockpit within which the armies wheeled and fought for several centuries. It was a battle by Carham in 1018 which fixed the Tweed as the line in the east. Subsequent attempts by David I to extend his hegemony as far south as the Tees were defeated at the great Battle of the Standard in 1138, when the Saints' sacred banners brought both relief and victory to the northern lords. A clutch of major clashes occurred in the breadth of these border shires – Halidon Hill 1333, Neville's Cross 1346, Otterburn 1388, Homildon 1402, Solway Moss 1542, Ancrum Moor 1545, Pinkie 1547 and of course Flodden itself, bloodiest by far. If southerners showed scant interest in events on these distant marches this was partly due to incomprehension. In the sixteenth century when gentlemen were abandoning their ramparts for the blessings of civilised comfort, their northern contemporaries were frantically throwing up more. Northumberland had become an embattled landscape.

In the course of three long centuries of strife the Anglo-Scottish borderland and its people adapted to the reality of endemic warfare, be this major cross-border incursions from either side or the endless cycle of raids from hardened denizens of upland dales. Northumberland was anchored in the east by the great bastion of Berwick-upon-Tweed, forcibly and savagely wrested from Scotland in 1296 and hotly contended ever since. To recover Berwick for Scotland would be a feat worthy of a true Renaissance king. Norham was a grand prize but Berwick infinitely more so.

Since the mid-thirteenth century, contending shires, on both sides of the line, had been overseen by border officials, state appointees known as wardens; one each plus a deputy for East and West marches with latterly a third for the centre or middle sector. These officers were responsible for the administration of cross-border justice but also for harnessing their marches in time of war and maintaining efficient espionage networks. Their task was an unenviable one and many like both Home and Dacre were enmeshed in the petty politics of their fiefdoms. All too often the warden was as much a part of the overall problem of endemic lawlessness as he was the solution to it.

North and central Northumberland could boast some impressively fortified holds. That long and lordly strand of sandy coast was guarded by the ancient seat of the kingdom at Bamburgh, by the Fortress of Earl Thomas of Lancaster at Dunstanburgh, the great Percy holds of Warkworth and Alnwick, down to Tynemouth and the solid, square keep of Newcastle. Vulnerable areas such as Tynedale were covered by castles at Bywell, Dilston, Hexham and Prudhoe. Baronial towers stood at Thirlwell, Chipchase, Belsay, Aydon and a host of others. Latterly, peles and bastles spread like a rash over the upland dales. It was, in every sense, a defensive landscape. The upland dales, Tynedale, Redesdale and Coquetdale, the latter sealed by the distant fortress of Harbottle, were particularly troublesome, haunt of the riding names, descendants of the earlier hobilars whose trade was war and thieving and for whom the arts of peaceful living had no relevance whatsoever.

Glendale, down whose fertile valley James' host would advance, was defended not just by the queen of border fortresses at Norham but by lesser manorial holds such as Etal and Ford, proof against reivers but not against siege guns. When James deployed his formidable train he altered the dynamic. Hitherto, defenders could resist casual raids and sit out larger incursions from behind stout walls; each individual strength part of a network of positions that threatened the rear of any attacker who simply sought to bypass them. With the emerging dominance of the gunner's art and the great weight of shot the Scots could deploy in 1513, this tried strategy was no longer viable. The face of war was changing and James could take any position he chose, leaving only rubble behind.

A _List of Castles and Fortalices_[24] prepared in anticipation of Henry V's invasion of France in 1415,[25] reveals an impressive array of fortified dwellings. One commentator has suggested that,

> Northumberland's gentlemen builders were anxious that their edifices should be graced with the name of 'castle', to be classed alongside noble, time-hallowed fortresses such as Alnwick, Warkworth and Bamburgh. The commissioners who compiled the 1415 survey may well have been subjected to lobbying

by the owners of these buildings, who would have been anxious to ensure that they were accorded the 'correct' status; the marginal annotations perhaps reflect the more considered opinions of the commissioners, after the process of compiling the survey had been completed, and they were somewhat removed from the pressures of their peers.[26]

At this time many of what we know as bastles were simply timber blockhouses not rebuilt in stone till much later in the sixteenth century. Traces of these bastions stud the upland dales, like rough-hewn outcrops sprung from the very stone. They are not pretty, entirely functional, almost resembling their Second World War successor, those ubiquitous concrete pillboxes reflecting much later defence considerations.

By 1513, nearly two centuries of war had shaped the northern dales with the fury of a glacier, moulding the inhabitants into a martial and independent breed. Many contemporary commentators complain of the depredations carried out in particular by the English borderers during the campaign of 1513. MacDonald Fraser quotes the Bishop of Durham, writing to Henry VIII in the aftermath, who offers some pithy observations on the habits of English marchers during the campaign:

> The borderers … be falser than Scottes, and have doon more harm at this tyme to our folks than the Scottes did … I wolde all the horsemen in the bordours were in France with you for there schulde thay do moche good, where as here they doo noone, but muche harme, for, as I have wretyn byfore, they never lighted from thayr horses, but when the battaylis joined then felle thay to ryfelying and robbing aswelle on our side as of the Scottes, and have taken moche goods besides horses and catelle. And over that they took diverse prisoners of ours, and delyverd theym to the Scottes, so that our folks as moche feare the falsued of thaym as they do the Scottes.[27]

This pejorative view, whilst undoubtedly accurate, takes no account of circumstances. These upland families had no concept of patriotism. Their contemporaries disdained them in war and forgot them in peace. Their fierce and ruthless code bound them only to affinity and name and demanded blood for blood in deadly *feid* (feud). For them killing was a necessity, incidental to the business of raiding, 'reiving', as it would become known.[28] Blood once spilt had to be avenged so murder begat murder in an endless cycle of retribution that echoed down through generations like a curse. Borderers on both sides were well aware, as were their respective wardens,[29] that whichever army triumphed on the field the loser's territory would suffer grievously.

And it was hard ground these dalesmen rode and fought over, wild valleys such as Coquetdale, Redesdale and Tynedale on the English side, Liddesdale and Teviotdale on the Scottish. More densely populated than today, a necklace of squalid hamlets clinging to stone tower or bastle, few roads, little arable cultivation, hills shrouded by ancient forests of bog oak, ash and myrtle, deep unfathomable marshes or mosses, like primeval swamps, offering handy refuge when the warden's raid appeared. Here the riding names clung to bare subsistence, living only by stealing from their neighbours, these uplanders were as content thieving from their own as from the Scots. Indeed it was far from uncommon to find criminal alliances being formed by reivers from both sides with a common view to plunder. If they felt they owed their country little, they had received far less.

Millfield Plain where Surrey hoped to give battle was, in prehistoric times, the bed of what has been called Glendale Lake.[30] It was the scene of the first clash in the 1513 campaign, the 'ill rode' where Home's marchers were bested by their English ambushers. Northwards, the land slopes towards higher ground which dominates the plain below. Flodden itself, 'this high ridge which frowns over Millfield Plain', was settled in prehistory, the highest point is crowned by an ancient earthwork wherein it was said James pitched his royal pavilions.[31] Archaeology is already beginning to illuminate this corner of the field. Fresh water was available from the north-east flank, the 'Sybil's Well' immortalised by Scott in *Marmion*, a fountain 'where water, clear as diamond spark … in a stone basin fell'.[32] From this higher ground, the land dips to the north, falling into an easy saddle from which it rises northward toward Branxton Edge, at a distance of little more than a mile.

This second, north-facing ridge overlooks the hamlet of Branxton and the Pallinsburn below. Once on the crest of the ridge the Scots would not be able to see their enemy deploying below as the gentle nature of the initial decline prevents this. They would in fact move a short distance down the slope till they reached the rim of the sharper fall. From here all was clear – or appeared to be. Appearances, as ever, can be deceptive. The slope is everywhere gentle and would appear ideal ground for the deployment of large bodies of foot wielding the cumbersome if potent pike.

What is not evident is the nature of the water obstacle which the burn, running at the foot of the ridge presents; nor the steepness of the rise beyond which those Scots' formations, attacking in the centre, would be obliged to ascend. Recent, pioneering and fascinating studies by Dr Paul Younger have added considerably to our understanding of the the hydrology. Rather than sweeping down upon their foes with irresistible momentum, essential for success, they would falter, flounder and then struggle. For English bills, hungry as hawks, sharp as razors, this would be all the opportunity needed.

# On the matter of devolution and the independence debate

Flodden has, in part passed into the mythology of Scotland. It could be said that Scott kicked off the nationalist debate beginning with the state visit of George IV in 1822. If the sight of their obese monarch cavorting like a mountebank in outrageous tartan pushed Scots towards a nationalist agenda then it's perhaps not to be wondered at. It was, ironically perhaps, the Scottish conservatives who began to raise the issue of 'Home Rule' in the 1850s, alarmed at the extent of subsidy heading towards Ireland at that time. The whole business then rather dragged however, overshadowed by events over the water. A Scottish Home Rule Bill did not appear before Parliament till 1913 and the Scottish National Party (SNP) was not formed till 1934, during the great post-war depression.

It is possible that Harold Macmillan's 'Winds of Change' speech in the post-imperial epoch, heralded by the Suez fiasco of 1956, added fresh impetus and this was further fired by the discovery of North Sea oil. There is, however, widespread agreement that the major driving force of nationalism in the last forty years has been economic. The loss of heavy industry and the battle to replace it provided a new focus for Scotland's polity. A polity which had honed its skills in the trade union and labour movements of the early twentieth century. Attempts to tackle recession by reducing spending on infrastructure left Scots with a sense of isolation, a perception that England was pulling resources in to the centre to cope with the restructuring demanded by new economic realities.

The McCrone report of 1974 confirmed that oil revenues would facilitate a viable, independent Scottish economy. A subsequent referendum in 1979 produced a small majority favouring devolution and a Claim of Right, calling for a Scottish Assembly was advanced a decade after. It was not, however, until 1998 that this became a reality when the Scottish Act of that year was passed. The Scottish parliament now controls most domestic matters within Scotland. In the 2007 elections, the SNP became the single largest party albeit by a narrow margin.

The nationalist debate has gathered significant momentum in recent years. It is interesting to reflect what part Flodden plays. The answer will always tend towards the subjective but it is fair to assert that the battle is now part Scottish consciousness. Scots are, quite rightly, proud of their history. It is an astonishing and vibrant voyage through turbulence, divisiveness, violence and singular achievement. James IV sought a place in Europe. It might be said he failed yet within two-and-a-half centuries Scotland became the cultural and intellectual powerhouse of Europe, the shining beacon of enlightenment. A recent, accomplished chronicler of this dazzling pinnacle has commented

'... the Scottish Enlightenment created the basic idea of modernity ... It is the Scots more than anyone else who have created the lens through which we see the final product'.[33]

Scott then offered a romantic alternative to the spring tide of materialistic modernism:

> He saw more clearly than most of his contemporaries that the Scotland of even recent memory was passing into oblivion, and that the loss was not just a matter of regret. It was a cultural tragedy ... He offered modernity its self-conscious antidote; a world of heroic imagination, to balance the world of sober, and sometimes dismal fact[34]

Our memory of Flodden then and its place in the nationalist pantheon derives in no small measure from Scott's re-awakening. This was the world of Lochinvar and Ivanhoe, heroic, comfortable and oddly safe. James IV fell straight into the pit of romantic revival, the doomed hero of glorious defeat.

Disaster below Branxton Hill revived as Homeric tragedy. Defeats generally are more easily borne in national consciousness if there is some element of glory to fixate upon. Dunkirk in 1940 perhaps serves as a case in point. The evacuation from the beaches is hailed as a form of triumph, a national deliverance (as indeed it was). But the campaign which had gone before was an unmitigated disaster. And so with Flodden, the worst single defeat the Scots sustained at the hands of the northern English amongst the many which occurred in three centuries of conflict. With Scott's tampering, this debacle became identified as a source of national pride, sublime courage pitted against impossible odds, Scotsmen dying in large numbers as willing sacrifice to protect their homeland. This, of course, ignores the more uncomfortable realities. The campaign was in fact one of aggression rather than defence. The Scots enjoyed a significant numerical and technological advantage and many of those who took the field did so unwillingly and fled when the clash occurred.

Myth is seldom deterred by historical realities, especially when the fictionalised account is more palatable. In time, Flodden became a symbol not of pointless and costly disaster but of heroic failure, a key bastion in the fortress of romance which time and social/political imperative continue to drive. In 1995 Mel Gibson's film *Braveheart* – pure Hollywood hokum – was released. This proved highly successful at the box office, affording a view of Scottish history which history itself would not otherwise support. *Braveheart* entered upon the nationalist manifesto at popular level. Historians might affect to sneer at such insubstantial escapism and yet the importance of Flodden as a symbol of contemporary Scottish nationalism is an important part of the legacy of events from 1513.

Nor can such considerations be entirely divorced from our objective study of the battle. None of the combatants would have recognised Scott's view or the current debate, except for the overriding cause of Scottish nationalism. It was, after all, the 'Great Cause' which had kick-started the entire process of extended conflict from 1296. It is quite right we think upon the resonance on the campaign thereafter – provided we see clearly that Scott's view is that of the nineteenth-century romantic revivalist with a very clear agenda. Those who survived the events of 1513 would not ever have recognised the great man's portrayal of them and their perception of the battle would have been very different. Their voices are almost entirely mute, yet it is our job to tease what we may from what remains.

NOTES

1. Scott, *Minstrelsy* (London, 1892), p. 86.
2. The conflict is now often referred to as the Three Hundred Years War from 1296–1603, resolved with supreme irony when a King of Scots ascended to the throne of England.
3. Scott, *Minstrelsy*, note p. 87.
4. Norham formed part of North Durham, a fief of the Prince Bishops.
5. Fishes Steads, at that time, was a 'vill' or small settlement.
6. This was consistent with prevailing Swiss pike tactical doctrine.
7. The precedents were unhappy; three kings of Scotland had come to grief in Northumberland, one killed and two captured.
8. Robert Lindsay of Pitscottie (c. 1532–80), Scottish chronicler and author of *Historie and Cronicles of Scotland*.
9. Pitscottie, *Historie and Cronicles of Scotland*, p. 272.
10. Macdougall, p. 272.
11. Loyd, A., *My War Gone by, I Miss it so* (London, 1999), pp. 152–3.
12. The dynastic conflicts between Valois and Hapsburg fought out mainly in Italy from 1494–1559.
13. This arose after Alfred's grandson defeated a Norse-Caledonian confederation at the Battle of Brunanburh in 937.
14. Malcolm in fact came once too often, being killed at Alnwick in 1093 and a cross was subsequently erected to mark the spot where he fell.
15. Balliol whose unhappy tenure as king of Scotland thus concluded was so known as his coat of arms was ceremoniously ripped from him.
16. Berwick was savagely assaulted and sacked in 1296, thus setting the tone.
17. See Rose, A., *Kings in the North* (London, 2002), p. 56.
18. The 'Shameful Peace' otherwise Treaty of Northampton 1328 had failed to deal with the thorny question of those English magnates who had lost cross-border estate – the 'Disinherited'.
19. David was captured by Sir John Coupland, at the cost of several teeth knocked out and the enmity of his neighbours who finally killed the parvenu knight.
20. Dupplin Moor (1332) was not fought by English Crown forces but by a mercenary company organised by the 'Disinherited'; Edward III was strictly neutral though clearly partisan.
21. Halidon Hill (1333) just north-west of Berwick was considered ample revenge for the humiliation of Bannockburn.

22. Moffat, A., *The Borders* (Selkirk, 2002), p. 211.

23. It seems likely that James III was murdered after Sauchieburn rather than killed in the skirmish; in any event his death went largely without mourners.

26. King, A., 'Fortress and fashion statements: gentry castles in fourteenth-century Northumberland', *Journal of Medieval History*, vol. 33 (2007), pp. 396–397.

27. Fraser, G.M., *The Steel Bonnets* (London, 1971), p. 21.

28. The borderers contribution to the development of the English language comes in the form of bereaved ('be-reaved', having been robbed) and blackmail (or black-rent) as it was known, what we might now term a protection racket.

29. The wardens were government officers, each responsible for a district or 'march', initially two on each side, latterly three. Frequently as much a part of the problem as any glimmer of a solution, theirs, nonetheless was a singularly unenviable task.

30. Tomlinson, W.W., *Comprehensive Guide to Northumberland* (Newcastle, 1863), p. 512.

31. *Ibid.*

32. *Ibid.*

33. Herman, A., *The Scottish Enlightenment* (London, 2001), p. VII.

34. *Ibid.*, p. 279.

# 2

# GREAT UNDERTAKINGS:
## THE ROAD TO WAR

But that the Scot in his unfurnish'd kingdom,
Came pouring like the tide into a breach,
With ample and brim fullness of his force;
Galling the gleaned land with hot assays,
Girding with grievous siege castles and towns;
That England being empty of defence,
Hath shook and trembled at the ill neighbourhood.

Shakespeare, *Henry V*

Edward Hall, on writing of the marriage of Margaret Tudor to James IV celebrated in August 1502, observed that the English found their Scottish hosts somewhat vulgar and the overly ostentatious excess of the court distasteful. Doubtless this form of snobbery was commonplace and had probably not inhibited the guests from taking their fill.[1] James was out to impress but the southerners were disposed to sneer. Any amity between the two nations at this juncture was entirely skin deep. The Treaty of Perpetual Peace, business end of the marriage deal, was not the brave new world many subsequent writers have perhaps imagined. The chance for such a beginning lay more with James III's earlier accord in 1474. That James' reign, inglorious and unhappy as it was, became marked by the king's anglophile obsession, not at all popular with his people. Peace may have seemed like a good idea but it was not high on anyone's agenda. Even James found himself obliged to fight in 1480 and, again, two years later, when Gloucester's brilliant campaign recovered Berwick, previously bargained away by Margaret of Anjou in 1460. Worse, it saw English standards hoisted over the nation's capital.

## The Pretender

This James had learnt from his father's errors and, though he was prepared to enter into terms with England, there was no suggestion that he was inclined to adopt his unlamented parent's hopeless anglophile policy.[2] Perkin Warbeck[3] at various times claimed to be Richard III's bastard, the Earl of Warwick finally, Duke of York, Edward V's younger brother. Not the most convincing of pretenders, he was nonetheless useful to those who sought to embarrass Henry VII. Henry, himself a usurper, was right to be mindful of others. After all, he'd already had to deal with Lambert Simnel, tool of the disaffected Earl of Lincoln, an episode which had ended in a major battle at Stoke.[4] Warbeck's adventures put Henry to a deal of difficulty.

Flirtation with displaced Yorkists had not been unknown at the Scottish court. In March 1492, the would-be king sent a message to the Scottish polity, recommended to James by the Earl of Desmond.[5] Warbeck, despite his basic implausibility, had some connection with European rulers, most notably Margaret of Burgundy, last real Yorkist paladin. The pretender might prove useful in aiding James to gain a foothold in the counsels of Europe. He could also balance the pro-French and pro-English elements amongst his own advisers. Warbeck attempted a landing in Kent in the summer of 1495 backed, in a desultory fashion, by the emperor-elect. The sub text for Scottish support, purely nominal, was a possible wedding alliance, with Warbeck's flimsy cause as cement for the accord.

As was so often the case, this putative understanding was drowned in the mire of European power politics and led nowhere. Rather like Warbeck's expedition which was easily rebuffed, survivors sailed for Ireland where fresh catastrophe awaited and the pretender found himself on the run. Perhaps Scotland's king might offer some hope of succour. Warbeck might prove a handy pawn in his current initiative, a hoped-for alliance with Spain. Ferdinand and Isabella needed Henry VII as an ally against France.

Setting Warbeck loose on the Anglo-Scottish border supported by James' power would divert the English king's attention to his troublesome frontier. The Spanish favoured a substantive truce to fix Henry's attention across the Channel. James happily gained access to the ambassadors' sealed orders before they did and saw that Ferdinand and Isabella had no lasting interest in Scotland. James now decided to play his trump card. After consulting his council (where opinion was likely divided),[6] he decided to offer Warbeck asylum. That November, the pretender was made welcome at Stirling, hailed as 'Prince Richard' of England.

Having browbeaten the hapless Spanish ambassadors, James arranged for his new puppet to be married to Lady Gordon, a fair match for the son of a Flemish bourgeois. Moreover, the king funded Warbeck's motley crew of hangers on, who flooded into the new host country like a plague, plus arranging a generous stipend for their leader.[7] Outwardly, James appeared to be offering significant endorsements, though this was more from policy than conviction. Even the advantageous marriage, whilst a step up for Perkin Warbeck, would have been way beneath a titular Prince of England.

The Fleming was simply an investment in diplomacy, a tool to persuade the wily Spanish to reconsider their position. The sought-after marriage link was payback for an alliance with Henry VII. In fact Spain had a dearth of suitable candidates but it is clear James was simply using Warbeck as an investment in leverage. Ferdinand and Isabella decided to rely upon prevarication and falsehood, cornerstones of productive intrigue.[8] James, however, was a quick learner and, even before his embassy returned he was mustering forces for a raid into England. Don Pedro de Ayala, the new Spanish ambassador, failed to fool James but formed a distinct liking both for the young king and his kingdom; his letter to his sovereigns describing the King of Scots provides an invaluable and insightful pen portrait.

By 15 September, the Scots' army was concentrating at Ellam Kirk.[9] Henry was right to worry but his tireless diplomacy beforehand had eliminated any prospects of support for the pretender beyond Scotland. The King of England whilst agreeing to join the Holy League,[10] attached conditions; he would take no overt action against France whilst his northern border remained threatened. Sir Henry Wyatt, Captain of Carlisle, had written in rather unflattering terms, suggesting the loyalties of numerous border officials were by no means fixed. Henry, therefore, had no cause to relish war with Scotland. He decided to try persuasion, instructing his envoys, the bishops of Durham and Carlisle, to offer the substantive inducement of a Tudor marriage. Despite Bishop Fox of Durham's skilful diplomacy, James was not immediately open to conversion. Admittedly, Princess Margaret was only six and the contract could not be solemnised for some time. James understood his future father-in-law. The offer could be used as bait to persuade the king to dump Warbeck and then be as easily withdrawn.[11]

In fact, what James had in mind was not a bid for conquest in the north where any real prospects of support for the pretender were likely to prove illusory but simply a major raid which the inhabitants of both sides of the line understood only too well. Bashing the English, provided the sport did not end in disaster, always guaranteed a popular press and would establish the young monarch's military credentials, hitherto untried. Henry was not lacking in potential allies in Scotland. Some of the losers of 1488 were already on his payroll.[12] The Earl of Buchan and Lord Bothwell both prominent amongst these, were suborned to do away with Warbeck and thus save everyone a deal of trouble. Indeed, Bothwell had provided a most detailed account of the Scottish preparations and of the bargaining between king and pretender. After hard wrangling, Warbeck had agreed a fee of 50,000 marks[13] over five years and the return of Berwick as a price for intervention.[14] Even the French were moved to offer a substantive bribe for Warbeck's head to keep Henry from Spanish coils.

James remained adamant, citing a catalogue of past grievances and omitting mention of the compensation he'd already received,[15] though the Scots may already have tired of the burden of maintaining Warbeck and his 1,400 chancers. Detailed plans were made for the kidnap and/or murder of the pretender but, in the event, came to nothing. Ramsay did, however, confirm Henry's earlier mistrust of some of his border officers; Lord Dacre's brother Randall had sent a courier to communicate directly with Warbeck in Edinburgh.[16]

The Scottish king had assembled his artillery train, including some experienced master gunners from the Low Countries and unleashed a short, fourteen-day campaign.[17] Much time was consumed with a lumbering march to the Tweed, heavy ordnance being dragged over atrocious roads. James' vanguard had already reported that no significant opposition was mustered against him. Once the river had been successfully crossed, the Scots proceeded with fire and sword in traditional manner, 'the natives who resisted he cruelly killed'. Once byres and fields were emptied and purses filled, the Scots decided they had done enough and, in Vergil's words 'he would have gone even further but for his troops being so laden with spoils that they refused to follow him'.[18]

Warbeck's introduction to daily life on the northern frontier of his kingdom caused him considerable upset. Needless to add, no supporters had come forward. Vergil tells us he protested to James who dismissed his feeble complaint brusquely, pointing out the noticeable dearth of support. After barely a day in the field, Perkin Warbeck slunk back over the border. James proceeded to business, slighting a handspan of towers by Tweed and Till and laying siege to Heton Castle.[19] Despite vigorous operations, the place was still holding out when the king, apprised of an English force on the march from Newcastle, decamped smartly and re-crossed the Tweed. This was the end of the 1496 campaign.

It had been a most inglorious affair, nothing more than a typical cross-border raid, scant return for so costly an investment and not an ounce of glory. Certain minor English holds such as Twizel, Tilmouth, Duddo, Branxton and Howtel had been slighted,[20] thus leaving a scorched balcony for further offensive operations down the valley of the Till. The campaign, however minor, does show that James was not foolhardy and obsessed with seeking battle. Quite the reverse, it rather demonstrates the king's caution and willingness to focus on limited objectives. It was during this foray that De Ayala made his famous observations as to the king's personal bravery. The ambassador had accompanied the army and saw matters at first hand, very much so, as numerous of his own retainers were killed or wounded.[21]

The canny Spaniard observed that James clearly loved war and yet there was policy in the whole business. At little risk, if some expense, James had shown his people he was a valiant war leader and not affected by his father's squeamishness. He had reminded Henry of the vulnerability of his northern frontier and that he, James, could strike as he chose and at will. Henry was not impressed. He regarded the raid as a declaration of war, a material and fundamental breach of the previous truce. Parliament granted significant resources, some £120,000,[22] to pursue hostilities on both land and sea. James had stirred a hornet's nest. It was necessary to ensure the borders were defensible and this task occupied the Scottish king over the autumn and winter. He did, however, find time to make Warbeck's shabby entourage redundant, leaving the pretender alone and isolated, effectively on ice until, or indeed if, a further use could be found for him.

## The campaign of 1497

James was not the man to sit idly on the defensive whilst his enemies mustered unchecked. In February 1497 he launched a pre-emptive strike, scourging the border as before. This, the Raid of Home, was a brief, though for the victims no doubt, a costly affair. Henry, his rage intensifying, had already sent instructions to Dacre to make ready. The warden would need little persuasion. James had by now ordered a general muster and *wappinschaws* – the host to serve for 40 days whilst his gunners remained stationed on the border.[23] Ominously for the English, Mons Meg, that great and venerable leviathan was refurbished for service in the forthcoming campaign. Cast probably in the 1430s, this greatest of great guns was still the most formidable in all Britain. No conventional walls could hope to withstand her Olympian blast.[24]

If Warbeck was no longer a player, his continued presence was still Henry's prime *casus belli*. Further attempts by Spanish envoys to mediate foundered on this particular rock. James might have largely dispensed with the pretender but he was still a useful pawn on the board. De Ayala, by now a bit of a James groupie, was impressed by the young king's sangfroid as he carefully made ready whilst visibly maintaining a façade of sport and pleasure; 'as though he were lord of the world'. Henry, meanwhile, was distracted by rebellion in the west as disaffected Cornishmen marched upon London. His normally well-tuned antennae had, for once, let him down. His focus upon the north had caused him to miss the peril from the west. In the event this was effectively countered in a scrimmage at Blackheath and the threat evaporated.

With such alarums in England, Henry was not as willing to march his host against Scotland. The resourceful Bishop Fox of Durham was sent to negotiate, ideally for the surrender of Warbeck, but in reality for whatever he could bargain for. James had the edge and knew it. He launched two more forays in mid- and late June, beating up the marches and showing his Scottish subjects he was indeed a leader most fit for war. At Duns the Homes saw off an English riposte. With the initiative in his palm, James took the chance to rid himself of the surplus pretender who was packed off back to Ireland,[25] appropriately in a ship named *Cuckoo*.

Bishop Fox had need of all his considerable finesse for James had decided to attempt the reduction of Norham, jewel in the Prince Bishop's crown. The king held his muster at Melrose where he could deploy a very substantial train, exceeding anything seen previously on the borders. Mons Meg, the pride of his artillery ignominiously broke down just south of Edinburgh and several days were lost in necessary repairs. In August the siege began in earnest, James' great guns pounding away at the citadel whilst strong fighting patrols beat up the environs. Despite all this fine show, the leaguer achieved nothing. A spirited defence and pressure on James' already overstretched finances caused him to abandon his lines by 10 August and march the host back to Edinburgh.

By now, Thomas Howard, Earl of Surrey was hastening north to relieve Norham. Finding the Scots already decamped he crossed the line and sat down before Ayton Castle – a Home hold in the Merse.[26] James now had to marshal his forces once again and march south to confront Surrey. A standoff ensued and the usual formalities were exchanged. James challenged the earl to single combat to decide the fate of Berwick. This was mainly show, given the difference in ages, Howard would hardly be likely to accept, though indeed he very nearly did.[27] In the event, James withdrew rather than commit to battle. Surrey, of course, portrayed this as poltroonery. In fact it was sound policy. James had nothing to gain from a fight and much to lose. Whatever his chivalric notions, the king was clearly not prepared to allow these to rule his head. The Ayton incident shows us that James was not the reckless chevalier of legend: here was a display of tactical flexibility and *realpolitik* that Machiavelli would surely have applauded.

King Henry was not best pleased. He unfairly regarded Surrey's campaign as a dismal waste of time and precious resources. The year 1497 was turning out to be a difficult one. For the Scots too, James' belligerence had consumed much treasure and yielded few gains, other than to establish the king as an accomplished war leader and one who could hold his own against England. Both sides, by the end of August, were effectively played out. Henry had expended somewhere between £60,000–£90,000 on Surrey's campaign at a time when the west was still rumbling[28] and he urgently needed peace.

Accordingly, he sent a delegation including Dacre and the Bishop of Carlisle to treat with the Scots, beginning a series of negotiations which would culminate in the treaty of 1502. By September, diplomats from both sides had brokered a seven years' truce. This was a beginning though such arrangements were notoriously flimsy and the indefatigable de Ayala rounded off his Scottish service by acting as James' ambassador to London that autumn. The treaty was amended to provide it should endure for the period of one year after the death of the last surviving of the two rulers. Ferdinand and Isabella would act as arbitrators from now on.

What, if anything had James achieved? In fact, rather a lot; he had wiped out the inadequacies of his father's dismal reign and shown his people they had a dynamic young ruler capable of standing up to the English. He had demonstrated his capacity as leader in war and as knight in battle. Both were important and, though de Ayala might fret, Scotsmen expected their king to shine in arms. Bruce had taken similar risks, engaging the English knight de Bohun in single combat before the hosts on the first day of Bannockburn. Logically, this was madness for the lynchpin and fount of Scottish hopes to brawl like a common soldier, not even fully harnessed. The effect of the win repaid the hazard, a Scottish Achilles.

To be led by such a man was surely a harbinger of victory. As Norman Macdougall observes, James had shown himself to be a man worthy of a king's daughter in marriage.[29] He had also demonstrated that well prepared and rapid military action secured results. His earlier and subsequent campaigns in the Highlands in 1494 and 1495, with that of 1498–99 had also achieved tactical successes. Though the events of 1513 were to be on a far larger scale, it would be untrue to assert that James was completely without some degree of military experience.

## A 'Perpetual Peace'

Since the onset of the Great Cause in 1296, relations between Scots and English had been characterised by hostility. James' raid in 1496 celebrated 200 years of bitter strife and endemic warfare. The negotiations, begun in the autumn of the following year, had been brought on by dire necessity on the part of Henry VII. His policy was dictated by expediency rather than any desire for peace, indeed only the hapless James III had sought a lasting accord. It is said that de Ayala was considered remarkable for having endured a full twelve months in the northern kingdom, as though he had spent that time in the midst of a barbarian horde.[30] Even as talks continued, there were fresh disturbances at Norham where the Scots were worsted in a fracas with garrison troops there.

Despite this mutual detestation and suspicion, the 1502 accord was based on more solid foundations than that of a generation earlier. On this occasion, the proposed dynastic union did indeed take place. Moreover, the treaty embodied a revised legal code for cross-border redress, obliging any injured party to bring his complaint, in the first instance, before the warden having jurisdiction. The notion of perpetuity was also built in: every succeeding monarch of both realms was obliged to re-affirm these terms within six months of coming to the throne. By the time the marriage was solemnised Henry's eldest boy, Arthur, had died followed not long after by his mother. Only King Henry's younger son, the future Henry VIII remained as heir. For James, this offered the dazzling prospect of the greatest prize of all should young Henry not live to inherit. Needless to add, the younger Tudor was to prove a very robust specimen indeed.

James had demonstrated with telling clarity that he was not his feeble father. This was important. The failures of the older James' rule, the humiliations of the war of 1482 and the loss of Berwick, allied to the king's anglophile obsession had demeaned the martial ardour of his magnates and subjects. In a short space of time his son had rebuilt the northern kingdom's military prestige and restored self respect. He had campaigned aggressively and brought Henry to the negotiating table. All of this had been achieved without his having to fight, attaining his goals without the hazard of battle. Despite any chivalric impulses, he was well aware of the dire precedents and allowed caution to prevail. Even the treaty of 1502, sound and statesmanlike as it was did not commit the king to an anglophile policy. He had treated with Henry as an equal, a free and independent prince. The accord with England did not inhibit James from seeking amity with France and Denmark.

In 1504, James cooperated with Dacre in a joint raid or 'rode' against the thieves of Eskdale and the Debateable Land.[31] Malefactors were strung up in satisfying numbers whilst monarch and warden gambled and hawked together. Again, and rightly, the king's biographer sees policy in this[32], James stamping his authority on the ever-troublesome marches. This pattern of short, sharp shocks was to set the mould for much of the sixteenth century. For much of the time the royal writ simply did not run on the troublesome marches. Not all cross-border matters proceeded as smoothly or with such a degree of amity. One of the most notorious breaches of the standard conditions of truce days occurred in the spring of 1508 when Sir Robert Ker of Cessford was killed by no lesser rogue than Bastard Heron. Whether this was, as the Kers contended outright murder or the consequence of a duel is unclear. This incident still rankled by 1513 and James regarded the killing, or more particularly, the failure of the English administration to hand over Heron, as a significant breach of the terms of the treaty.

More incidents followed. Even before the Ker/Heron business, the Earl of Arran had been detained by English authorities on his return journey from a mission to France. This seems to have arisen from fears James was about to renew the French alliance. If so, such highhandedness was not the remedy. The king was understandably furious over Arran's arrest. The earl had indeed been engaged in matters of diplomacy, for Louis XII had been soliciting James for military assistance. The war in Italy was draining French resources. James responded cannily, he had not the slightest intention of getting drawn into the whirlpool of continental wars[33] but wished to remain on cordial terms with Louis. The king advised he was always willing to assist his traditional ally but rather more notice would be needed. This was most tactful. His ambassador Robert Cockburn, postulate to the Bishop of Ross, was instructed to reinforce this assurance. James was playing a skilful game, keeping the idea of the traditional French connection alive whilst not actually entering into any formal undertaking.

This did nothing to allay English suspicions which struck deep. Matters on the border, in the words of the later English Middle march warden Sir John Forster, as practised a reiver as ever was, continued 'very ticklish'. Henry remained fearful that the Scots still entertained designs on Berwick and that James persisted in flirting with Louis XII. Arran's detention had been a clumsy manoeuvre designed to frustrate renewal of the Franco-Scottish accord of 1492, when King Louis dispatched the capable Bernard Stewart, Sieur d'Aubigny[34] as ambassador. Henry sent north young Thomas Wolsey, the coming man, already marked for advancement. The future cardinal's observations, contained in his subsequent reports, are telling. James played an astute hand, advising Wolsey that he was under pressure from all sides of the Scottish polity to renew the French alliance and that he, and his council, were exasperated by the cavalier manner the English had adopted towards their treaty obligations. The English envoy rather cynically remarked that the Scots 'keep their matters so secret ... that the wives in the market knoweth every cause of my coming!'[35]

Wolsey picked up on the prevailing anglophobia and correctly deduced the policy behind it. Only Arran's release would ease the tension. Some Scottish counsellors suggested that a dual alliance with both France and England need not be to the detriment of either. James did offer some reassurance, opining that if the King of England treated him *kindly* and acted as a wise father should, then he should have no fear of enmity.[36] Arran was duly released. Despite this easing, D'Aubigny and his diplomatic colleague were treated with a far greater show of favour than the workaday Wolsey.

Providentially for England perhaps, Bernard Stewart expired of natural causes in June 1508. Undeterred, James sent the highly capable Gavin Dunbar, archdeacon of St Andrews, on a mission to France, sailing in the royal barque *Treasurer.* As ill luck provided the vessel, on its return journey, ran aground on the east coast of England. Dunbar with the other survivors was briefly detained and questioned before being released. James viewed this, understandably, as a repeat of the Arran business and muttered threateningly; sufficiently so for Henry to put the Berwick garrison on a war footing.[37]

But the English king was failing, his fears over Berwick and the border festered. He clearly viewed any increased amity between Scotland and her old ally France as damaging English interests. As had been pointed out to Wolsey, this did not have to be the case and, in any event, any such understanding was not an ostensible violation of the terms of the 1502 agreement. Suffice to say that when the old king died on 21 April 1509, relations were strained. Oddly, in the light of subsequent history, the accession of the brash young ruler, Henry VIII, did not result in further deterioration.

There was a brief honeymoon period and by the end of that November James, as he had undertaken to do, had solemnly ratified the Treaty of Perpetual Peace.[38] All well and good except that, as events would show, this Henry was cut from a very different cloth to his parsimonious father. With a secure throne and full treasury, proof of the effectiveness of his parent's cautious accrual, Henry VIII sought, from the very outset, to be a 'player' on the wider European stage. He was more influenced by the successes of his Plantagenet predecessors, Longshanks, Edward III, the Black Prince and Henry V.[39] After all, where was the glory in careful accounting and good housekeeping?

Henry's own biographer takes a dim view of the young king's aspirations:

> Henry VIII would lead England back into her past, into Europe and its endless
> squabbles, into another round of that conflict misleadingly defined as merely
> a Hundred Years War. He would reject his father's notion of a king's function,
> quickly dissipate his inherited treasure[40]

## Slide into war

By the closing months of 1511, Henry had thrown off the shackles of his more
conservative advisers, temperate residue of his father's council, and formally
joined the Holy League. The king was rewarded by Pope Julius II with the
grant of the order of the Golden Rose,[41] seasoned with a consignment of
fine wine and cheeses. If Henry can be criticised for falling back into the old
ways of warmongering, his subjects were unlikely to disapprove, Edward Hall
least of all:

> The King of England wrote often to King Louis of France to desist from per-
> secuting the Pope, his friend and ally: to which correspondence he [Louis XII]
> gave little regard, whereof the king sent him word to deliver to him his lawful
> inheritance, both the Duchy of Normandy and Guyenne and the counties of
> Maine and Anjou and also of his crown of France, or else he would come with
> such a power, that by force he would attain his purpose.[42]

The young king was now allied to Emperor Maximilian and Ferdinand of
Spain, not perhaps the most reliable of confederates, notoriously skilled in
dazzling with empty promises. Henry's youthful impetuosity was not yet
the equal of their practised cynicism. For James this promised difficulties.
To Scotland, the French alliance was a valued combination of longevity and
expediency. Trade connections were essential and booming, diplomatic links
long established. After extensive consideration James renewed the French alliance in 1512. Whilst this was not necessarily bound to conflict with the terms
of the English treaty, it put both brothers-in-law firmly in opposing camps.

As Professor Macdougall ably points out, this decision was based upon
sound policy rather than romantic impulse. James, at this point, did not desire
war with England. He employed the able Andrew Forman, Bishop of Moray,
in a Kissinger-like role attempting to reconcile the King of France with the
Pope. In part, the renewal of the French accord was a gambit in this wider
game. James was attempting to punch well above his weight in the councils
of Europe and exercise a degree of influence only made possible by the

presence of two larger armed camps, presently circling each other's wagons. By allying himself with France he might apply the brakes on Henry VIII's headlong ambition.

This was England's Achilles heel. If English armies crossed the Channel, a Scottish army might cross the border. This eventuality carried considerable risks for both parties. Numerous Scottish armies had attempted this and come to grief. David II had failed and been captured at Neville's Cross, Douglas had blundered and his forces bled at Homildon. Prior to the Hundred Years War, Malcolm III had been killed at Alnwick, King David defeated beneath the Standard and William the Lion come to grief, again before Alnwick.

If the business of Ker and Heron was not sufficient, the killing of Andrew Barton though unquestionably in a fair fight, added fuel to the creeping flames. Both James and Henry had experienced dynastic upset and personal grief when their respective infant heirs died. In Henry's case this left his brother-in-law as heir presumptive and he reacted with childish and dangerous spite by withholding his sister's legacy from her late father, a wholly unjustified and unnecessary provocation.

A series of diplomatic manoeuvres ensued. James assured Louis he had begun hostilities when he had not done so, the Frenchman responded that he would send to Scotland his client Richard de la Pole, the last Yorkist pretender. Henry had already taken the precaution of killing Richard's younger brother Edmund but Louis was unlikely to surrender so valuable a pawn as the elder de la Pole.[43] When James' herald delivered the king's ultimatum to his brother-in-law before the walls of Therouanne, the caustic rebuff featured a revival of the ancient claim of overlordship, dragging up the root of the Great Cause.

In the previous year, on 2 October, 1512 Louis XII had written to James:

He trusts the King of Scots more than any other prince because they are near of kin and because he has found in him cordial and loyal affection as in no other prince. He bids him to consider the ancient enmity which the English have borne to France and Scotland and still bear, and that it is necessary to diminish their pride and rashness because they intend to fight both countries at once and think nothing of it. Also they are allies of the King of Aragon, who, hiding his ambition under cloak of the Church, and founding in the Holy League a sect most dangerous to the Church, has joined the Pope, who approves his enterprises ...

To resist the schismatic sect the King of Scots must do all he can, which is much, for he is powerful, has good soldiers and many valiant men in his kingdom. Equally the King will make his effort and yet will be glad to help the King of Scots as time and his affairs permit, and at the beginning of their campaign against the English will send 50,000 francs, artillery, cannon-balls and powder. He begs the King of Scots to approve this offer in which there will be no failure. De la Mothe will tell what was done by the Spaniards at Florence and at Prato, at the capture of the latter town such cruelty was seen as was never done by the Saracens. They killed men, women, and children, priest and monks, besides committing other nameless crimes, and the greater part of these Spaniards were circumcised persons not Christians, at least unbelievers in God and the Christian faith.

The editor cites Brodie who quotes the warrant by Louis XII for payments when sending de La Mothe to Scotland to present 100 puncheons of wine, 800 iron cannonballs and 15,000lbs of powder. The arrival of the ships carrying these goods was noted by Dacre on 8 December who also tells us that eight serpentines of brass had been sent as well. Wood also asserts that the aid promised by the French was misleading. The money was never to materialise 'in spite of the later assertion of the King of England after the battle: of the rest, a part arrived in time; another part too late to be of any service.' The wine, however, did make its way to James![44]

Then, on 8 May 1513, Louis significantly upped the ante by making James a substantive offer of aid. He would bear the costs of maintaining the Scottish fleet on a war footing and provide cash subsidies to the value of £22,500 Scots, a most attractive inducement.[45] James would also enjoy the services of the accomplished admiral Pregent de Bidoux leading a squadron of seven galleys.[46] For his part, James would be required both to launch a land invasion of England and to lend the emergent Scottish navy for French service. Henry had no counter offer and the piled grievances, Ker and Barton's deaths, Arran's arrest and Margaret's dowry remained outstanding.

Henry's rather superfluous ambassador, Nicholas West, Dean of Windsor, was kept dangling. He had nothing to give and received as much in return. Even the queen, who might have been sympathetic, remained outraged over her brother's spite. By 13 April, West had had enough; his mission was a fruitless one, the king of France made a much more attractive offer. James' biographer speculates intriguingly about what might have been had Henry been prepared to proffer a substantive inducement. Even at this stage, war with England was not a foregone conclusion.

It happened in part because Henry VIII attached no importance to Scotland. James does not appear as the romantic or quixotic figure of his legend, quite the reverse. He is astute and worldly, vying for a place on the top table, and with a deal more finesse than his brother-in-law! One inevitable consequence of his French alliance was the enmity of Pope Julius who, virtually from his death bed, had excommunicated James on 21 February 1513.

This was a serious matter, though the king may have drawn comfort from the knowledge that Robert Bruce had been similarly cast out of Christendom after the killing of Red Comyn and had triumphed nonetheless.

James sent the indefatigable Forman on yet another mission to Julius' successor Leo X, begging he refrain from confirming the expulsion. This was to no avail for, in August, the new pope confirmed, by correspondence, that any abandonment of his treaty with England would justify a sentence of excommunication. James had in fact previously written to the late pontiff claiming that because of the various violations, he should be free to regard the 1502 treaty as void. Clearly this would not wash. Conversely, Julius II had made Henry VIII an astonishing offer. He would strip Louis XII of his crown and bestow the same upon Henry, the coronation to be carried out in Paris. All that was required of the king of England was that he first win his new kingdom by force of arms.[47]

Meanwhile and for no better reason than to provoke James, Henry had used alleged breaches of the treaty to resurrect the old chestnut of feudal superiority which the English parliament had confirmed in January 1512, when it voted for war subsidies:

> After that it was concluded by the body of the Realm in the high court of Parliament assembled, that war should be made on the French king and his dominions, the king with all diligence caused new ships to be built and repaired and rigged the old, caused guns, bows, arrows and all other artillery and instruments of war to be made, in such number and quantity, that it was wonderful to see what things were done[48]

Nearer the border, Dacre was offering pragmatic advice, suggesting that simply paying across Queen Margaret's legacy would suffice to defuse the rising tension. Sage advice from an old campaigner and successful border warden; needless to add it went unheeded. Dacre, unlike his sovereign, could not afford the luxury of complacency. His position was rather closer to the firing line and he was only too well aware of the weak state of the marchers' defences – many towers slighted in 1496–97 had not yet been refurbished. To add yet further insult, the instrument chosen for delivery of the papal ban was Christopher Bainbridge, Cardinal of York, a noted Francophobe. The See of York had claims over the whole establishment of Scotland and Bainbridge was the least acceptable of messengers, one who had already meddled in Scottish ecclesiastical affairs.

James may have felt that Henry VIII was something of an innocent abroad in the Byzantine coils of European power politics. His two previous interventions, Darcy's expedition to Cadiz and Dorset's foray, had both ended in costly and humiliating farce.[49] Even before the first shots of the campaigning season in 1513 had been heard, the League was already creaking. Venice had defected and patched matters up with Louis. Ferdinand, doyen of fair-weather allies, whilst expressing belligerence, had in fact concluded a year's truce. In a sea fight off Brest against the formidable de Bidoux, Edward Howard, boarding with reckless gallantry, was flung lifeless into the sea from the Frenchman's galley. Towards the end of May, James wrote to his brother-in-law, observing that his gallant admiral might have lived longer had his talents been employed against the Turk![50] No reply was forthcoming. War was probably now inevitable.

## NOTES

1. Macdougall, p. 252.
2. *Ibid.*, p. 251.
3. Perkin Warbeck (1474–99), after leaving Scotland the pretender finally landed in the disaffected West Country and, though he gathered a substantial following, lost his nerve at the critical moment, bolted and was finally captured. A sojourn in the Tower followed by a final journey to the noose awaited him.
4. The Battle of Stoke 16 June 1487.
5. Macdougall, p. 118.
6. *Ibid.*, p. 122.
7. *Ibid.*, p. 123.
8. *Ibid.*, p. 124.
9. *Ibid.*, p. 125.
10. This was Pope Julius II's intended alliance against France, including Spain, the Empire, England and Venice – more formidable in concept than action, signed at Rome in October 1511.
11. Macdougall, p. 127.
12. *Ibid.*
13. One Mark = 13s 4d (c. 67p).
14. Macdougall, p. 128.
15. *Ibid.*
16. *Ibid.*, p. 130.
17. *Ibid.*, pp. 130–1.
18. *Ibid.*, p. 131.
19. Heton Castle, since much rebuilt, the oldest surviving portion dates from c. 1580.
20. Phillips, G., *The Anglo-Scots Wars 1513–1550* (Suffolk, 1999), p. 107.
21. Macdougall, p. 133.
22. *Ibid.*
23. *Ibid.*, p. 135.
24. *Ibid.*,
25. *Ibid.*, p. 138.
26. Ayton Castle, the current rather grand baronial structure dates only from the mid-nineteenth century.
27. Macdougall, p. 139.
28. *Ibid.*, p. 140.
29. *Ibid.*, p. 141.
30. *Ibid.*, p. 249.
31. The 'Debatable Land' was a narrow strip of land stretching from the infamous Tarras Moss in the north to the Esk Estuary, no more than 3.5 miles wide, bordering on wild

Liddesdale. It was a lawless threap and is first mentioned around 1450, its somewhat
colourful renegade denizens continuing to cause trouble throughout the sixteenth century.

32. Macdougall, p. 251.
33. *Ibid.*, p. 252.
34. Bernard Stewart, Sieur d'Aubigny (1452–1508), a Scot by descent but one who rose high
in the French service and commanded the royal bodyguard in addition to a series of
important diplomatic missions.
35. Macdougall, p. 254.
36. *Ibid.*, p. 255.
37. *Ibid.*, p. 256.
38. *Ibid.*
39. Scarisbrick, J.J., *Henry VIII* (London, 1990), p. 23.
40. *Ibid.*, p. 21.
41. The Golden Rose is a sacred papal ornament blessed annually, and conferred as a token
of respect or reward.
42. Edward Hall, *King Henry VIII*, vol. 1, p. 39.
43. The de la Pole brothers were nephews of Edward IV. The fact Richard fought for
France (in whose service he was to die at the Battle of Pavia in 1525), sealed his captive
brother's fate.
44. Wood, Marguerite (ed.), *Papers, Diplomatic Correspondence between the Courts of France and
Scotland, 1507–1517* (Scottish Historical Society, Edinburgh, 1933; University Press by
T. and A. Constable Ltd); Brodie, *Letters and Papers of the Reign of Henry VIII., Foreign and
Domestic, 1372* (National Library of Scotland, Adv. MS. 34).
45. Macdougall, p. 259.
46. *Ibid.*
47. Scarisbrick, pp. 33–4.
48. Edward Hall, *King Henry VIII*, vol. 1, p. 41.
49. In May 1511, Lord Darcy was dispatched with 1,000 troops to Cadiz ostensibly to
accompany Ferdinand in a raid against the Moors. The expedition ended in ignominy
and fiasco, Ferdinand as ever proved duplicitous and the English running riot, created
mayhem. Dorset's adventure was on a grander scale aimed at combining with Spain in
an attack on Gascony. Again Ferdinand failed to deliver, see Scarisbrick, pp. 28–30.
50. Macdougall, p. 262.

# 3

# VALIANT CAPTAINS:
## ON THE ART OF WAR IN THE SIXTEENTH CENTURY

Lo! Bursting from their common tomb,
The spirits of the ancient dead
Dimly streak the parted gloom
With awful face, ghastly red;
As once, around their martial king, they closed the death-devoted ring,
With dauntless hearts, unknown to yield; in slow procession round the pile
Of heaving corpses, moves each shadowy file,
And chants, in solemn strain, the dirge of Flodden field.

'Ode on Visiting Flodden'

Over a decade after his great victory, Thomas Howard, 2nd Duke of Norfolk died at Framlingham Castle in Suffolk on 21 May 1524. He was then 81 years of age, a fair accomplishment in any era, remarkable in the sixteenth century. The old duke was something of a national hero and the manner of his send-off entirely commensurate. His body lay in state for four weeks, surrounded by candles and an honour guard of twenty-eight Howard retainers. The sumptuous state rooms lining the castle bailey were draped in 440yds of black fabric. Not until 22 June did the duke's coffin leave the chapel borne in a hearse of black and gold, horses in gilded tack, sombre mourners in a long, doleful column. It took a full two days for this winding tail to progress 30-odd miles to Thetford Priory. It was a damn good show; clergy and gentry at the head, next a company of heralds, liveried in black and bearing the great man's banner and knightly helm. Next the catafalque, followed by a long train of mourners, arrayed befittingly according to rank. Thomas Howard's last journey proved quite a crowd-puller, demonstrating that mawkish sentiment is not a purely modern concept.[1]

After resting for one night in Diss, the procession reached Thetford on 23 May and the duke was laid in a vault before the high altar, appropriate to his status, honours and patronage of the Cluniac Priory. His fine helm, which would have born its share of scars, had been re-fashioned as a funerary device, proud lion crest emblazoned, carried by Windsor Herald and dubbed 'the Flodden Helm', proud relic of the old man's finest hour. The oration from Revelations 5:5, 'Behold the lion of the tribe of Judah triumphs', was delivered with such fire it terrified half the congregation. Nearly 2,000 guests attended the splendid wake which followed.[2] None other of the many thousands who fell at Flodden received such a lavish burial, most lie in unknown, mass graves beneath pasture and peat, the sudden violence of their passing erased by nature's balm.

## The armies

> The smallest detail taken from an actual incident in war is more instructive to me, a soldier, than all the Thiers and Jominis in the world. They speak for the heads of state and armies, but they never show me what I wish to know – a battalion, company or even platoon in action. The man is the first weapon of battle. Let us study the soldier, for it is he who brings reality to it.
>
>                                                    Ardant du Picq

By 1513 English monarchs had long abandoned the feudal levy – a tradition still maintained in Scotland. In order to provide a reliable supply of trained fighting men, Edward III had developed the contract system. The monarch, as commander-in-chief, entered into formal engagements, indentured contracts in writing with experienced captains, who were then bound to provide an agreed number of men at established rates for a given period.[3] Frequently it was the magnates who acted as main contractors, sub-contracting knights, men-at-arms and archers in turn.[4] This provision of indentures and annuities was as it appears, also employed by lords to bind their retainers. Humphrey Stafford, 1st Duke of Buckingham, killed at Northampton in 1460, had ten knights and twenty-seven esquires in his service. One of the former, Sir Edward Grey, was granted a life annuity of £40 in 1440. Those further down the social scale might receive annual emoluments of £10–£20.[5]

This period of the early sixteenth century was one of transition but evidence of new developments, certainly on the English side, were barely discernible by 1513. Hand-held firearms which were to transform the face of battle and the art of war are not a recorded feature at Flodden, though they had been in use for decades. Commentators have observed that handguns were adopted primarily because they required minimal training as against the many years it took to train an archer.[6] Nonetheless, there was at least one more compelling reason why firearms should come to supplant the traditional bow and this lies in the penetrative power of shot.

By the dawn of the sixteenth century, armourers who had been seeking to render their expensively harnessed clients immune from the cloth-yard shaft had largely succeeded. It is one of history's ironies that they did so precisely at the moment when firearms were about to make the product redundant on every field bar the tilt yard.[7] It has also been argued that the adoption of the pike was in some ways a retrograde step, a system of mass armies rather than more elitist or specialist forces. It could be suggested this was the very effect James IV was aiming for prior to Flodden, using mass tactics to overcome perceived deficiencies in quality.

In addition to his professional retainers, a lord could call out his tenants, many of whom might also have military experience. To these he might, if numbers were sought, round up a following of master-less men happy to have the protection of a great man's livery. A surviving indenture, though dating from much earlier (1452), entered into by the Earl of Salisbury and his tenant Walter Strickland, knight of Westmorland, lists the complement which Sir Walter was to muster: Bill-men – 'horsed and harnessed', 74; mounted bowmen to the number of 69; dismounted bill-men 76, with 71 foot archers, an impressive total of 290.[8] Archers, still the predominant arm in most companies, outnumbered bills by anything from 3>1 to 10>1. This is, of course, six decades prior to Flodden but practice in England does not, in the intervening years, necessarily appear to have altered overmuch.

In the 1470s, as Sir John Paston was preparing to sail for Calais, he begged that his brother recruit 4 archers: 'likely men and fair conditioned and good archers and they shall have four marks by year and my livery.'[9] In short, these were to be permanent retainers, paid an annual wage. A particularly skilled archer belonging to a lord's household might command equal remuneration to a knight. In 1475 Edward IV was raising an army to intimidate France and the great magnates each contributed to his muster as follows:

| | | |
|---|---|---|
| Duke of Clarence; | 10 knights, | 1,000 archers; |
| Duke of Gloucester; | 10 knights, | 1,000 archers; |
| Duke of Norfolk; | 2 knights, | 300 archers; |
| Duke of Suffolk; | 2 knights, | 300 archers; |
| Duke of Buckingham; | 4 knights, | 400 archers.[10] |

The king still had the power to issue what were termed 'Commissions of Array' which empowered his officers to call up local militias who, in theory at least, were to be the best armed and accoutred men from each village in the county. This system, though time honoured, was much open to abuse. The antics of Falstaff provide a comic parody.[11] Surviving muster rolls from the period also provide an insight into local levies. One held at Bridport in Dorset on 4 September 1457, before the king's officers, reveals that a man was expected to possess a sallet, jack, sword, buckler and dagger. Of those on parade that day around two-thirds carried bows and had arrows; other weapons on show included poleaxes, glaives, bills, spears and axes, staves and harness.[12] Dominic Mancini has left us a vivid, eyewitness account of the appearance of the troops Gloucester and Buckingham brought into London in 1483 to provide encouragement for any citizen who might be tempted to think of resisting the usurpation:

There is hardly any without a helmet, and none without bows and arrows; their bows and arrows are thicker and longer than those used by other nations, just as their bodies are stronger than other peoples, for they seem to have hands and arms of iron. The range of their bows is no less than that of our arbalests; there hangs by the side of each a sword no less long than ours, but heavy and thick as well. The sword is always accompanied by an iron shield ... they do not wear any metal armour on their breast or any other part of their body, except for the better sort who have breastplates and suits of armour. Indeed the common soldiery have more comfortable tunics that reach down below the loins and are stuffed with tow or some other soft material. They say the softer the tunics the better do they withstand the blows of arrows and swords, and besides that in summer they are lighter and in winter more serviceable than iron.[13]

Long years of cross-border strife and the English involvement in France had led to a system where the levy was divided between north and south, with the northerners responsible for meeting any Scottish incursion. This practice had come into being during the reign of Edward III. His father's defeat at Bannockburn had ushered in a period of Scottish military hegemony, genesis of the hobilar, when the northern shires had been ravaged by successive raids. By re-settling the upland dales and creating, effectively a northern army, Edward could be assured the back door was always well guarded. The outcome at Neville's Cross had been sufficient proof the exercise had been worthwhile. As for the marchers, well they were always ready! When Edward III had re-populated the upland dales it had became normal for these marcher families to hold their threadbare estates on military tenure.

Fifteen years before the campaign of 1513, clergy from both Tynedale and Redesdale were reminded by correspondence that their mettlesome flocks were expected to bear arms on behalf of the sovereign.[14] In 1538, the county muster for Northumberland lists 'Northe Tyndell Theiffs', near 400 of them, as a tactical unit 'able with horse and harness'.[15] Gervase Phillips is of the view that the levy system, still in practice in 1513,[16] remained effective in times of national crisis, particularly so when those called up were not required to venture overseas.[17] This is clearly very much the case before Flodden. To northerners, service against the Scots was second nature. Long years of bitter and bloody divide had hardened attitudes. The Northern English had ample cause to be wary of Scottish armies but there was scant respect, as the old doggerel derides – 'as for those Scots I rate 'em as sots'. Despite the many common bloodlines, there was a marked ethnic element to the conflict.

Even for more effete southerners, warfare was the gentleman's natural vocation. In his work *Le Jouvencel*, the chronicler Jean le Beuil, writing around 1466, and, moving somewhat up the social scale, gives an insight into the mind of the fifteenth-century gentleman:

What a joyous thing is war, for many fine deeds are seen in its course, and many good lessons learnt from it … You love your comrade so much in war. When you see that your quarrel is just and your blood is fighting well, tears rise in your eyes. A great sweet feeling of loyalty and pity fills your heart on seeing your friend so valiantly expose his body to execute and accomplish the command of our Creator. And then you prepare to go and live or die with him, and for love not abandon him. And out of that there arise such a delectation, that he who has not tasted it is not fit to say what a delight is. Do you think that a man who does that fears death? Not at all; for he feels strengthened, he is so elated, that he does not know where he is. Truly, he is afraid of nothing.[18]

It is unlikely the marchers of the same era thought in quite such flowing terms, such '*Bobinantes Boreales*'[19] were less appreciated the further south they ventured. When they did so, as with Queen Margaret's great northern host which swept southwards in early 1461 in the aftermath of victory at Wakefield the experience, in southern eyes, proved traumatic. It would have been remarkable if some excesses had not taken place, and undoubtedly these did occur. Whether such depredations were quite on the biblical scale depicted by the shrill accounts of contemporary writers is less certain. The Croyland Chronicler probably articulated the fears of southerners, when the Prior, hysterical over the depredations wrought by these wild men from the north, wrote:

> The duke [York] being thus removed from this world, the north-men, being sensible that the only impediment was now withdrawn, and that there was no one now who would care to resist their inroads, again swept onwards like a whirlwind from the north, and in the impulse of their fury attempted to over-run the whole of England.[20]

Actual details of particular horrors are remarkably lacking; without doubt the northerners plundered as they went; as much through necessity as inclination. To the countrymen and townspeople this apocalyptic vision of a great northern invasion as murderously rapacious as Tamerlane, would have been terrifying enough. The Prior of Croyland waxed lyrical in his well-rehearsed outrage:

> When the priests and the other faithful of Christ in any way offered to make resistance, like so many abandoned wretches as they were, they cruelly slaughtered them in the very churches or church yards.[21]

## On strategy and tactics

Strategy tended to be based purely upon the offensive, conversely tactics often assumed the defensive. Command was most frequently exercised by the magnates themselves. Divisional commanders would often be family or high-ranking members of the commander-in-chief's affinity – thus Richard of Gloucester commanded a wing of his brother's forces at Barnet and Tewkesbury in 1471. Nonetheless, commanders might and did rely upon the advice of seasoned professionals. Campaigns were inevitably of short duration, avoiding the need to keep forces victualled and in the field through the harshness of winter. Commanders tended to seek a decisive encounter. It was Surrey's intention from the outset to bring about a general engagement with the Scots' army, for only by inflicting a decisive defeat could he free Northern England from the spectre of Scottish intervention. James, rather contrary to popular belief, was cannily disposed to avoid contact until the English flanking march forced the issue.

Knights and men-at-arms dismounted to fight on foot. Horses were sent to the rear, to be mounted only when the enemy was in rout. Pursuit of a beaten foe was rigorous and merciless, the slaughter indiscriminate. A wealthy captive in the French wars could have been the making of a yeoman's fortune but a Scottish lord, whose lands were like to be very much poorer, had no commercial value. Hobilars[22] or light horsemen; sometimes called 'prickers', were deployed for scouting and vedette[23] work but, once battle was joined, there was little direct control a commander could exercise. English armies were still marshalled into three divisions or 'battles', the van, or vaward, main battle and rear or rearward.

Deployment was in linear formation, knights and men-at-arms as heavy infantry, archers moving to the fore to shoot, all beneath the banner of their captain or lord. Battle was a most hazardous enterprise. In the early sixteenth century a commander had limited forces at his disposal. One single, significant defeat in the field would likely ruin his cause. Communications were dependent upon flags. Supply remained a constant headache and the spectre of treachery as omnipresent as Banquo's ghost. Surrey's men suffered inordinately from the predatory tendencies of their own English Borderers throughout.

If the armourer's art had developed to a point where good-quality harness could deflect a cloth-yard shaft, the commons, relying on jacks, were less protected. At the Battle of Stoke in 1487 the Earl of Lincoln's ill-harnessed, Irish kerns were shot down in droves. Improved armour did not render a knight invulnerable. When Lord Clifford unwisely removed his bevor to gulp water in an extended skirmish prior to the Battle of Towton in 1461, he was pierced through the throat.[24]

A similar fate befell Lord Randolph Dacre next day. It has been estimated, with reference to the Battle of Towton that, if each archer loosed four dozen arrows, then over 1 million shafts with a gross weight of 40 tons fell across the field.[25] In all probability archers, like billmen, remained posted with their own companies, rather than being formed into a separate arm. Most likely, at the commencement of the fight, all would advance a few paces from the line to shoot and then retake their places for the melee which was bound to follow. As a contemporary chronicler observed: 'After the third or fourth, or at the very most the sixth draw of the bow, men knew which side would win.'[26]

Although armies deployed in line with opposing divisions aligned, this neat arrangement could go awry, depending upon weather and terrain, as in the fog of Barnet in 1471. A commander with a good eye for ground might try to deploy an ambush party for a flank attack. The Duke of Somerset may have attempted this at Towton. A Scottish flanking move at Otterburn in 1388 had proved decisive. Late-medieval captains were, for the most part, literate and familiar with the tenets of their trade.

Many, if not most, would have read the classical authors, such as the late Roman theorist Vegetius, who's *Epitoma Rei Militaris* was revised in the fifteenth century by Christine de Pisan. She also wrote the *Livre des faits d'armes et de chevalerie*, subsequently translated and popularised by Caxton as *The Book of the Fayttes of Armes and Chyvalrye*. Companies were led by captains and formed up according to their chosen arms. Banners were important, as morale boosters, signalling devices and rallying points. The use of liveries did, at least, promote some degree of uniformity. In practice this consisted of a loose tunic or tabard which the soldier wore over his jack or harness in the lord's colours. The Percys for instance fielded a livery of russet, yellow and orange with the badge of the Percy Lion rampant sewn onto the shoulder.

In the campaign of 1513, the Earl of Surrey was at a constant disadvantage of numbers and supply. What he did possess were officers with experience. He himself had fought at Bosworth, his elder son had seen action at sea; many of his unit commanders had endured trial by battle. The Scots, in contrast, did not enjoy this wealth of experience – Lord Home was active in the hurly burly of border raids but most of the magnates had borne arms relatively rarely. There had been police actions against Donald Dubh and recalcitrant chiefs but no 'serious' warfare. The Scots therefore would be using unfamiliar tactics and led by officers devoid of much battle experience.

For several centuries the mailed and mounted knight had been the arbiter on most medieval battlefields though, in English armies of the fourteenth and fifteenth century, knights and men-at-arms fought dismounted. Such tactics had proved highly successful in battle against the Scots. Halidon Hill in 1333 being a case in point, when timely intervention from a body of mounted knights, the 'Disinherited' under Edward Balliol had averted disaster on the English right at Neville's Cross thirteen years later. Scotland was traditionally short of heavy cavalry yet both sides could deploy Border light horse, or hobilars. By now the border lances were specialists.

They rode light and could ride far. Their sure-footed garrons[27] could pick a path through treacherous mosses and over uncharted moors, their lances served equally well as cattle prods. They wore jacks instead of harness, long leather horseman's boots, lance, sword and perhaps a light crossbow or 'latch'. They were fleet and expert in the saddle, formidable if handled well, led by their wardens or local 'heidmen'.[28] Such local forces were vital for scouting and foraging though, as the Bishop of Durham's observations suggest, the borderers could generally be relied upon to serve no interest other than their own. Dacre's men would nonetheless do good service at Flodden.


## Sinews of war

There is some argument as to what extent, if indeed any, armies in Britain, both English and Scottish had, by the early years of the sixteenth century begun to adopt continental practices. As ever the process is more gradual than sudden, though as Gervase Phillips points out, foreign mercenaries had regularly been employed in Britain during the Wars of the Roses and internecine conflict in Scotland.[29] James was attempting to modernise his forces quite radically, certainly more so than his opponents who, in appearance, would have closely resembled their fathers and grandfathers who'd stood beneath the pounding sleet at Towton, half a century before.

Armour was reaching the very zenith of technical and stylistic perfection. Italian harness of this era was skilfully and beautifully constructed to maximise deflection. Defences for the vulnerable areas at the shoulder, elbow and knees were strengthened, fashioned ribs on exposed parts were constructed to deflect a killing blow.[30] German armourers moved this concept toward the angular perfection of the Gothic style with its emphasis on uncompromising lines, swept by heavy fluting. A harness of this period might weigh around 60lb (30kg) and would not greatly inhibit the mobility of a robust man, trained since boyhood to move and fight in armour.[31]

Medieval knights, even when fighting on foot, frequently bore a less onerous burden than the average 'Tommy' of World War One, loaded with rifle and pack, ammunition bandoliers, wire and tools. The Italian and German styles came together in Flanders, a flourishing centre of manufacture where Italian armourers produced a hybrid style featuring flexible, fluted plates of the Gothic combined with more rounded pauldrons (shoulder defences) and tassets (thigh guards) of their native style. Such armours were sold in quantity in England, as evidenced by their regular appearance in funerary monuments.

For head protection, the sallet form of helmet was popular from mid-fifteenth century onwards. The rear of the elegantly curved brim swept downwards into a pointed tail to provide extra deflection to the vulnerable areas at the back of the head and neck. Usually provided with a fixed or moveable visor, the sallet was accompanied by a bevor which afforded protection to the throat and lower face. Although knights could move freely, even in full plate, thirst and heat exhaustion were constant threats. That swift end meted out to Butcher Clifford by an alert archer was the penalty for unstrapping his bevor in the heat of battle. Dressing for war was best achieved at leisure, before the enemy was in the field, as a contemporary author, writing *c.* 1450 explains:

> To arme a man. Firste ye must set on Sabatones [armoured over shoes] and tye hem up on the shoo with small points [laces] that woll not breke. And then griffus [greaves, plate defences for the calves] and then cuisses [thigh defences] and ye breche [leggings] of mayle. And the Tonlets. An the Brest and ye Vambras [upper arm defences] and ye rerebras [lower arm] and then gloovis [plate gauntlets]. And then hand his daggere up on his right side. And then his shorte sworde on his lyfte side in a round rynge all naked to pull it out lightli [the sword is carried without a scabbard, hung in a ring for quick release]. And then put his cote upon his back. And then his basinet [Bascinet – a form of helmet in use prior to the sallet] pyind up on two greet staples before the breste with a dowbill bokill [double buckle] behynde up on the back for to make the basinet sitte juste. And then his long swerd [sword] in his hande. And then his pensil in his hande peynted of St George or of oure ladye to bless him with as he goeth towarde the felde and in the felde.[32]

Whilst knights and men at arms would wear full harness, archers tended to favour padded jacks or brigandines, as the account from Dominic Mancini, quoted earlier, suggests. This fabric garment was finished with plates of steel or bone riveted between the inner and outer layers or, in the cheaper version, simply padded and stuffed with rags and tallow. The ubiquitous jack was far cheaper, lighter and, for many purposes, more practical. Some were fitted with sleeves of mail to afford protection to the arms. Though archers traditionally eschewed leg harness, bill-men and men-at-arms would wear whatever they could afford or were able to loot, a seasoned campaigner augmenting his kit from the spoil of the dead or captives.

As an alternative to the expensive sallet, foot soldiers might still rely on the basic 'kettle' hat. By the time of Flodden, the favoured form of helmet might now be an 'armet' worn with a 'wrapper'. The armet consisted of a hemispherical skull, fitted with two hinged flaps which locked beneath the jaw, the joint protected by a narrow section of plate, a small visor fitted over the side pieces. Vision was afforded through the narrow slit formed between the rim of the visor and the lower edge of the skull. The front of the helm was reinforced by an additional plate defence called a wrapper. Those beneath the top tier of Scottish society might wear imported armours known as 'almain rivet'. These were essentially munition quality harness comprising breast and back, a sallet-type helmet, possibly Italian and tending to feature a rounded or 'bellows faced' visor. Articulated tassets covered the thighs though the lower legs were normally unprotected, save for stout leather boots.

Highlanders would most probably go bare foot and bare legged with a long shirt, dyed saffron. Over this their gentry would wear a padded aketon and perhaps a full-length mail shirt, for the most part the rank and file, armed with bow and spear, would be un-armoured. The early sixteenth-century Scottish chronicler John Major has left us with a description of the Highland warriors of his day:

> From mid leg to the foot they go uncovered; their dress is, for an overgarment, a loose plaid and a shirt, saffron dyed. They are armed with a bow and arrows, a broadsword and small halbert. They always carry in their belt a stout dagger, single edged but of the sharpest. In time of war they cover the whole of their body with a coat of mail, made of iron rings and in it they fight. The common folk amongst the Wild Scots (Highlanders) go out to battle with the whole body clad in a linen garment sewed together in patchwork, well daubed with wax or with pitch, and with an overcoat of deerskin.[33]

By this time, the knightly sword had reached the apex of its development prior to its eclipse, later in the sixteenth century, by the rapier. Blades were designed for both cut and thrust. Long and elegantly tapering, with a full grip that could be hefted in one or two hands, in section resembling a flattened diamond; simple quillons, curved or straight, a wheel, a pear or kite shaped pommel. This was the hand and a half or 'bastard' sword, the very 'King of Swords'. Such precision instruments were reserved for the gentry and were extremely expensive to buy.

The commons carried a simpler, lighter and considerably cheaper side-arm, a short single-edged blade with the quillons curving around up to the hilt to provide a form of crude knuckle guard. Gentlemen and commons both bore daggers. The long-bladed rondel with tapering triangular blade, hardwood grip, disc guard and pommel, was a popular style. Ballock knives, who's wooden handle featured two rounded protuberances of suggestive form, rather resemble the later Scottish dudgeon dagger. As handy as a tool as weapon, daggers were carried by all ranks and might be used to stab an opponent or plant vegetables as the situation required. In battle, the thin-bladed knife could be used to deliver a coup de grâce to an armoured enemy, either thrust directly through the eye slit of the steel visor or into the more vulnerable areas of armpit or genitals.

Descended from an agricultural tool, the English bill was neither crude nor inelegant. Bill-men, deployed in companies, had contributed mightily to an impressive string of victories won in France and the bill, on the field, was to prove more than a match for the puissant pike. It was a perfect killing implement with a long head tapering to a point, cutting blade fixed with a hook and spike to the rear. Well-drilled companies of billmen would move and fight in formation, using the weapon as a spear for thrusting or as fearful axe for an overhead slash or 'hack'.

Only during the later sixteenth century, did the term 'longbow' come into usage. A plainer expression, 'bow' or 'livery bow' was more commonplace during the fifteenth. Retained or liveried archers normally carried their own bows but, in the long continuance of the French wars, the Office of Ordnance began issuing standardised kit on campaign to replace those lost or damaged. Thus, quantities of bows were manufactured to a standard or government pattern, like the infantry musket of following centuries. Yew was the preferred timber, though ash, elm and wychelm were also favoured. The weapon was usually between 5ft 7in (1.675m) and 6ft (1.850m) in length, the cross section corresponded to a rounded D with a draw weight of 80–120lb (40–60kg). A modern target bow has an average draw of around 45lb (22.5kg).

Arrows were crafted from a variety of woods. Roger Ascham, tutor to Elizabeth I and a noted sixteenth-century authority, advocated aspen as the most suitable, though ash, alder, elder, birch, willow and hornbeam were also utilised. The shafts were generally around 2ft 6in (75cm) in length, fletchings formed from grey goose feathers. Arrowheads came in a variety of forms, flat, hammer headed, barbed or wickedly sharp needle pointed piles or bodkins, designed to punch through plate and mail. Livery quality arrows were issued to retainers, 'standard' grade was just that and 'sheaf' arrows came in bundles of two dozen.[34] At each extremity the bow was tipped with cowhorn, grooved to take a linen string and, when not in use, the stave was carried unstrung in a cloth cover.

To draw, an archer gripped the bow with his left hand, about the middle, where the circumference of the wood was around 4.5in (22.5cm). Then he forced the centre of the bow away from him to complete the draw, using the full weight of his body to assist, rather than relying on the strength in his arms alone. Such strength, stamina and expertise demanded constant drill. Practice at the butts was compelled by statute. The bow could kill at 200yds; every archer wore a leather or horn 'bracer', strapped to his wrist to protect against the vicious snap of the bowstring.

## Artillery (see also Appendix Four)

By the early years of the sixteenth century, artillery had become the dominant arm in siege warfare and indeed had been so for nearly a 100 years. These monsters were fired from ground level and from behind a hinged, timber shutter rather like a very much larger version of the archer's mantlet. This provided some cover for the gunner, his mate and matrosses. Most guns loaded at the breech, having a removable block shaped not unlike a commodious beermug. From the 1460s trunnions had come into use and even the heavier pieces were being equipped with wheeled carriages. Elevation was achieved by the use of wedges.[35]

Transportation was an area of major difficulty. Large teams of draught horses or oxen were required. A section of pioneers had to be added to the train, their task to level and fill the generally appalling roads over which the guns must pass. Larger pieces were still manufactured on the hoop and stave principle (hence the term 'barrel'), though casting in bronze was, by mid-century, commonplace.[36] Another arm, growing in significance and potency, was the smaller handgun or 'gonne' which would soon become predominant.

It was one thing to drag the great guns to fixed positions and batter castle walls; the handling of field artillery was an altogether different matter. Using lighter guns on the field was a relative innovation and Flodden was the first British battle in which the deployment of field artillery was to have a marked effect upon the outcome. Even that earnest advocate of modernity Machiavelli had little faith. He regarded guns on the field as being more of a distraction, soon prone to being knocked out by enemy cavalry. The Italian cites the Swiss as the very model of steadfastness under fire; 'they never decline an engagement out of fear of artillery'.[37]

In this he was overly contemptuous. During Bull Talbot's last doomed battle at Castillon as the Hundred Years War closed in 1453, the English had been badly mauled by guns firing from redoubts. The Lancastrians attempted similar tactics at Northampton seven years later but were foiled by a mix of torrential rain and treachery. Flodden would be the first fight in Britain to begin with an artillery duel as opposed to an archery exchange. The Earl of Warwick had deployed guns at Barnet but his efforts were frustrated by mist. His rolling, roaring cannonade which thundered blindly through the long hours of darkness did little but rob those on both sides of rest.

## Face of Battle

Time and romance have, over the intervening years, cast a shroud of pageantry over the harsh realities of late medieval/early Renaissance combat. The truth is somewhat less attractive. Though lacking the scale and widespread devastation of modern wars, devoid of the full horror of industrialised conflict, warfare, in the early sixteenth century, was every bit as frightful. English battles of the Wars of the Roses generally opened with the archery duel, regular volleys thudding home into tightly packed ranks, inflicting numerous fatalities and wounds.

These preliminaries probably lasted only a short time before that side which was suffering the most was compelled to advance. The movement would be ordered rather than swift, sergeants bellowing orders to keep the ranks dressed. Cohesion was all-important. Those divisions which could maintain both order and momentum stood the best chance of breaking a more disordered foe. A commander with an eye for ground would always seek the position of best advantage, though elements in the topography, adverse weather, mist and darkness could combine to upset the best laid plan.

In the melee men, half blind in plate, soon assailed by raging thirst and swiftly reaching exhaustion would become disorientated. Dust and the steam from thousands of sweating men would further obscure any wider view. Few would be killed by a single blow, but a disabling wound, bringing the sufferer to his knees, would expose him to a further flurry, his skull then shattered, pierced through the visor or groin by daggers, hacked by bills, stamped on, kicked and slashed. Not a swift death, nor an easy one; the heaving field garnished by a slew of severed limbs, and blood in great, bright rivulets.

Once one side broke in rout, casualties would begin to mount. Armoured men trying to flee towards horses tethered at a distance would be easy prey. Those less encumbered or not enfeebled by wounds might survive the race, others would not. The victors, their horses brought forward by grooms, would be swooping and circling like hawks. The English chronicler, Abbot Whethamstede, who may have been an eyewitness, graphically chronicles the fate of some of the Earl of Warwick's men, fleeing from the debacle at the Second Battle of St Albans in 1471:

> The southern men, who were fiercer at the beginning, were broken quickly afterwards, and the more quickly because looking back, they saw no one coming up from the main body of the King's army, or preparing to bring them help, whereupon they turned their backs on the northern men and fled. And the northern men seeing this pursued them very swiftly on horseback; and catching a good many of them, ran them through with their lances.[38]

By contemporary standards available medical services were rudimentary and sparse. The perceived presence of evil humours was the source of copious bleedings, quacks cast horoscopes and peddled bizarre potions. Wounds, sensibly, were cauterised with hot pitch. Anaesthesia, with solutions mixed from herbs, was by no means unknown, however, and surgical techniques perhaps more sophisticated than might be assumed. Gerhard von Wesel, travelling in England in 1471, has left an eyewitness account of the army of King Edward IV as the survivors of Barnet trudged wearily back into London: 'Many of their followers were wounded, mostly in the face or the lower part of the body, a very pitiable sight'.[39] These, it must be remembered, were the victors.

When two sides came to close contact and the melee erupted, many would suffer wounds; cuts to the head, body and lower limbs. If a man fell he was lost, snuffed out by a flurry of blows. The noise would be terrific, a lunatic cacophony of grinding blades, shouts, exhortations, curses, screams of injured and dying men. The mounds of dead which contemporary illustrators show piling on fields of battle[40] would build up as the fight burned brightly in various sectors. It would not be at all tidy, the neat precise coming together of opposing lines. Knots of men would eddy and swirl as with the ebb and suck of the tide, temporarily disengaging as the ranks were thinned or disordered. The very press of dead would form a considerable barrier so that the living must fight atop heaps of slain, adding their entrails to the pile.

We cannot now fully understand, nor perhaps even imagine, the nature of late medieval/early Renaissance combat. Most contemporary military actions come no closer than perhaps a couple of hundred metres. Modern firefights are very rarely decided by cold steel. When one side does launch a bayonet charge, the other will almost invariably fail to stand; superior morale of the attacker as decisive as his weapons. A medieval gentleman was trained in the use of arms from an early age. To be a knight was his profession and, however exalted his status, be he a great magnate or humble gentleman of the shires, he would be judged on the field according to knightly virtues.

Gentlemen would be taught by their seniors and by professional fight masters, a fifteenth-century version of the gentlemanly personal trainer.[41] This was not polite fencing but the essential art of killing. Survival in battle depended on rendering your foe incapable as quickly as possible, dead for preference. For this reason the head blow would be favoured. Mortal wounds to the body might still afford an opponent the chance for a final lunge of his own.[42]

Fighting in harness swiftly leads to dehydration and heat exhaustion even in a fit young man, accustomed to the weight and proficient with his weapons. Wearing a helmet was deemed essential; the penalty for carelessness on the field was very often death. The narrow eye slit of a sallet or armet, closed up, greatly reduces the wearer's field of vision. He must therefore be trained to keep his focus on the opponent's eyes and yet judge movement of his blade. At the same time he has to maintain a degree of spatial awareness as to what is going on around, for the threat comes not just from the fellow in front.

Even in twentieth- and twenty-first-century eyewitness accounts, participants gain only a limited and often distorted view of events around them. In the heat of battle, with adrenalin pumping and senses deafened, it is highly unlikely any individual would remain so detached as to glean a wider understanding of tactical developments. On the field courage, like its opposite panic, is collective. Men who have fought steadfastly may give way in rout once fear, like a contagion, spreads. Often, if not invariably, the rot will begin in the rear.

Those in front are too much occupied with the business of survival to initially contemplate flight. Once the fear spreads, it consumes like wildfire and it will be then that the great killing begins. As they flee, men will cast aside helmets, too restrictive as they struggle to find breath for flight. The enemy, released from the tension of combat, his vision blurred by the red mist, will have leisure to strike at will. Moreover in battles of this period where combatants fought on foot, those gaining the advantage, seeing their foe dissolve, would have their horses near enough to hand.

A magnate would have his retainers and household men around him, trained to fight as a unit, weapons honed by long practise, sealed with the bonds of comradeship. Once battle is joined the higher sentiments are sharp forgotten. What counts on the field is your fellowship, 'mates' – it is these you fight for and it is they you do not wish to let down. The feudal bond between retainer and lord, knight and magnate is also telling. The social contract bound by oath is important. This business of oath taking was onerous.

Take a purely notional contest which pits an English bill-man against a Scottish pikeman, who has dropped his stave and drawn sword. The bill-man delivers two fast blows to his opponent's head, disabling him and causing his body to begin to fall. The Englishman is being pushed forwards by the press of comrades behind. He must therefore brush aside or step over his fallen foe before meeting the next threat. He has no time to pay the other any heed. Should the luckless man show any sign of vitality, those coming behind will finish him off, almost certainly with a further blow to the skull. Daggers thrust into armpit or groin might be employed for swift despatch but, by virtue of the relative shortness of blade, would bring the attacker so close to his victim as to further restrict his already limited vision.[43] Sword or polearm, where the killing blow could be given from a greater distance, were safer.

The former has the ability to deliver cut or thrust. For a sound killing blow the thrust is always to be preferred hence the old fighting maxim 'the point will always beat the edge'. However, the thrust has to be aimed carefully or the point will glissade off harness. It needs be inserted into the join between plates and driven home far enough to inflict mortal damage without becoming lodged in the victim's torso. The killer does not have the luxury of extended leisure in which to disentangle his blade.

Polearms and maces were less sophisticated weapons than blades, but swinging percussive blows would suffice to bring an opponent down without entanglement, shattering bone and tissue. And there would be blood. The level of exsanguination would be truly horrific. Men in battle die noisily and messily. In this fight they were dying in great numbers and the walls of dead which swiftly arose would act as a barrier to combatants. Of necessity there would have been lulls in the killing frenzy. Not any form of ordered truce but where the lines drew apart as if by tacit consent to clear the dead, order the ranks and, above all, take on water.

Dehydration, even in cold weather, is a marked feature of armoured combat. Men could only keep going if they were given drink. Great clouds of steam would rise from the overheated carapaces and the unsung water carrier was a feature of every fight. Much of this work would be done by women, so the field was by no means an exclusively male preserve.[44] It appears to have been the convention that, as non-combatants, these women were not targeted. They would also act as stretcher bearers and, effectively, paramedics. A wounded man's chances of survival would, then as now, be dependent upon how swiftly he could be got off the field. Many of those struck down, despite the best attentions of their enemies, would not be dead and the mounds of fallen would neither be still nor silent but would rather writhe and moan as though stirred by an invisible hand, smells of blood garnished with ordure and urine.

There are no modern comparisons to fearful rout. None of those thousands caught up in the horror left accounts. We may get some flavour from later battles. From Culloden, fought in 1746, eyewitness testimony confirms the fury and murderous intensity of a bloody pursuit 'after receiving many cuts of the sword on the face, and many stabs of the bayonet'.[45] The cavalry, in this instance did the work, the foot too exhausted to move, they 'pursued vigorously, and killed great numbers without distinction; for being newly raised men they were more willing to exert themselves'.[46]

Numerous of those slaughtered in the wrack of the Jacobite army were mere bystanders, those who had simply come out to watch the fight. War might be bloody but it was still entertainment. In an age where public executions were accepted spectacles, battles might offer a rare treat. Whether at Flodden there were those who simply watched as the melee unfolded is a question that cannot be answered. Such practice was common throughout history and perhaps this fight too had its spectators. If so, their position in the rout will have been a precarious one. Soldiers have no pity for those who've come to watch them die for sport.

## Of blood and bile

A mysterious fraternity born out of smoke and danger of death …

Stephen Crane

Perhaps the holy grail of Flodden scholars has been the location of grave pits. These have so far eluded researchers. A similar obsession guided those who have studied Towton and here a startling new revelation came to light in July 1996 when building works were underway at Towton Hall. Contractors unearthed a shallow pit which contained nearly two dozen skulls. Once it was clear this was not a crime scene the archaeologists, mainly from Bradford University and West Yorkshire Archaeological Service, took over and, that September, digging was extended to reveal the full extent of inhumation. When finally fully investigated, the burial chamber was some 10ft 8in by 6ft 6in (3.25m x 2.00m) with a depth of 2ft 1in (0.65m).[47] The remains of no less than fifty-one male skeletons aged 16–50 were uncovered. Aside from a trio of silver rings and other traces,[48] there was no data from which to identify a date for the burial. However, the remains exhibited significant evidence of serious battle-related trauma. That these are the dead of Towton can scarcely be doubted.

Some of them, the shortest being 5ft 2.5in (158.5cm), were small men. These were typically from the younger age range. Those who were older attained heights of 6ft 0in (183.5cm) with an average height measurement of 5ft 8in (171.6cm). They were thus a shade taller than the average for this era.[49] The remains, as far as could be determined, showed little signs of disease, though most had lived lives involving hard physical labour.[50] Dietary traces and dental evidence were consistent, though latterly these men had neglected their basic dental hygiene, perhaps due to the strains of campaigning.[51]

At least two of the dead, older men, had evidence of previous trauma, suggesting seasoned veterans, perhaps of the French wars who had finally met their deaths at the hands of fellow Englishmen. Three exhibited signs of development associated with the practice of archery and the level of physical evidence clearly indicated numerous others had undergone prolonged physical labour. Whether this was occasioned by arduous military service or simply by working on the land could not be determined. Others were very much less robust and perhaps represented 'scraping the barrel' in recruiting terms.

That their deaths were shockingly violent was soon obvious. The Towton mass grave tells a very different story from any of our more stylised and glorious views of medieval warfare. The bones cannot lie. Given the location of the grave it has been surmised that the dead were adherents of Lancaster, cut down in the rout. Skull injuries strongly suggest the victims were not wearing protective headgear at the moment of death. This gave rise to some initial suggestions that these were revenge killings, cold-blooded murder enacted after the fight. This now appears unlikely. Possibly the fleeing men threw aside their helmets as they ran. Dumping kit and harness to facilitate flight is natural. There is no reason to suppose Flodden would be in any way markedly different.

In medieval conflict, head wounds are generally the most common, identifiable cause of mortality. Of the twenty-eight skulls which could be successfully examined twenty-seven had suffered trauma to the head. Interestingly, nine of these had suffered prior, healed damage to the skull, one individual had no less than five, a hitherto very lucky fellow whose good fortune, like that of so many others, had run out on Palmsunday Field. One particularly battered individual exhibited no less than nine injuries[52] and thirteen in total had identifiable wounds to the body. Obviously many more such injuries might have been inflicted without leaving archaeological traces. Abdominal wounds, penetrative strikes entering lungs, general damage to soft tissue would all have occurred though there is a general absence of traces of any damage to ribcages which may suggest the men had been wearing jacks or harness.

Scoring of bones is suggestive of blades rather than blunter weapons such as the mace or poleaxe. Most prevalent traces were cuts to hands and arms, defensive wounds typically occurring when the victim was attempting to parry or deflect. This would further account for injuries to the left side of the neck and collarbone, inflicted by a right-handed opponent. More wounds to the back of the neck would have occurred whilst the victim was in flight or already on the ground. The angle of some blows clearly suggests they were inflicted by a mounted assailant. There was nothing pretty about this fight.

One victim's skull was so mangled it required a near-complete reconstruction.[53] He was one of those who'd survived an earlier injury (a depressive fracture to the left parietal region). Death had resulted from a series of eight wounds, 'multiple penetrating and non-penetrating', sustained in the course of hand-to-hand combat facing a right-handed attacker swinging a blade, probably a fair-sized weapon, perhaps a hand-and-a-half, or 'bastard' sword. One massive swinging cut to the rear of the skull had inflicted catastrophic and probably fatal, certainly disabling, damage. This was delivered with a 'large bladed instrument in a slightly down-to-up motion'. In the frenzy of battle a further two blows were added. It is unlikely our victim noted these.[54]

None of these men died nobly. They fell in a frenzied hacking melee of pure and prolonged horror. Bones show the dire nature of their wounds. They cannot reveal the faces of the victims as they died, the sounds, animal cries and screams, the great gushing streams of bright arterial blood, stink of sweat and excrement; in short, the face of war. On average, each victim had sustained four wounds. One was dispatched with a single stroke, the unluckiest required thirteen. Some 65 per cent of injuries were inflicted by cuts of the blade, some sheering along the bone, others biting deep or through.

Most seem to have been inflicted from the front, suggesting combat rather than rout. Although percussive wounds were less frequent, they were more damaging, most delivered against the face or side of the head, smashing blows;

crushing bone. Of the total skulls, eight had suffered stabbing wounds, a dozen in all, delivered to the side or rear of the head. These were more surgical in nature, the point of the sword or dagger driven home then twisted free. Sword thrusts were the minority, only three; the others were caused by points or beaks of staff weapons. One unfortunate had been prone when at least two of his three hurts were delivered.[55] The shape of some of the wounds suggested those made either by bodkin pointed arrows or the chunkier penetrations from crossbow bolts.

In common with other periods, men would also die from disease and want. Dysentery was a major killer as was typhus. Plague also stalked armies. The late-medieval era has been described as 'the golden age of bacteria'[56] with perhaps thirty-odd outbreaks of pestilence occurring prior to 1487. French mercenaries in the service of Henry Tudor were blamed for introducing the 'sweating sickness' that, in 1485, killed off two mayors of London with six aldermen in barely a week.[57]

## Innovation – Pike tactics

Man is intolerant and fearful of solitude, physical or mental … He is more sensitive to the voice of the herd than to any other influence … He is subject to the passions of the pack …

Wilfred Trotter

James IV, King of Scotland, was acutely aware that Scottish armies had fared badly in the past. Spears had proved unequal to English bills and their lack of quality armour left them horribly vulnerable to the hurricane arrow storm. As early as 1496 James had established a 'harness mill' at Stirling to produce munition-quality armours for the commons whilst his nobles were investing in fine plate from Milan. In the second half of the fifteenth century a military revolution had been taking place on the continent. The Swiss had emerged from their mountain fastnesses as a force to be reckoned with. Serving as mercenaries they had come to dominate the many battlefields of the Franco-Imperialist conflict raging in northern Italy. These Swiss had largely re-invented the famed Macedonian phalanx of antiquity. Their pike columns deployed in dense formation, stiffened by ferocious discipline and superb morale, wielded an 18ft pike, the sarissa of Alexander's day.

Using mass bodies of spears was not an innovation. Robert Bruce, in 1314, a dozen years after the Flemings had routed a conventional force of mounted chivalry at Courtrai, utilised traditional Scottish formations (the *schlitron)* employing 12ft staves to win a dazzling victory. He delivered his attacks in echelon, combining mass, momentum and cohesion in ways the Swiss would certainly have recognised. Wallace had tried the *schiltron* at Falkirk in 1298 and failed, defeated by a superior, all-arms force which combined the shock of heavy cavalry with sustained missile power. Edward II was not the master of war his father had been and it could be argued that such victories as Bannockburn and Courtrai were won because the losing side were badly led and misunderstood the ground.[58] In the fourteenth century soldiers of the emergent Swiss cantons had employed halberds to great effect winning significant victories at Mortgarten (1315) and Laupen (1339). Gradually, and partially in response to a defeat at Arbedo in 1422, the Swiss began to increase the ratio of pikes to halberds in their ranks.[59]

This unstoppable mass of resolute points could smash through enemy formations like a steamroller, movement, mass and cohesion welded together into a formidable instrument of war. Swiss armies were characterised by relentless discipline, constant aggression and swelling confidence. Charles the Bold of Burgundy, that rash adventurer, confronted the Swiss in the 1470s and suffered a series of catastrophic defeats, at Grandson, Morat and, finally, Nancy, where his last army was decimated and his own life forfeit. Since then the Swiss had turned war into a trade, selling their genius for wages, which, if not forthcoming, would produce immediate defection. These Swiss fought wars as an industry, not for glory. Machiavelli was certainly impressed:

> The Swiss regiments at present are also based upon the model of the ancient phalanxes and follow their method both in closing up their order of battle and relieving their ranks; when they engage they are placed on each-other's flanks, not in a parallel line. They have no method of receiving the first rank, should it be thrown back into the second; in order to relieve each-other, they place one regiment in the front and another a little behind on the right, so if the first is hard pressed, the second may advance to its assistance, a third is placed behind both these and also on the right, at the distance of an arquebus shot. They have adopted this disposition so that if the other two are driven back, the third can advance to relieve them, and all have sufficient room either to retreat or advance without falling foul of one another.[60]

Pike columns, as they deployed for the advance, would, from the right, comprise the van or *vorhut*, this division was followed by the main body, the *gewaltschaufen* and this, in turn supported by the rear or *nachut*. The phalanxes were fronted by arquebusiers or crossbowmen to provide covering fire together with picked swordsmen wielding hefty double-handers. Their role was to secure the vulnerable flanks of each column and act as a strike force if the main advance faltered. Momentum was the key. If this could be sustained the rush was unstoppable but, if halted, the densely packed ranks provided a massed target. It was weight of shot that finally beat the Swiss at the decisive Battle of Bicocca in 1522. Once stationary the pikemen were mown down in droves. On the borders the English achieved a comparable outcome at Pinkie in 1547.

As early as 1471, the Scots Parliament had passed an ordinance making the traditional spear redundant in favour of pikes. In 1513, their French allies were particularly keen to see Scots adopt these winning tactics. A cadre of French officers, which disembarked at Dumbarton either late in July or early the next month, comprised some forty captains under the Sieur d'Aussi. Their role was to instil Swiss tactics into raw Scottish levies. This was an unenviable task, to convert such untried material into the equivalent of elite Swiss mercenaries was a formidable assignment. The time and complexity of training required to bring men up to the required standard was very considerable.

For the Swiss this was their trade. They regarded war as a career. Could the companies of potentially unwilling Scottish conscripts be turned, in a matter of weeks, into a battle-winning instrument? The message from Swiss victories was clear, this offensive doctrine could produce victory in the field. James was aware of the number of defeats Scottish spear formations had suffered in battle against the English, winnowed by bows, hacked by bills. Only an army trained and drilled in such tactics could hope to triumph.

Furthermore, to succeed the phalanx needed to be deployed on suitable ground where the momentum of an attack could be sustained. Pike columns had to comprise men familiar with their weapon, extremely well disciplined, commanded by officers who knew their business and fired by high morale. It was common practice for commanders to attempt to use terrain to delay the rush until the enemy was at hand. A rash advance over open ground would expose the Swiss to the weight of enemy missile fire and risk fatal loss of both impetus and cohesion. Their ruthless and experienced captains appreciated the weaknesses of the puissant pike and they had developed their supporting arms accordingly. This had taken a generation, not a mere matter of weeks.

Once Swiss brigades had been committed to battle there was little individual captains, or indeed a commander-in-chief, could do to further influence the outcome of the fight. Tactical flexibility was, therefore, lacking and it was customary for the officers to charge home with their men, sustaining discipline and morale being prime considerations. James has been excoriated for doing just this at Flodden. However, the decision to lead his division in person should be viewed in the light of the prevailing doctrine. James does not appear to have attempted to throw out a skirmish line of missile troops ahead of his pike formations. These were typically used to pick off targets of opportunity and disrupt enemy lines. Charles V, a dozen years after Flodden, demonstrated their effectiveness at Pavia as the armies closed to contact.[61]

It is generally recognised that drill, so much resented by so many generations of perhaps not too willing warriors, is a military essential. It provides the weld to cohesion and no amount of sporting or natural martial instinct can cover the deficit. This routine aspect of training is doubly essential in those who manoeuvre in mass where momentum, precision and esprit largely depend upon drill instilled through months if not years of seemingly endless 'square-bashing'. It was this all important cement that was lacking from the fabric of James' army. The men were conscripts and they had only weeks in which to train. True, the puissant pike was not so very far distant from the Scottish spear but it was different enough to warrant serious and repeated drilling. This could not occur. Such a deficiency would tell.

## War and the law

One could assert that a primary casualty of war is the rule of law. Juvenal was of the view that civil law had little application once the dogs of war had been let loose.[62] What passed for military or martial law, the *jus armorum* (laid down as a compendium of convention), provided for conduct of dealings between combatants.[63] The plain fact was, most civilians had no legal protection whatsoever. Canon or ecclesiastical law allowed for safeguarding clergy and of course church lands. Towards the end of the fourteenth century a canon lawyer, Honore Bouvet, attempted in his *L'Arbre des Batailles* ('Tree of Battles'),[64] to set out legal principles which might offer some succour to hapless civilians. His argument was that canon law, and the protection it afforded clergy, might be extended to all non-combatants, a doctrine of 'proportionality'. This obligation extended to princes and men of rank who might command forces in the field and who were thus responsible for the actions of their troops.

Bouvet accepted that the peasant might be plundered according to the exigencies of war but his person should remain unmolested as long as he had not taken up arms himself. Travellers engaged upon peaceable journeys and the ploughman, whose endeavours allowed the combatants to maintain their armies, should also be inviolate. In the wake of Agincourt (1415), Alain Chartier in his *Livre do Quatre Dames* ('Book of Four Women') considered the plight of womenfolk affected by the outcome of battle.[65] Whilst lawyers and poets might be coming to a realisation that civilians needed and were entitled to be protected from the worst excesses of soldierly misconduct, few on the Anglo-Scottish border would have cause to notice the difference. Warfare along the frontier had been characterised by savagery since the outbreak of hostilities in 1296 and earlier. Nothing that occurred in 1513 would represent a diminution of the scale of habitual atrocity.

NOTES

1. Ferguson, J., *The Flodden Helm and events linked to the death of Thomas Howard in 1524* (Cold Harbour Press, 2009), p. 8.
2. *Ibid.*, p. 9 – the Priory fell into ruin after the dissolution but a plaque still commemorates the former location of Surrey's tomb.
3. Phillips, p. 47.
4. Wise, T., *The Wars of the Roses* (London, 1983), p. 22.
5. *Ibid.*, p. 23.
6. Phillips, p. 9.
7. *Ibid.*, p. 13.
8. Oman, Sir Charles, *The Art of War in the Middle Ages* (London, 1924), vol. 2, p. 408.
9. Wise, p. 27.
10. *Ibid.*, p. 27.
11. *Henry IV Part One* act IV scene I – [Falstaff] 'If I be not ashamed of my soldiers I am a soused gurnet I have misused the king's purse damnably.'
12. Wise, p. 27.
13. *Ibid.*, p. 27.
14. Phillips, p. 48.
15. Tuck, J.A., 'War and Society in the Medieval North' in *Journal of Northern History*, vol. 21 (1985), p. 51.
16. A revised system of 'General Proscription' did not come into being until 1522, see Phillips, p. 48.
17. *Ibid.*
18. A.W. Boardman, *The Medieval Soldier in the Wars of the Roses* (London, 1998), p. 173.
19. Literally 'Roaring Northerners' – this was not a term of endearment.
20. Riley, H.T. (ed.), *Croyland Abbey Chronicle* (1854), p. 531.
21. *Ibid.*, p. 531.
22. Hobiler-(ar) – essentially light cavalry, the term may have originated in Ireland in the thirteenth century.
23. Vedette (or vidette) from the Latin videre (to see), refers to mounted sentinels or outposts.
24. Wise, p. 29.
25. Boardman, p. 167.
26. *Ibid.*, p. 167.
27. A garron (or garran) was an undersized, rather poorly regarded animal though still within the breed standard. Scottish or Irish term can be applied to a warhorse.
28. 'Heidman' was the leader or patriarch of a riding family or grayne.
29. Phillips, pp. 42–3.
30. Blair, C., *European Armour* (London, 1958), p. 77.
31. Norman, A.V.B., and Pottinger, D., *English Weapons and Warfare 449–1660* (London, 1966), p. 114.
32. Oakeshott, R.E., *A Knight and his Weapons* (London, 1964), p. 51.
33. Major, John, *History of Greater Britain* [1521] (Scottish History Society, 1892).
34. C. Bartlett, *The English Longbow-man 1330–1515* (London, 1985), pp. 23–30.
35. Rogers, H.C.B., *Artillery through the Ages* (London, 1971), p. 19.
36. Norman and Pottinger, p. 141.
37. Phillips, p. 30.

38. Riley, H.T. (ed.), *Registrum Abbatis Johannis Whethamstede 1872*, vol. 1, pp. 388–92.
39. Bartlett, *Op. Cit.*, p. 51.
40. Norman and Pottinger, p. 141.
41. John Waller in Fiorato, V., Boylston, A., & Knusel, C.H. (eds), *Blood Red Roses – the Archaeology of a Mass Grave from the Battle of Towton* (Oxford, 2007), p. 148.
42. *Ibid.*
43. *Ibid.*, pp. 149–50 (this notional scene is developed from that created by John Waller, a true sword-master).
44. There is anecdotal evidence from the field of an earlier Scottish battle 'the 'Red Harlaw' of 1411' where there is a tradition that separate grave pits were dug for female dead killed during the battle.
45. J. Prebble, *Culloden* (London, 1961), p. 119.
46. Fiorato, Boylston & Knusel, p. 33.
47. *Ibid.*, p. 29.
48. Aside from the aforementioned rings the principal finds were a series of copper 'aiglets' – these are the tips of the laces called points and used to fasten clothing and perhaps as in one instance sections of harness.
49. Fiorato, et al., p. 55.
50. *Ibid.*, p. 74.
51. *Ibid.*, p. 88.
52. *Ibid.*, p. 153.
53. *Ibid.*, skeleton 41.
54. *Ibid.*, skeleton 25.
54. *Ibid.*, p. 100.
55. *Ibid.*, skeleton 41.
56. Thrupp, S.L., *The Problem of Replacement Rates in Late Medieval English Population*, ECHR, 2nd Series, 18 (1965–66).
57. *Ibid.*
58. Phillips, p. 17.
59. *Ibid.*, p. 18.
60. Niccolo Machiavelli, *The Art of War* [1521] (New York, 1965), p. 86.
61. Phillips, p. 23.
62. Keen, M. (ed.), *Medieval Warfare – a History* (Oxford, 1999), p. 267.
63. *Ibid.*
64. *Ibid.*
65. *Ibid.*, pp. 268–9.

# 4

# ABLE SOLDIERS
# AND MARINERS:
## WAR AT SEA

Here are two people almost identical in blood ... the same in language and religion; and yet a few years of quarrelsome isolation – in comparison with the great historical cycle – have so separated their thoughts and ways, that not unions nor mutual dangers, not steamers or railways, nor all the king's horses and all the king's men seem able to obliterate the broad distinction.

R.L. Stevenson, *Essays of Travel*

## Restless Natives

When James IV finally embarked upon abolition of the Lordship of the Isles in 1493, he calculated the move as one enabling him to cement royal power in the west. In this he was mistaken. The fall of Clan Donald ushered in an age, not of centralised authority but of murderous, internecine strife; the *Lin na Creach* – 'Age of Forays'.[1] In the same year he kicked away the last supports of the tottering Macdonald hegemony in the west, James' Parliament enacted that all coastal burghs should provide a well-founded vessel (of not less than 20 tons) with able-bodied mariners for her crew. To reinforce awareness that the ending of Clan Donald's sway was but the beginning of a new extension of the business of the state, James led a fleet to the Isles in August, accompanied by Chancellor Angus and a fine train of magnates. At Dunstaffnage, where he stayed a mere eleven days, James may have accepted the surrender of some chiefs, re-affirming their holdings by royal charter. The MacDonalds were not completely over-reached; both their chiefs, Alexander of Lochalsh and John of Islay, received knighthoods.

In 1495, accompanied by Andrew Wood, commanding *Yellow Carvel* and *Flower*,[2] James cruised down the Firth of Lorn, through the Sound of Mull to MacIan of Ardnamurchan's seat, Mingary Castle,[3] where a quartet of powerful magnates bent their collective knee. These included such noted seafarers and pirates as MacNeil of Barra and Maclean of Duart. Whilst James was diverted by his flirtation with the posturing Perkin Warbeck, this policy of treating with the chiefs was undone, largely by the avarice of Argyll, who preferred force to reason. Inevitably, this merely served to alienate the Islesmen, whose galleys conferred both force and mobility. In 1496 Bute had been taken up and disorders reached a level where the king felt obliged, once again, to assert his authority by launching a naval expedition. Indeed, this was the only means whereby the chiefs could effectively be brought into line. A land-based expedition would accomplish nothing: Islesmen counted wealth and power in the number of their keels.

The king's expedition of 1498 proceeded by way of Arran to his royal castles of Kilkerran, where he spent two months, then on to Tarbert. James, though he wished to impress his authority on the west, did not necessarily have much enthusiasm for the chore. For the royal writ to run in the west and to fill the gap in authority left by the collapse of the Lordship, power needed to be exercised by loyal and respected subordinates. Argyll had succeeded in alienating a number of the chiefs, including his own brother-in-law, Torquil MacLeod of Lewis,[4] who was to become a fierce opponent. MacLeod had secured, by uncertain means, the keeping of the boy, Donald Dubh,[5] would-be claimant to the defunct Lordship. Argyll was no more loved by Huntly, his successor as lieutenant in the north west and one who proved equally hungry for personal gain.

James was briefly diverted in 1501 by the near fiasco of his Danish adventure and did not turn his gaze westwards again until the following year. That Torquil MacLeod should control the person of Donald Dubh was fraught with risk. MacLeod was summoned to appear, failed to do so and consequently outlawed. Huntly was commissioned to take up Torquil's confiscated estates, doubtless to Argyll's fury, he being sidelined for failing to keep a grip on his own kinsman. Both Mackintosh and Mackenzie managed to escape from confinement, though the first was soon re-captured and the second killed. By 1503, disturbances had become widespread and Huntly was engaged in wholesale dispossessions of those who refused to submit. With Donald Dubh lending legitimacy to their cause (the last of the Lords of the Isles, old John died in January 1504), the rebels under Torquil struck back. Bute was again extensively despoiled

Parliament, sitting in March 1504, commissioned Huntly to retrieve Eilean Donan[6] and Strome castles, whilst a naval command, assembled under the ever-vigilant eye of Sir Andrew Wood, was entrusted to Arran. The fleet was to reduce the rebels' stronghold of Cairn na Burgh, west of Mull in the Isles of Treshnish. These capital ships, with a full complement of ordnance, soon proved their worth. Naval gunnery swiftly reduced Cairn na Burgh. Few details of the siege have survived but the operation would clearly have been a difficult one. The ships would come in as close as the waters permitted and deliver regular broadsides, essentially floating batteries. What weight of shot the rebels possessed is unclear, most likely it was not very great. Several rebels-chiefs, Maclean of Lochbuie, MacQuarrie of Ulva and MacNeil of Barra, presently found themselves in irons. Gradually the power and authority of the Crown was restored. These captured chiefs saw little prospect in continued defiance. Argyll was forcefully abetted by MacIan of Ardnamurchan, a ruthlessly effective pairing.[7]

Argyll, now restored to his lieutenancy, was prepared to be more diplomatic and, from 1506, returned to a more conciliatory policy, rewarding those chiefs prepared to submit, even some of those who'd been implicated or involved in the recent disturbances. MacIan too did well enough, though he had few friends in the Isles and his own advancement had to be checked to avoid the greater alienation of others, especially the MacLeans. Torquil Macleod kept the dissident flame firmly alight and his example helped to inspire potential rebels. Parliament, summoned for early 1506, convicted him of treason.

An expedition sent against him was to be led by Huntly and involved the hire of captains such as John Smollett and William Brownhill, with ordnance supplied from the royal train. The king and his advisers had planned on a campaign of two-months duration to wrest Lewis from Macleod. In September James paid £30 to Thomas Hathoway as a fee for the hire of *Raven* which had been engaged for the campaign. By September it also seems likely that Huntly had succeeded in reducing Stornoway Castle and capturing Donald Dubh, though the wily MacLeod slipped the net and remained a fugitive until his death in 1511.

By now, James IV was losing interest in the Isles. Control was best exercised through local magnates like Argyll even if the Campbells, for all their avarice, were not possessed of an effective fleet of galleys. This deficiency was partly corrected by the cordial relations the earl enjoyed with the MacLeans, anxious to see the ruin of Clan Donald fully accomplished in order that they might assume the mantle of a naval power amongst the clans. James had by now set his heart upon and his mind towards the creation of a Scottish national navy.[8] In August 1506, he'd written to the King of France intimating that this naval project was a key objective. Scotland was a small kingdom, disturbed by the fissiparous tendencies of the Islesmen and magnatial factions. It was also a poor nation, lacking the resources of England. Nonetheless, during his reign, James bought, built or acquired as prizes taken by his buccaneering captains, nearly two score of capital ships, a very considerable total for the day.[9]

## Towards a Scottish navy

This proposed Scottish navy was not a complete innovation. The king's predecessors had been possessed of ships. As early as 1457, Bishop Kennedy of St Andrews owned the impressive *Salvator* – at 500 tons a very large vessel.[10] Developments in naval architecture, influenced by advances in the science of gunnery, had necessitated the final differentiation between ships of war and merchantmen. The Crown could no longer count upon assembling an effective fleet by hiring in merchant vessels and converting them to temporary service as man-o'-war. Nations that sought to strut upon the wider stage required a navy as a tool of aggressive policy and a statement of intent. The fifteenth century had not witnessed any serious English interference before 1481–82 and the prime consideration, in terms of sea power, was to protect Scottish ships against the unwelcome attention of privateers, for the most part English, infesting the North Sea like hungry sharks.

Richard of Gloucester's campaigns showed how exposed the Firth of Forth and indeed the whole of the east coast were to amphibious attack. Here, in the east, the problem was wholly different from that of the west. No Hebridean galleys disturbed the peace but the Forth and Edinburgh were horribly exposed to English hostility. Whilst Henry VII proved less inclined to attack Scotland than his predecessor and actually ran down the navy he'd acquired, the Perkin Warbeck crisis of 1497 highlighted this continuing exposure.[11] Even when a more cordial atmosphere prevailed, the activities of privateers continued regardless, Andrew Wood and the Bartons persisted in their piratical activities as did their English opposites.

In 1491 the Scots Parliament empowered John Dundas to erect a fort on the strategically sited rock of Inchgarvie.[12] Wood had already thrown up a defensive work at Largo. Conversely, the legislature had previously ordered the slighting of Dunbar Castle, an English occupation being the requisite spur. Later, after 1497, the ubiquitous Wood was to oversee its rebuilding. Such defensive measures and the encouragement of privateers, were entirely sound but, of themselves, insufficient to undertake coastal defence and the wider protection of the sea lanes. For this greater task, only a fleet would suffice.

With James, the creation of a navy rapidly rose to become a near obsession; policy was overlaid with prestige. For the first ten years of his quarter-century reign James spent under £1,500 Scots in total on his ships, a very modest outlay. This climbed to something in the order of £5,000 per annum after 1505 and by the end of the reign he was spending over £8,000 on his new navy. To give a comparison, during the years he was on the throne, the king's income roughly trebled but his expenditure on the navy increased sixty-fold![13]

A switch of emphasis from west to east characterised James' policy toward ships and shipbuilding. Dumbarton remained both as a base and a shipyard but he considerably improved the facilities of Leith's existing dockyards, constructed a new yard at the New Haven (Newhaven) and, latterly another at the Pool of Airth. Not only did Scotland lack adequate facilities for the construction of larger man-o'-war but she lacked the requisite craftsmen and these had to be imported, primarily from France. In November 1502, Treasurer's accounts reveal the hire of a French shipwright, John Lorans, working at Leith under the direction of Robert Barton. This first importation was soon complemented by others. Jennen Diew and then Jacques Terrell were engaged and, due to a shortage of hardwood, obliged to source timber for their new keels abroad.

In June 1506, the great ship *Margaret* (named after the king's Tudor consort), slid into the placid waters of the Forth. This vessel was a source of great pride to the king. As indeed she might be, the cost of her construction had gobbled up quarter of a whole year's royal revenue. She was a four-master, weighing some 600 or 700 tons and bristled with ordnance. James' chivalric obsession with the panoply of war found a natural outlet in the building of his great ships. He dined aboard, appointed himself Grand Admiral of the Fleet, and wore the gold chain and whistle of his new office.[14]

That which had acted as a further spur toward creating a purpose-built navy had been the fiasco of the Danish expedition in 1502. This botched intermeddling represented an attempt by James, at least in part, to establish himself and his realm as a player on the wider, European stage. The result was scarcely encouraging and, despite the 'spin' placed upon the outcome, the affair proved something of a debacle. James' uncle, King Hans of Denmark, in 1501–02, found himself confronted by rebellious subjects in his client territories of Norway and Sweden and had lost control of a swathe of key bastions, including the strategically significant hold of Askerhus near Oslo. James was bound to the Danes by earlier treaty and the situation raised possibilities for a useful intervention.[15]

The king hurried to make preparations for an expedition – *Eagle* and *Towaich* were made ready, together with *Douglas* and *Christopher*. Total costs of the fleet and accompanying troops was a whopping £12,000 and the burden fell on Scottish taxpayers. From the start there were difficulties. Lord George Seton had been paid to make ready his vessel *Eagle* but his part ended in acrimonious litigation and impounding of the ship, which does not ever appear to have weighed anchor. Raising the requisite number of foot soldiers, ready to serve in the proposed campaign, proved arduous; far from the number of 10,000 postulated, it seems unlikely that the force amounted to more than a fifth of that total.

When the truncated fleet finally sailed, toward the latter part of May 1502 it comprised *Douglas*, *Towaich*, *Christopher*, together (possibly) with *Jacat* and *Trinity*, under the flag of Alexander, Lord Home, wily borderer and Chamberlain. In two months of campaigning, little was achieved. The Scots suffered losses in an abortive assault on Askerhus. Others sat down before Bahus and Elvsborg, a significant number simply deserted. For James, who'd had equal difficulties in securing payment of the taxes due to fund the business. There was nothing but frustration, tinged with humiliation. This was not at all what he'd envisaged.[16]

Construction of *Margaret* was followed by the commissioning of *Treasurer*, built by Martin le Nault of Le Conquet at a further cost of £1,085 Scots. More vessels were purchased including Robert Barton's *Colomb* which was quickly engaged in the west, cruising from Dumbarton under the capable John Merchamestone to recover Brodick Castle, seat of the earl of Arran, seized by Walter Stewart. When King James wrote to Hans of Denmark in August 1505, he had to concede that he had no capital ships available, such were the demands of home service, making good storm damage, wear and tear, with other vessels detached on convoy duty.[17]

In part, this deficiency could, and had to be, made up of hire or joint-venture agreements with merchants/privateers such as the Bartons but it was clear more capital ships were needed. By 1507, work on the construction of the New Haven was already far advanced, the king now considering the potential of Pool of Airth, well to the west of the fort at Invergarvie and thus far more sheltered from attack. By the autumn of 1511, three new docks had been built under the direction of Robert Callendar, Constable of Stirling Castle, who had received £240 Scots to meet the costs involved. Norman Macdougall makes the highly apposite observation[18] that James' fascination with his nascent navy and the trappings of high command mirrored that of his brother-in-law, Henry VIII of England.

Impressive as the construction of the great ship *Margaret* had been and as much as she represented the best in contemporary warship design, she was insufficient to satisfy James' obsession with capital ships. As early as 1506 the king had engaged James Wilson of Dieppe, a Scottish shipwright working in France, to begin sourcing suitable timbers for a yet larger project. This new vessel, *Michael*, was to define the Scots navy of James IV. A later chronicler estimates its cost as not less than £30,000 Scots, a truly vast outlay. Finding adequate supplies of timber to build her hull and furnish the planking gobbled up much of Scotland's natural resource with much else imported besides. She would have weighed at least 1,000 tons with a length of 150–180ft.

Her main armament probably totalled twenty-seven great guns with a host of smaller pieces, swivels and handguns. Henry VIII, not to be outdone in what was developing into a naval arms race, commissioned *Great Harry* which went into the water a year later. For James this was imitation as flattery, the fact that *Michael* was afloat, moved Scotland into the first rank of maritime powers. A Scots navy had now fully 'arrived'. The new ship took to the water for the first time on 12 October 1511. She had been nearly five years in the building and carried a full complement of around 300 of whom 120 were required to serve the great guns.[19]

James took an enormous pride in his flagship. At that moment she was likely the most powerful and advanced warship that had ever sailed. Her very existence heralded Scotland as a European power. His nascent navy now comprised in addition to *Michael* and *Margaret*, the capital ships *Treasurer* and *James* with smaller but still potent man-o'-war in *Christopher* and *Columb* plus a couple of substantial row-barges and lesser craft. This royal squadron could be further up-gunned by the private vessels of the Bartons and seafarers such as Brownhill, Chalmers, and Falconer with, of course, Sir Andrew Wood. Not only had the king created a navy but the sea was his passion, to a far greater extent than appears to have been the case with any of his forbears.


## Actions at sea

Andrew Wood, notable as his career was, never quite achieved the renown of the Bartons. John, the father was an experienced mariner from Leith. His three sons, Robert (Hob a Barton to the English), John and, most famously Andrew, carved a niche as the most active privateers of their day. The brothers had a singular enmity toward the Portuguese who, aside from discommoding John the younger, had plundered their father in 1476. All three sons had distinguished and energetic careers both as merchantmen and sea-thieves. The combined proceeds made each of them wealthy. Intimates and trusted servants of King James IV, numerous of their more outrageous acts were simply winked at. It has been suggested that issuing the brothers with letters of marque[20] was a handy and cost-effective means of bestowing patronage, for the burden fell upon those despoiled in consequence. Robert was heavily involved in the king's shipbuilding programme, entrusted with the sourcing, acquisition and transport of materials.

It was he who James chose to escort Perkin Warbeck when the Pretender was conveyed from Scotland. The letters of reprisal authorising the brothers to prey on the Portuguese, whilst being issued, were not actually authorised and thus not effective prior to 1507. Robert promptly scooped a fat prize only to find himself under arrest in the port of Veere, his release being procured only after an energetic exercise of royal diplomacy.[21]

Robert's career significantly outlasted that of his two siblings. Andrew died famously in battle in 1511, John, of natural causes, whilst serving the French two years later. Robert survived to become an important figure in Albany's regency administration and, thereafter, in the government of James V, holding the offices of treasurer, comptroller, great customar, master of the coin, master of the ordnance and conservator of the mines of Scotland. Despite his many sinecures with the combined proceeds of trade and piracy, Robert fell into serious financial difficulties and died, probably in late 1540, still beset by creditors.

Andrew was born around 1470 and did service in the business of the pretender, Perkin Warbeck. By 1505 he had risen to the command of a capital ship *Margaret*. Like his brothers, he was active in pursuing Portuguese targets after 1507, using the letter of reprisal as carte blanche to take up merchant shipping at will. Something of a swashbuckler, he was accused of plundering a Breton ship and found it expedient to cruise to Copenhagen where the King of Denmark, impressed by his fame for derring-do was anxious to procure his services. The king may have been disappointed for Andrew accepted his wages but did little in return, sailing for pickings in the Channel on board *Lion* (probably of around 120–130 tons) and the lighter pinnace *Jennet of Purwyn*, notwithstanding that the smaller ship had been a gift from James to Hans of Denmark! By now his depredations were causing serious embarrassment in Edinburgh and, following loud protests from the Portuguese, James, in the spring of 1511, suspended the letters of reprisal.

His luck finally ran out toward the end of June that year. The two Scottish craft had been cruising in the Channel seeking prizes when the Scots encountered, off the Downs, two superior English keels *Barbara* and *Mary Barking*. These were commanded by Sir Edward Howard and his younger brother Lord Thomas, sons of the Earl of Surrey. The Howards' vessels were both capital ships and the Scots were outmatched. Whilst not detailed to hunt pirates but engaged primarily to protect merchant convoys, the English captains hoisted sail and gave chase.[22]

Edward Hall, the English chronicler, and no ally to the Bartons, gives a rather coloured but dramatic account of the epic fight which followed. The weather was vile, high seas and wind hampering both hunters and quarry. The ships became separated with Thomas Howard taking the smaller *Jennet* whilst his brother closed with the *Lion*. Broadsides thundered over the darkening waters, round shot crashing. With the waves riding so high, there was little that long-range gunnery could achieve and the two ships closed to grapple and board. Barton directed his men with, as even the English chronicler was prepared to concede, magnificent élan. One of his singular tactics was to unleash a heavy boulder or weight from the yard arm to come crashing down onto and through an enemy deck.

Howard, aware of his peril, detailed his most efficient archers to shoot any Scot seeking to clamber up and release the great weight. Two brave Scots tumbled to the bloodied decks, before Barton, who had the benefit of harness, refused to sacrifice more sailors and attempted the job himself. A first shaft glanced harmlessly from plate and it seemed the day might yet be his but a second struck home under the arm, sending the pirate plummeting to the deck, mortally wounded. Facing death, his courage did not waver and, like Grenville of the *Revenge*, he continued urging his men on to continue the fight for as long as he had breath. Once their captain had expired, however, the survivors succumbed to instant loss of zeal and hauled down their colours.[23] James lodged a series of protests with Henry VIII, who responded with some clemency, releasing the surviving Scottish crew. The killing of Andrew Barton still seems to have rankled with James. Thomas Howard, seeking to goad the king into fighting before Flodden made specific, gloating reference to his part in the pirate's end.

## Naval tactics

References to guns mounted on board ship can be traced to the early 1400s but the art of navel gunnery only began to flower in the closing decades. Initially, lighter pieces were mounted in the fore and aft castles, essentially

intended as anti-personnel weapons, flensing the enemy decks with shot. As the weight of guns and shot increased, castles needed to be constructed in a sturdier manner to bear the sharp recoil, ordnance being mounted on the internal elevations as well to clear the between decks of enemy boarders.

Cannon were to have a considerable effect upon the development of naval architecture and the changes would effectively exclude the all-purpose merchantman/man-o'-war. At the start of the fifteenth century the cog or nef was a single-masted, single-decker with only the one square sail. By the close, it had grown into a much larger vessel, possibly three-masted, with a bowsprit, five sails and double-decked. Ordnance had become both heavier, throwing a greater weight of shot, and more effective, capable of doing significant structural damage to an opposing ship. Initially, naval guns were of the cast iron, hoop and stave, breech-loader variant. These were the only guns that could be easily reloaded at sea, firing as they did from a fixed, wooden carriage. The sections of iron were held in place by iron rings or hoops sweated on around the external circumference. Crude carriages were finished with a heavy timber baulk at the breech, which not only held the wedge securing the removable breech, but soaked up the crashing recoil.

This primitive form was superseded late century by an improved design, which featured a series of lengths of iron tubing, the lip being shaped like a cotton bobbin. These were secured together by a series of rings beaten around the barrel at the joints. Nonetheless, these still loaded as before, at the breech. A surviving example, salvaged from the wreck of the Tudor warship the *Mary Rose*, is of this type and the barrel is fitted with lifting rings, probably used to lash it to the frame. As gun-casting techniques improved a wheeled carriage was developed, which greatly facilitated loading from the muzzle. Heavier guns were placed on the main or lower deck and ships sides were now fitted with gun ports, through which the great guns were run out to fire. These heavy deck guns might have a barrel length of 10–13ft (3–4m) and throw a shot weighing 11lb (15kg).

Powder or 'serpentine', was milled from a mix of sulphur, saltpetre and charcoal, being consistent neither in quality or effect. Fifteenth-century gun barrels needed to have strength equal to 80 times the weight of their shot. As milling techniques improved and within a century, this would increase to a ratio of 400. One advantage of a bronze barrel was that it would 'bulge' before bursting, a timely warning for the gunner. Iron was less accommodating, being prone to a sudden, catastrophic burst. On land this was bad, for those like James II, who had the misfortune to be in the immediate vicinity, frequently fatal. At sea it would be worse for powder and flame added greatly to the risk of shipboard fire, a sailor's nightmare.

The plain fact is that sea raiding and privateering were highly profitable activities for successful captains and the niceties of diplomacy could not be allowed to intrude upon such lucrative enterprise. At Bamburgh on the Northumbrian coast, Bishop Kennedy's fine ship *Salvator* came aground in March 1473 and was relieved of her cargo by James Ker, despite his Teviotdale name, an Englishman. It required negotiations spanning a year and a half before James III, who may have been a stakeholder in the vessel, managed to lever any compensation. Gloucester's cog *Mayflower* had taken *The Yellow Carvel*, a ship later to be associated with Andrew Wood of Largo. Sir John Colquhoun of Luss was also despoiled of shipping by Lord Grey. John Barton, brother of Andrew, had one of his vessels taken by Portuguese pirates off Sluys, who stripped the valuable merchandise and murdered a number of those on board.

The war with England of 1481–82 had seen a considerable amount of action at sea. In this, the advantage lay heavily with the English. In 1481 Lord John Howard took his squadron into the Firth of Forth and secured a number of valuable prizes, eight Scottish vessels, taken from Leith, Kinghorn and Pittenweam. He then took up Blackness which was thoroughly spoiled and torched, capturing another and larger vessel. This aggression did not go unopposed for Andrew Wood led a flotilla which engaged the English, apparently giving a very good account of themselves and inflicting numerous losses.

Next year, to support Gloucester's invasion, Sir Richard Radcliffe, an intimate of the duke's who was to rise in his administration, led a second expedition, probably placing his flag on the capital ship, *Grace Dieu*. He was able to occupy Leith and contributed significantly to the English victory on land and the recovery of Berwick – the final time that much beleaguered town was to change hands. Dunbar, an important bastion on the coast of Lothian, was handed over to the English in 1483 by James' traitorous sibling the Duke of Albany and remained in their possession for a couple of years. Being a coastal fortress, the English could rely on their maritime supremacy to facilitate resupply.

Andrew Wood had been rewarded for his zeal in opposing Howard with the feu-charter of Largo, granted in 1483. The king needed Sir Andrew within his affinity. In the campaign which led up to the king's defeat and subsequent death in the spring of 1488, it was Wood's ships, *Yellow Carvel* and *Flower*, which twice transported royal forces across the Firth of Forth and carried the battered survivors back. James may well have been in flight toward these ships when he was overtaken and killed. Each of Sir Andrew's ships was around 300 tons. Sizeable vessels both and he was soon in action again against the English when, in 1489, his squadron took on five English raiders in a brisk engagement off Dunbar and captured them all. Wood was well rewarded for his victory, but Henry VII resented the humiliation of so sharp a reverse and commissioned Stephen Bull, an experienced mariner who commanded three competent vessels, to take up the gauntlet.

Bull took his ships into the Firth of Forth, believing, correctly that Wood, was beating back from Flanders and keeping his squadron well hidden in the lee of the Isle of May. To identify his prey he kidnapped local fishermen who, when sails were sighted were obliged to climb to the topmast and identify the vessels. At first the locals temporised but, with the incentive of their release dangled, confirmed the ships were indeed *The Yellow Carvel* and *Flower*. Confident of success, having numbers and weight of shot on his side, Bull broached a cask and offered his officers an additional stimulus before engaging. Undeterred by the sudden ambush, Wood cleared for action. He was surprised, outnumbered and outgunned, but like his opponent he broke out the grog before the great guns thundered. With the wind steady from the south-east the longer English guns had the advantage. Wood then beat to windward before closing the range to unleash his own broadside.

The fight which followed was both long and hard. In the constricted waters of the Firth there was little scope for extensive manoeuvring and the battle became a slogging match. Both sides sought to grapple and board, pounding each other beforehand. Amidst shrouds of foul, sulphurous smoke, seamen strove to bring the opposing vessels together, cloying air quickened by the rattle of musketry, the crash of spars and rigging as round shot tore through sails and cordage.

Battle continued all day, the combatants, like punch-drunk fighters, lurching into the open sea. Newer weapons, ordnance and handguns were deployed alongside crossbows and broadswords. Guns added to the fury of battle with their diabolical roar and great clouds of filthy, sulphurous smoke. Vast clouds of the stuff, whipping and eddying in the breeze, one minute obscuring the combatants, then lifting as though with the parting of a veil. As the ships closed to grapple and board marines spat bolts and leaden balls from handguns.

Then, it was down to hand strokes. Knots of fighters boiled over gunwale and deck, screams and shouted orders bellowed in the dense-packed melee. No one had anywhere to run, axes, mallets and the lethal thrust of daggers competed in the stricken space. Darkness brought a brief lull, shattered masts and rent sails were cut free and either cobbled together or ditched overboard. Decks were littered with debris from the fight, gunwales, in several instances, awash with gore and spilt entrails, groans of the wounded and dying. In the quiet hours, many a man slipped away and was quietly heaved toward a watery grave.

Next day, trumpets sounded and the great guns thundered again as battered vessels re-joined the fight. As Wellington would have observed, it was a very close run thing. Losses and damage were considerable on both sides but it was Bull's Englishmen who struck their colours. A crowd of Scots had dashed along the shoreline as the battle reached the mouth of the Tay, cheering on the home side! Sir Andrew had wisely stayed to windward, herding the

Englishmen toward the Fife shore, unaware of the risk, till too late, all three of Bull's ships ran aground. The fight was over, the stranded keels boarded and towed in triumph to Dundee. James, delighted with his victory, could afford to be magnanimous and the survivors were repatriated, but only after a spell as forced labour working on coastal defences! Wood survived into a comfortable retirement and even ordered the construction of a canal between his fine house and the parish church so that, as he journeyed to mass he might be conveyed in his barge in a manner befitting so venerable a sea dog.[24]

## To sea – the naval campaign of 1513

We tend to focus on the land campaign in 1513. Obviously this is where the main and most dramatic action occurred but there was also a naval involvement. Since James had developed a maritime capacity this afforded him the opportunity to strike a blow at sea, to reverse the traditional English domination and free the eastern seaboard of Scotland from fear of attack. If James could summon a joint Franco-Scottish fleet with the possibility of additional Danish assistance then he might do much more, destroying English hegemony in the Channel and interdicting Henry's supply line.[25] The English king had antagonised Charles, Duke of Gueldres, James' cousin whilst Hugh O'Donnell of Ulster[26] had, from 25 June 1513, been enlisted as an ally. The Irish earl's main preoccupation appears to have been with war against English garrisons in Ireland, notably the great fortress of Carrickfergus.[27]

As James' biographer points out, possibilities vastly exceeded realisation. The looked-for Danish involvement was little more than a pious hope, dashed for good when King Hans died in February 1513. It is a part of Scotland's tragedy in 1513, that her magnificent ships of war, upon which so much labour and treasure had been lavished, should achieve so little. Men who might have been recruited for land service had to be sent to man the ships; there is a suggestion that service at sea was by no means popular.[28] One who was certainly not laggard was Robert Barton. War provided a handy platform for both revenge and profit. By the time the Scots army was ready to march Barton, sailing his fine new vessel *Lion* of 300 tons, was already lying at the mouth of the Seine, with supplies for a force of seamen and marines totalling 260.[29]

Nor were the French themselves idle. Their own ships were being provisioned, additional sailors and fighting men levied and a full muster of the combined fleet planned for Honfleur, where Louis de Rouville would be appointed as grand admiral of the combined squadrons. Meanwhile, the King of Scots had appointed his cousin Arran[30] to lead his own vessels and those of the privateers into French waters.[31] This involved a circuitous route as English man-o'-war prowled the Downs. When the Scottish ships weighed anchor in the dying days of July, James sailed aboard his flagship *Michael* up to the north coast of Caithness where they bore westwards via Pentland Firth, sweeping down past the Hebrides and England's west coast toward the haven of the Seine.[32]

Despite fair winds, the Scots reached the Seine only in mid-September as Arran had detoured into Belfast Lough to turn his ordnance against the bastion of Carrickfergus. Pitscottie sees this as nothing more than a frolic of his own, and requiring the fleet to return to Ayr for supplies and, presumably, repairs.[33] The king, outraged at such gross insubordination, replaced his wayward cousin with the experienced Sir Andrew Wood, accompanied by Angus who was to act as admiral, presumably under Wood's advice. Arran cannily weighed anchor and made sail for France before his nemesis could catch up.[34] This time the weather proved to be on the side of England and the Scottish fleet was battered by late summer gales as the ships tacked towards the haven of Honfleur.

Norman Macdougall takes the entirely logical view that Arran might in fact have been acting on orders and in pursuance of the earlier agreement with O'Donnell. This seems entirely reasonable but he might have rather botched or extended the diversionary attack, necessitating a return to Ayr. Obviously, attacking Carrickfergus was a legitimate objective in a war against England.[35] Very likely the weather, as is often the case in the Channel, proved the deciding factor both delaying the junction of squadrons and, in September, scattering the combined fleet and frustrating any plans to attack Henry's own ships as he sailed for home a month later.

*Michael*, the pride of James' new navy, ran aground and ended the campaign as a beached footnote. Returning Scots complained of their poor treatment by French allies.[36] The English were not disturbed, nor even mildly deterred. The potential for successful maritime intervention had appeared considerable and James' logic cannot be faulted. As ever, operations at sea are more fraught than campaigning on land, particularly in the age of sail, and the king could not really have expected too much from allies such as the Danes and Irish. Still, the French were clearly serious and the concept of attacking English supply lines was both appealing and strategically sound.

NOTES

1. The Age of Forays was synonymous with internecine violence as the influence of the Lordship disappeared and royal rule through surrogates proved a poor substitute.
2. Pitscottie, *Historie and Cronicles of Scotland*, pp. 226–31.
3. Mingary Castle also survives in a most dramatic coastal location by Ardnamurchan, though at the time of the writer's last visit in 2009, in a rather parlous state.
4. Torquil Macleod of Lewis (*c.* 1460–*c.* 1510), was the principal champion of Donald Dubh – see Macdougall, pp. 175–90.

5. Donald (Domhnall) Dubh (d. 1545) was the grandson of the last Lord of the Isles, John of Islay, Earl of Ross, his doomed life a final knell for the Lordship – see Macdougall, N., 'Achilles Heel: The Earldom of Ross, Lordship of the Isles and the Stewart Kings 1449–1507', in Cowan, E.J. & MacDonald, R.A. (eds), *Alba: Celtic Scotland in the Medieval Era* (Edinburgh, 2000), pp. 248–75.

6. Eilean Donan Castle in Loch Duich is perhaps the most familiar of Highland fortresses; most of what survives dates from the twentieth century however.

7. See Macdougall, pp. 223–46.

8. *Ibid.*, p. 228.

9. *Ibid.*

10. Hector Boece described this vessel as *the biggest that had been seen to sail upon the ocean.*

11. In 1497, Henry VII was diverted from an attack on the East Coast of Scotland by the Cornish Rising.

12. Macdougall, p. 227.

13. *Ibid.*, p. 228.

14. *Ibid.*, pp. 176–95.

15. *Ibid.*, p. 229.

16. *Ibid.*, pp. 230–1.

17. *Ibid.*, p. 233.

18. *Ibid.*

19. *Ibid.*, pp. 236–7.

20. The letter of marque empowered the captain to act as a privateer on behalf of the state, licensed piracy in effect.

21. Macdougall, p. 239.

22. *Ibid.*, p. 241.

23. Hall, *King Henry VIII*, vol. 1, p. 38; the Englishman's account of the fight may be biased, Norman Macdougall thinks so (p. 241) but the essential facts need not be questioned.

24. Pitscottie, *Historie and Cronicles of Scotland* pp. 226–31.

25. Macdougall, p. 266.

26. Knighted by Henry VIII in 1511.

27. Macdougall, pp. 266–7.

28. *Ibid.*, p. 267.

29. *Ibid.*

30. James Hamilton, Earl of Arran, 2nd Lord Hamilton (1475–1529). He had ample experience of naval operations, having commanded those Scottish ships sent to assist Hans of Denmark. Later he cruised the Western Isles during disturbances there and remained active in regency politics.

31. Macdougall, p. 268.

32. *Ibid.*

33. Pitscottie, *Historie and Cronicles of Scotland*, p. 256.

34. Macdougall, p. 269.

35. *Ibid.*

36. *Ibid.*

# 5

# UPON THE SIDE OF A HIGH MOUNTAIN:
## THE SCOTS' INVASION

When the king of England was determined in his high court of Parliament to pass the sea, in proper person, for the recovery of his realm in France, he and his council forgot not the old pranks of the Scots which is ever to invade England when the king is out, or within age.[1]

English and Scots were no strangers to cross-border conflict. They had been intermittently at war for generations. Cross-border alliances and the pernicious customs of the vendetta or 'feid'[2] proliferated. Both sides carried out large-scale, cross-border incursions and this state of enmity had existed since Longshanks first made war on, as he perceived, his rebellious Scottish vassals in 1296. Since the development of English longbow tactics the southerners had generally held the advantage on the field, Dupplin Moor, Halidon Hill, Neville's Cross and Homildon had all been signal triumphs. To counter this, Scottish commanders had generally sought to avoid full-scale encounters and concentrated on a process of attrition.

## King James and his great guns

New infantry tactics were by no means the King of Scots only innovation. James could dispose a formidable artillery train and, whilst big guns had played an increasing role in siege warfare for decades, the king could field a greater weight of shot than any of his predecessors. Guns were now being cast often in bronze, rather than made up from iron sections banded together (a process akin to the manufacture of wooden barrels – (see Appendix Four). Despite these uncertainties, artillery ensured that the tactical advantage in siege warfare had passed from those who built up castles (who had predominated through the earlier centuries), to those who sought to knock them down.

Cast in Flanders, possibly around 1460, a notable survivor from this period is the great bombard 'Mons Meg'. The huge barrel is 13ft 2in (3.95m) in length and the bore measures 19.5in (4.87m). It threw a shot weighing some 549lb (249kg) which is reputed to have carried for a full 2 miles. A tempting, if unlikely, legend asserts that the gun was cast by Molise McKim the hereditary smith of Threave and that the weapon was named after his ferociously tongued wife![3]

This potent train which James had amassed comprised five heavy siege pieces, curtals, throwing a 60lb (27kg) shot, two 18-pounder culverins, four 6-pounder 'culverins pikmoyenne' or 'sakers', and half a dozen 'culverins moyenne', larger versions of English 'serpentines'.[4] Each of these great guns had its team of master gunner, matrosses and drivers, assisted by detachments of pioneers. In charge was Robert Borthwick,[5] the king's proficient gunnery expert and *master meltar*, though a number of his more experienced crews had been detached for service with the fleet and the complement made up from men of lesser capability. By contrast the English, although they could field more guns, could not hope to match the weight of shot. Their pieces were lighter, sakers and serpentines, intended for use in the field rather than the more static continuance of a siege. Nonetheless, Surrey's master gunner, Sir Nicholas Appleyard assisted by William Blackenhall, had a full complement of experienced crews and this greater expertise would, in due course, tell on the field.

It was on 24 July that King James ordered a general muster or levy, in accordance with prevailing feudal custom. His proclamation required that all those between the ages of 16 and 60 be ready within twenty days with supplies for twice as long.[6] Having issued the summons the king dispatched his herald, Lyon King of Arms[7] to deliver his ultimatum to Henry in France. Clearly this was mere formality and the dogs of war were already unleashed (see below). As the Scots levies began their mass muster on the Burghmuir of Edinburgh[8] from around the middle of August, some chroniclers estimated their numbers as high as 60,000. This is almost certainly a wild exaggeration and their actual strength was, most probably, rather less than half that. Home's borderers, at least 6,000–7,000 strong did not muster outside the capital but upon their own march, from where they initiated the first strike, a major probing raid that was to come rather badly unstuck.

Magnates and some of the gentry would be encased in fine plate, complete harnesses most probably from Flanders or Italy; contemporary illustrations show these armours as being more popular than the elegantly fluted German style. By contrast, the English army would have presented a far more traditional image, most of its soldiers resembling their fathers and grandfathers who'd fought in the Wars of the Roses and, in many cases, bearing the arms their forbears had handed down. A majority were raised by the system of contract or indenture. The royal purse also provided 'travelling expenses' at the rate of 8 pence for every 20 miles the soldier travelled to begin campaigning.

It is probable that something in the region of 80 per cent of the English army was raised by contract.[9] A great number, perhaps a third of the whole, served the Stanleys,[10] leading magnates of Lancashire and Cheshire. More were drawn from Yorkshire, perhaps 10,000 and a lesser number, perhaps a fifth of that, from Durham.[11] Thomas Howard, the Lord Admiral was able to contribute a full battalion of marines, perhaps 1,200 strong, from the fleet. In terms of appearance, this army could have fought for Lancaster or York, ranked in companies of bows and bills. The magnates would sport fine plate in the latest fashion, similar to their Scottish counterparts. Many of the lesser gentry and men-at-arms would be wearing more venerable armours, equipped with the older sallet. The humbler rank and file would either go unarmoured or rely on a brigandine with kettle hat or simple sallet.

In the years after the English debacle at Bannockburn, Edward III, angrily frustrated by the failure of mounted chivalry during the abortive Weardale campaign of 1327,[12] recognised the need to suit troop types to the terrain. Hobilars, known later in the reign of Henry VIII as the Border Horse and later still as the Steel Bonnets, were present in both armies. For these uplanders war was now a way of life. Mounted on swift, hardy garrons, lightly armoured with mail or 'jakke',[13] favouring the lance borderers acted as scouts, or 'prickers' and skirmishers for both sides. Their performance on the field was not calculated to win plaudits. Local alliances and the lure of loot, regardless of which side they plundered, considerably outweighed any exaggerated notion of patriotic fervour. Their cynicism was justified as inhabitants could be sure that whoever won on the field, the loser's borderlands would suffer accordingly.

## The Ill-Rode

A righteous judgement of God upon these barbarous wretches!

Oliver Cromwell

It was Home who struck the first blow, crossing the border on 13 August with some 3,000 riders.[14] In part his raid is said to be in response to an English incursion.[15] The warden was an old hand at this and torched seven settlements or vills. Many towers were still derelict or semi-derelict after the invasion of 1497, yet Home and his scavengers knew how to pick over any half-decent carcass and they'd soon amassed a haul. This did not go unchallenged. Surrey had anticipated such a move and sent a flying column of 200 archers north from Doncaster under Sir William Bulmer. It was his intention these would simply stiffen the local gentry but in fact they formed a nucleus for a small field force, perhaps 1,000 marchers who set up an ambush; bowmen concealed among tall broom covering Millfield Plain.

Home, for all his experience, rode straight into the trap and, before his riders had time to react, a hail of arrows emptied scores of saddles. The fight was still a hard one but the Scots were finally routed. As many as 500 fell, nearly as many taken captive. Home just escaped, leaving his standard and his brother, Sir George, in the hands of the victors.[16] English losses were perhaps a tenth of those of their vanquished adversaries. Most of the loot and livestock, including a fine herd of geldings was recovered: first blood to England.

It would seem that Surrey relied upon Dacre as his local spymaster, indeed espionage was very much one of the warden's functions. Hall tells us that the Cumbrian informed his commander of 'the numbering and preparing of men in Scotland'.[17] Cannily, Dacre goes on to advise that though Home's abortive raid was a clear breach of the prevailing truce Surrey should, for the moment, abstain from a wholesale muster of the marchers:

... lest if the Scots had perceived the English ready to fight they would have refrained from their purposes at that time, till the Englishmen were all returned to their regions, then suddenly appear again.[18] Thus, according to Hall, King James' muster began to swell by the day ... and assembled his people over all his realm, whereof the talk was they were two hundred thousand, but for sure there was a hundred thousand good fighting men at the least.[19]

## On the matter of numbers overall

The King of Scots had now marshalled an enormous host. However, the levy restricted the conscripts to forty days service and, during that time, they were expected to provide their own foodstuffs. On campaign, supply inevitably proved problematic. Once hunger bit, individual fighters were likely to disperse to forage or simply desert. We are unfortunate in that the Household Accounts from August 1513 to June 1515 are lost so that an exact tally is impossible. To this uncertainty must be added the discrepancy between those who were called out and who actually fought on the day. Many of these were the personal retainers and affinities of the magnates and as such would be less prone to defection.

Now to the chroniclers, the *Trewe Encountre* and Edward Hall both claim the Scottish host numbered 100,000. Thomas Howard, the Lord Admiral in his official dispatch (*Articles of Battle*), claims 80,000, still far too high and smacking more of politics than military reality. A contemporary letter, written by Brian Tuke to Richard Pace, reduces the claim to 60,000, a figure echoed by Polydore Vergil. Writing in the eighteenth century, George Ridpath says there were 60,000–100,000 Scots on the field.[20] Scottish writers of the sixteenth century, however, are more modest in their assessments: Buchanan says the Scots numbered no more than 15,000, Pitscottie gives double that figure; some twentieth-century Scots authorities maintain these much lower numbers.

Numbers for the English army are easier to quantify as the muster rolls apparently survived. Hall and most of the sixteenth-century authors agree on 26,000, only Vergil puts the English numbers at 30,000, Ridpath concurs with the lower figure. Respected military historians writing in the last thirty years, such as Donald Featherstone and Charles Kightly, plump for 40,000 Scots and 26,000–30,000 English. The matter cannot be satisfactorily resolved but we may assume that, with the English, most of those who mustered at Bolton in Glendale near Alnwick fought on the field.

The Scots remain more problematic. Sickness and desertion will have accounted for numbers of those who mustered on the Burghmuir and in the borders by Ellam Kirk. Peter Reese suggests that the proportion might be as high as 25 per cent. It is, of course, not possible to say. The campaign in the north of England to be initiated by the Scots in 1513 was recognised by both sides as a sideshow, essentially an attempt by the Scots to divert English troops from the main effort across the Channel and directed at assisting their allies the French. It is the supreme irony of Flodden that the sideshow would yield a decisive and bloody denouement whilst the vaunted continental campaign would achieve little beyond a minor English win in the rather overblown 'Battle of the Spurs' or Guingattes, fought on 16 August.

Surrey had been dismayed and angered that his role in the coming campaign should be limited to what he initially perceived as a police action on the inhospitable northern frontier whilst the spoils and honours accrued in France. Edward Hall expresses the matter rather more tactfully:

> And when the king should take ship at Dover, he took the Earl [Surrey] by the hand and said, my lord, I trust not the Scots, therefore I pray you be not negligent: then said the earl I shall so do my duty that Your Grace shall find me diligent and to fulfil your wish shall be my gladness.[21] Howard was less respectful toward his potential Scottish adversary: Sorry may I see him or I die, that is cause of my abiding behind, and if ever he and I meet, I shall do what lies in me to make him as sorry as I can.[22]

The earl was to make good his promise.

Henry regarded his brother-in-law's likely intervention as no more than an irritation, a distraction from the decisive results he anticipated in Northern France. In the event the Holy League was to prove the flimsiest of alliances and any gains negligible. Most of the dying was done in Northumberland. The English plans, therefore, were entirely defensive in nature. Surrey simply sought to prevent the Scots from conducting a large-scale raid into Northern England with impunity. He would also have been concerned over the security of Norham and, even more importantly, Berwick. During the campaign James made no overt move to attack this, the most important of the eastern border fortresses, but recovery of Berwick would have been bound to feature in his future planning.

## King Henry campaigns in France

By the later part of April the opening salvoes, delivered by the English fleet, had been fired in King Henry's campaign. This proved inauspicious because an engagement off Brittany cost Edward Howard his life, a misjudged feat of vainglory delivered with typical Howard panache. Thomas Howard, appointed in his brother's stead, stood ready but contrary winds kept his vessels confined to harbour. By the end of June both the van and rearguard of Henry's land forces were safely over the Channel, commanded respectively by the Earl of Shrewsbury and Lord Herbert.[23] Gleaming in burnished harness, Henry himself stepped ashore at Calais on the evening of 30 June. Like his grandfather, Edward IV, 'the Sunne in Splendour', he had arrived, with full pomp of chivalry, to reclaim the ancient right of his Plantagenet ancestors in France. Riding his warhorse, the king proceeded through the thronged streets to offer thanks to God for a safe arrival and in the hope the Almighty might look favourably upon his cause.[24]

He was not alone, for a vast retinue, including Wolsey himself, the highly efficient universal fixer of the king's affairs, followed by a glittering retinue of magnates came ashore as well. Surrey, remaining in England, for all his loyal protestations, must have been consumed by bitter gall. For where else should a Howard be than by the king's side, ready to share the hazard and glory of war? What hopes for such renown might be found in merely acting the sheriff against the despised Scots? By leaving the Howards to command available manpower from the northern shires Henry was following established custom. For two centuries, no king of England had raised his standard in France without first securing the back door. Opportunistic moves from Scottish kings had generally broken against this tried rampart of bows, bills and border lances. It had not entered Henry's calculation or Wolsey's that his royal campaign might ironically prove to be the sideshow after all and it was 'Dad's Army' and the marchers who would scoop the laurels that year.

When, on 21 July, the English marched from Calais the men received only a miserable drenching, any other evidence of God's approbation was absent. Henry's objective was the town of Therouanne in Artois, a relatively modest objective. By the time the English began their siege, August and blistering heat had arrived. The march, no more than 40 miles, had been enlivened by some aggressive moves from the French but, though the king hopefully deployed his forces in full battle array, his enemy proved disinclined. King Henry's lavish pavilions provided a suitable background for the king to welcome his ally the Emperor Maximilian who came fully armed with flattery, if little else. The emperor offered to place himself plus the threadbare force he'd brought, beneath Henry's banners and serve under him for the duration of the operation, a small price for a gain that could offer him rather a lot and Henry remarkably little.[25]

As he lay before the walls, Henry received via James' Herald, Lyon King of Arms, correspondence by way of an ultimatum. This could not have been entirely unexpected and Hall includes the full text in his narrative. James upbraids his brother-in-law for the numerous wrongs done to him, the failure to apprehend Bastard Heron, withholding Queen Margaret's legacy, the killing of Andrew Barton and now this invasion of France. 'Therefore we write to you this time at length with plain speaking and desire you to desist from further invasion and utter destruction of our brother and cousin the most Christian King'.[26]

Henry wasted no time in sending an urgent copy to Surrey for here was proof of James' intentions. He also penned a reply to his brother-in-law in terms that were scarcely conciliatory. He denied any of James' allegations and rehearsals of previous wrongs, though there was no question that he had improperly withheld his sister's portion of her father's estate which was clearly due to her. The matters of the Bartons and Heron were perhaps rather greyer in texture. His response in relation to the nub of their differences, the invasion of France was unequivocal:

> Finally, at touching upon your request we desist from further attempts against our enemy the French king, we know you for no competent judge of so high authority to require us in that behalf; wherefore God willing, we purpose with the aid and assistance of our confederates and allies to prosecute the same ...[27]

This was a declaration of war. Henry also wrote to Queen Katherine as regent charging her with responsibility for defending the homeland 'to prepare in all haste for defence of [against] the said king of Scots'.[28]

Henry had also delivered a stinging riposte to the Scottish herald lambasting James 'for we never esteemed him to be of any truth and so now we have found it, for notwithstanding his oath, his promise in the word of a king ... yet now he has broken his faith and promise to his great dishonour and infamy for ever'.[29] In case this was not sufficiently inflammatory, Henry went on to remind his brother-in-law that; 'I am the very owner of Scotland, and that he holds it of me by homage, and in so much as now contrary to his bounden duty he, being my vassal, rebels against me'.[30] If anything could be guaranteed to raise the ire of the Scottish king it was this ancient contention of feudal superiority, the 'Great Cause' which had seen so much blood spilt already.

On 16 August, a body of French horse, aiming at a relief, blundered onto the guns of the Allied force and was scattered by shot. Jubilant English and Burgundian cavaliers sped in pursuit. There was no real battle as such, a mere skirmish, though a profitable one as the haul of captives was impressive, including several magnates. Some days later, on 24 August, the town submitted. This insignificant brush was dubbed the 'Battle of the Spurs' and, such as it was, proved Henry's only triumph. An interesting footnote is provided by Edward Hall for Henry, like his brother-in-law, was anxious to lead his men in person but allowed himself to be dissuaded – 'the king would fain have been at the front with his horsemen, but his advisers persuaded him to the contrary, so he remained with the foot, accompanied by the Emperor'.[31] It would have been better for Scotland had James been willing to heed such sage advice.

Therouanne was duly handed over to the emperor and Henry moved on to a fittingly royal welcome from the citizens of Lille before advancing his banners towards the next strategic objective, the town of Tournai. Maximilian had razed Therouanne as a warning against obstinacy and Tournai lowered its colours after a mere eight days. Outwardly, this was a substantial prize and one destined to remain in English hands, like Calais a balcony for further offensive operations. Henry's exertions were crowned with success and yet real strategic gains were meagre and the king was no nearer his expressed goal of winning the Crown of France. He was indeed strutting upon the European stage though the drain on his treasury was prodigious and he was acting as little more than the tool of mercurial allies.

Tournai fell on 24 September, fifteen days after Flodden and by which time the extent of Surrey's great victory was known. After tumultuous celebrations, amidst all the pageantry of chivalry, ably and as ever organised by the industrious Wolsey, King Henry departed, firstly to Lille, thence to Calais and finally back to England. His campaign had been conducted in a blaze of ostentation and pomp, seasoned with a fair measure of hot air. The emperor had done rather well all round and for precious little outlay. Henry had conducted an outwardly successful campaign but one which had gobbled up his father's carefully hoarded resources and achieved nothing of strategic value. Meanwhile, those cold and hungry footsloggers, from their drab northern shires, had added great lustre to English arms and destroyed the most powerful host ever to sweep south of the border. This was not quite the outcome Henry had intended. We have to wonder how Wolsey now regarded his downgrading of the Howards!

## King James' plan of campaign

James IV of Scotland had achieved a great deal for his country in terms of economic growth, administrative and constitutional reform; the increasing centralisation of power, the navy and the arts. He had, however, never won a major victory in the field. To do so would set the seal on his reign; prove him to be the very model of Machiavelli's Renaissance prince. Not only would this be a significant coup on the purely domestic front and curb the ever-present fissiparous tendencies of his magnates but would mightily impress allies and secure a place on that glittering, wider stage of European politics.

It was not necessary for James to fight in order to secure his strategic aims. His artillery was swiftly able to reduce Norham, which had successfully defied him previously, and the mere presence of large Scottish forces in Northumberland would be sufficient to draw Surrey northward. If we accept that the earl's army numbered around 26,000 at the outset, a very substantial force by the standards of the day, James' intervention denied use of all of these men to Henry even if, as was the custom, the northern shires were never depleted in order to be ready to deal with any Scots' aggression. Nonetheless, the wage bill for Surrey's force was substantial, providing a further drain on the king's coffers which, if thanks to his father's parsimony were amply stocked, were not bottomless.

Given the scale of the forces deployed across the Channel, James may have considered, as has been suggested, that all that remained were *millers and mass priests*. It is unlikely the King of Scots would have so underrated the potential of the northern army or Surrey's capacity for dynamic action but he would have been justified in thinking that this army was essentially 'second best'. If he could fight on favourable ground where these new tactical doctrines could be properly employed then there was clear prospect of victory. Whether James deliberately courted battle or whether it was forced upon him must remain a matter of debate. There can be little doubt that his enthusiasm exceeded that of his nobles, only too well aware of past catastrophes.

Once Norham and almost certainly Wark castles had been secured then a logistical corridor across the Tweed several miles wide had been satisfactorily opened. The subsequent taking of Etal Ford and perhaps Twizel (see Appendix Four) covered the eastern flank of the invasion whilst the west was secured by impassable ground. When he then occupied and fortified Flodden Edge, James had created a strategic 'box' secured in depth. This was, of course, entirely prudent and we will argue that his careful digging of works at Flodden shows the influence of continental advisers.

This does not advance our understanding of the key question of whether it was his intention to fight a battle. We tend to the view that it was not his *prime* objective. As in any campaign, a successful commander has to be aware of opportunities as they arise and James would have been negligent had he not provided for such an opportunity should it present itself. In the past, as in 1497, he had shied away from confrontation when the possible outcome was very uncertain. That he was ready to fight if put to it, or if the English were sufficiently foolish as to attempt an assault on his inexpugnable position, made sound sense.

However sound his tactical doctrine appeared, the plain fact remained that James had never commanded an army in battle and the Scots still had bad memories from previous encounters. Nonetheless, the aphrodisiac of martial glory beckoned. James was neither rash nor reckless but he must have considered that his host was more than a match for any scratch force that Surrey could muster. With the pride of English chivalry in France, this opposition would be the residue rather than the substance of English might. To win a victory in plain field was a dazzling prospect. None other could ensure James' place within the pantheon of Scottish heroes or more pointedly win him a seat in the counsels of Europe. Success in war brought rewards both at home and abroad.

In practical terms, triumph in battle would expose the whole of northern England, an opportunity not witnessed since the halcyon days of Scottish military hegemony after Bannockburn. Norham would be secured and Berwick threatened. In strategic terms, Surrey's defeat would frustrate the main effort in France and surely force Henry to withdraw (please refer to *Map 1* for details of the invasion route). Popular pressure in England would demand that English arms concentrate on a retaliatory strike against the Scots, by now withdrawn over the border. James may even have envisaged a return to those remarkable times (from the Scottish perspective) when King Robert's able captains Douglas and Randolph had held the whole of northern England to ransom, maintaining hostilities at the enemy's expense.

If James chose not to fight and simply withdraw as he'd done sixteen years earlier, Surrey would be obliged to withdraw as weather deteriorated and his wage bill mounted. If the earl did attempt to mount a counter raid James could adopt the tactics of his predecessors, scorched earth and harrying the flanks. Let the English sweep through the Lothians, as they'd done so many times before, until hunger and dysentery compelled their withdrawal. It was just this eventuality that Surrey had to contain. His task was an unenviable one. It would be difficult for him to keep his forces in the field beyond the end of summer. Northumberland lacked the infrastructure and resources to support so large a host indefinitely. From a logistical viewpoint Surrey had to chastise the Scots as soon as ever possible. He had, from the outset, to accept the hazard of battle as the only sure means of doing so. For him there was never any other course open.

He would be aware how easy it would be for James to simply march his host back over the border. The English had not the means to mount a counter invasion. The Scots could then re-appear at the border when the English army had dispersed. A successful engagement was therefore the only means whereby Surrey could ensure the safety of the north, nothing less would remove the threat. When contemporary accounts fail us, as they do in relation to this campaign, we are forced to fall back upon Colonel Burne's theory of 'inherent military probability'. That is to say, what would a sensible commander of troops do in such a situation? This is not entirely satisfactory and tends to be disfavoured by academic authors. Nonetheless, those current writers who have focused on the battle including Charles Kightly (1975), Niall Barr (2001), Peter Reese (2003), and the present writer (2006) broadly agree.

As a general Scots-muster appeared imminent, Surrey, in mid-July, could not afford to be idle; nor was he. By 12 July, grain was being shipped up to Newcastle, intended as base of operations. This great northern city was the natural choice and had been a jumping-off point for many previous expeditions from the reign of Edward I onwards. Victorious Yorkists had used the city as a base for their campaigns against the Lancastrian–held border fortresses from 1461–64. A major port, foodstuffs and munitions could be sent ahead by ship rather than dragged over rutted highways.

Already the citizens of Berwick, in English hands since 1482, were becoming nervous and soliciting resources to put their much-tried walls in defensible order. Ominously, their Scottish neighbours in the Merse were seen to be moving livestock and valuables, invariably a sure portent of impending conflict. The earl first summoned his immediate retinue, 500 strong and drawn from his own East Anglian estates. Individual companies were officered by captains on 4s (25p) a day, assisted by junior or petty captains. Those heavy horse who rode with the colours earned 1s 6d (7½p), light cavalry, 'demi-lances' were paid 9d (3½p), the rump of the foot, 446 strong, comprising bows and bills and liveried in the white and green of the Tudors, received 8d (3p) per day. To assist him in his role of commander-in-chief, Surrey had an HQ staff of thirty-nine.[32]

His younger son Edmund was appointed as Marshal of the Host. The earl would also, in due course, be joined by his elder surviving son, the Lord Admiral. This was to be very much a Howard dominated army. Rouge Croix was to be the English Herald and the logistical 'tail' included six trumpeters, joiners and clerks. Sir Nicholas Appleyard[33] would command the ordnance which would comprise twenty-two great guns, eighteen of which were 2-pounders or 'falcons' and the remainder 5- or 6-pounder serpentines. Although the English train could not match the Scots for weight of shot these lighter field pieces were, by virtue of their manoeuvrability, far more suited to counter battery work than the heavy siege guns. Appleyard and his Clerk of the Ordnance, William Blackenhall, also had a full complement of trained and experienced crews.[34]

James would have been aware that England had not been completely denuded of defenders. It seems unlikely, therefore, that he would have been tempted to express the measure of contempt attributed to him:

> There's none at home left in the land but jault head monks and bursten freers,
> or ragged rustics without rules or priests prating for pudding strives or millners

madder than their mules, or wanton clerks waking their wives. There's not a lord left in England, but all are gane beyond the sea, both knight and baron with his band with ordinance or artillery.[35]

The king may have sought to boost his army's morale by denigrating the worth of likely opposition but neither he nor his magnates would be so blind.

James knew Surrey of old and he would have no illusions about the vigour of the English response. If he was to seek a precedent the dire consequences of David II's intervention in 1346 should have been sufficient warning. The Scottish king, in support of his French ally, defeated at Crecy, invaded northern England in an autumn chevauchee. He proceeded on the belief that the country was denuded of able-bodied defenders. He was much surprised therefore to be boldly confronted by a northern army, just west of Durham. The Scots were utterly defeated and the king himself captured. This King of Scots could, with reason, believe his train to be superior and he had confidence in the ability of his lords and their French advisers to instil new battle winning tactics into raw Scots levies. As the king gave orders for a general muster, 'each man made haste to mend his gear ... some made their battle axes bright ... some from their bills did rub the rust some made long pikes and lances bright'.[37]

By 25 July the Scottish fleet had weighed anchor to join with the French, the most impressive armada ever assembled in Scottish waters including the two capital ships *Michael* and *Margaret*. This was the king's play for a seat in the great councils of Europe, a daring and ambitious strategy. Whether subsequent tales of dire warnings given to the king are apocryphal, these may well reflect concerns of the magnates that their monarch might commit to battle at the earliest opportunity. One of the more enduring tells of a seer who approached James whilst at his devotions in the chapel at Linlithgow: 'Thou wilt [he advised the king] not fare well in thy journey nor none that passes with thee ... meddle with no women nor use their counsel, not let them touch they body nor thou theirs, for and thou do it thou wilt be confounded and brought to shame'.[37] It is suggested this was probably a ruse brought on by the queen and the anti-war faction, an idea supported by Pitscottie.

By late July or perhaps early in August, a cadre of forty French captains, under the Sieur D'Aussi had disembarked at Dumbarton; to them would fall the unenviable task of training the Scots in pike drill.[38] The bulk of these valuable supplies arrived too late to be deployed in the forthcoming campaign. Time was the commodity which both James and his new instructors lacked. To create pikemen as disciplined, hardy and ferocious as the Swiss took months of training, this on an assumption that the requisite will was present and no such assumption could be made of the Scottish conscripts.

Not only was the training schedule impossibly tight but the Scots' formations would be deficient in those supporting arms upon which the Swiss relied so heavily: a commanded body of halberdiers. The Swiss halberd being akin to the English bill, these were positioned within the pike block to deal with any dangerous obstructions, to aid their hefty swordsmen in softening up an enemy line, scything a bloody swathe. Crossbowmen and hand-gunners to mount guard upon the exposed flanks and pick off targets of opportunity were also lacking.

From the 13–20 August the levies mustered on the Burghmuir whilst the borderers began assembling by Ellem Kirk near Duns.[39] On the 17th, as these musters swelled toward their full complement, the great guns were removed from Edinburgh Castle and placed on their carriages. By next day, some were ready for the hard journey south, the rest following on the 20th. By then the army had already marshalled for the march, passing through Dalkeith to collect the border contingent, prior to crossing the Tweed, sweeping Rubicon of border conflict.

The Scots with all of their ordnance, baggage and inevitable swollen tail of ragged camp followers must have presented an unforgettable sight as they marched; proud panoply of knightly pennons fluttering in a light summer breeze, the tramp of many thousands of men trailing eighteen–foot shafts of the 'puissant' pike. In their wake, gasping in the great clouds of dust given off, scores of tradesmen, pedlars, whores and drovers. At their head, the magnificent figure of James IV, King of Scots, his surcoat, with fashionably slashed sleeves and embroidered with the royal arms. Around his neck, a beautifully wrought gold collar and, on his finger, the turquoise ring sent by Queen Anne.[40]

## The Scots march

We are but warriors for the working day;
Our gayness and our gilt are all besmirch'd
With rainy marching in the painful field.

Shakespeare, *Henry V*

This was to be the largest field army Scotland had ever mustered. It possessed a magnificent artillery train and had been drilled in tactics that could inflict a crushing defeat on any English army. James had placed great faith in his French captains but their task was an unenviable one. Raw levies were not Swiss pikemen and a few weeks drill could not hope to equal years of hard training. However, they were as ready as they could be. The Scots had, of course, traditionally relied upon spear-armed schiltrons, perhaps not so very different from the phalanx. Indeed, Swiss generals would have nodded approvingly at Bruce's plan of attack at Bannockburn, virtually a textbook precedent.

We have seen that James' herald Lyon King at Arms had already, on 11 August, delivered James' final ultimatum to his brother-in-law at the leaguer of Therouanne. Henry treated this threat with typical sangfroid, indifferent to the power of the Scots to intervene and trusting, as previous monarchs before him, the northern army to counter any invasion. Could James imagine that Henry would withdraw? Clearly this was not within the bounds of expectation. An invasion of the north promised no more than to attract the attentions of a northern army which was not otherwise destined to form part of the effort across the Channel. James was not therefore diverting forces from the French campaign. He might force Henry to further deplete his overstretched treasury by spending a deal more on soldiers' pay but he was unlikely to have any effect upon his brother-in-law's overall strategy.

The reasoning behind James' decision to invade was pure policy, a statement of intent that would cleave him to the King of France and win a seat on the councils of Europe. He did not show any intention of seeking to recover Berwick, clearly unrealistic whilst Surrey remained undefeated. A victory in the field would, however, almost certainly force Henry to abandon his continental project and seek a resolution on the border. James has been heavily criticised for his forward and aggressive leadership. There can be no doubt he craved martial glory, the aim of every Renaissance prince. In this, he was no different from his brother-in-law.

Nonetheless, his subsequent decision to 'lead from the front' was by no means entirely foolish or reckless in view of the nature of the army he was leading. Scotland was not a unified state. The Highlands had long evinced fissiparous tendencies and the borderers had a lengthy history of rugged individualism. To function, the army needed a vibrant figurehead. None other than the king himself could supply this. James has been compared unfavourably to Robert the Bruce at Bannockburn who retained tactical control throughout. Bruce did, however, possess the inestimable advantage of commanding an army that was both tried and tested and he had a number of vastly experienced and reliable subordinates in whom he could trust absolutely. James did not.

## The Earl of Surrey begins his muster

On 21 July Surrey had mustered his retinue at Lambeth and, next day, led them out through Bishopsgate onto the long north road. This was one he'd travelled many times and did so now, boiling with resentment against the King of Scots whose intermeddling he perceived had denied him his rightful place by Henry's side in France. In reality his exclusion probably owed much to Wolsey's politicking. By 1 August the earl had passed Doncaster and established temporary headquarters at Pontefract,[41] one of the chief fortresses in the north. Here he formed a council of war and marked out a network of north/south, trans-Pennine staging posts and relays that were soon carrying his summons to the northern gentry. He ordered his artillery train with its attendant supplies of powder and shot to proceed north initially to Durham and from there on to Newcastle. It is difficult to assess the relative mettle of the two commanders. Surrey was, of course, much older and also more experienced. This shows throughout the latter stages of the campaign and the final advance to contact. His flanking march is a masterstroke. But what of leadership, that indefinable spark that marks a true leader of men? This matter of charisma is the very essence of command. Correlli Barnet calls this a *psychological force* which he defines as separate from morals or ideals, a matter of will; 'a process by which a single aim and unified action are imported to the herd'. It would seem that Surrey, insofar as the limited sources can guide us, is possessed of this. Whether the same may be said of James is less clear, though his difficulties arise from inexperience, not lack of capacity.

Whilst we cannot, from the scanty chronicle evidence, establish a clear picture of Surrey's intentions at this stage we may be confident that he would be ready to offer battle to any Scots army that crossed the border. More than ready perhaps, for only a decisive victory in the field would compensate for the missed opportunities in France. Despite his age, very considerable for the period, and his numerous ills, the earl was both vigorous and determined in his outlook. He was to have two of his sons at his side and, if he could bring on a general engagement against the Scots, the Howard clan might yet win some glory and confound such jealous parvenus as Wolsey!

## The siege and fall of Norham Castle

Home's defeat offered an ill omen but, on 22 August, the main Scots army crossed the Tweed at Coldstream. Estimates of their numbers vary considerably. Allowing for the inevitable minor casualties, sick list and desertions beforehand, it may be that the army which crossed the Tweed numbered over 40,000, still a vast array. The first night was spent encamped by Twizelhaugh, the army's flanks protected by the waters of both Tweed and Till. The reduction of Norham was the Scots' first objective, the 'Queen of Border Fortresses', pride of the Prince Bishops, whose stout walls had defied James sixteen years earlier. The castellan, John Anislow, believed himself to be ready; his garrison could hold out until Surrey arrived with the relief.

Built in the early twelfth century by Bishop Flambard as a timber motte and bailey, the great stone bastion which was raised on the site by Bishop Hugh de Puisset, one of the most prolific builders amongst the Prince Bishops,[42] comprised both inner and outer baileys, the latter defended by a moat.[43] Much of this early work, particularly the enormous pile of the great keep, survived later alterations. The site itself forms a superb defensive location, standing high above the steeply rising banks of Tweed, dwarfing the pleasant settlement below, latterly immortalised in luminous oils by Turner. The original western gatehouse was sealed up at one stage but opened in the fifteenth century when a barbican was added.[44]

Norham had withstood a series of earlier sieges, most recently and notably of course in 1497, and its defenders remained confident. This was to prove misplaced for the great fortress was essentially of medieval construction, ill-suited to withstand bombardment – so great a train as King James was bringing had never before been seen on the border. Anislow, the castellan, had confidently bragged to Surrey that 'he prayed God that the king of Scots would come with his puissance [power] for he could defend the castle indefinitely till the time that the king of England came from France to its relief'.[45]

This braggadocio reassured Surrey who was anxious not to hazard so vital a bastion – 'which answer rejoiced the earl much'.[46] Regrettably so, for the English castellan was rather over optimistic in his assessment, even though Bishop Ruthal had steadily been building up reserves of powder and shot. This reassurance dissuaded Surrey from marching directly northward for, had Anislow appeared less certain, the earl would have ensured as he had sixteen years prior, that the relief of Norham became his first priority.

Scottish batteries were initially laid at Ladykirk bank on the north side of the Tweed. Their weight of shot vastly exceeded that available to the besiegers in 1497. These great guns pulverised the western gatehouse and punched a breach through a length of curtain wall running parallel to the river. Gunners having declared the entry practicable, the fortress was then subjected to infantry assault. Though the attackers gained the outer ward their attempts on the inner ring were repulsed. James was anxious to secure the prize. Perhaps, here we see evidence of his inexperience, launching costly attacks and squandering lives when the business was best left to his gunners.

Ancient walls, great square keep rising above, wreathed in smoke, acrid sulphurous odours choking damp summer air. Waves of Scottish foot, long pikes levelled would be flung into the breaches. Their gunners would aim to collapse the wall from the base and outwards so clattering rubble formed a ramp for the foot. For their part the defenders would seek to seal off the entry as soon as possible and defend the gap with every ounce of their resolve.

It would be bloody and exhausting work for both sides, broken stones soon slippery with spilled blood.

Nonetheless, after five days of intensive bombardment and three major attacks 'three great assaults three days together',[47] the garrison found themselves critically short of powder and missiles. Anislow, on 29 August, felt obliged to capitulate whilst his men could still expect the courtesies of war. Hall believed Anislow's profligacy with his ammunition stocks was to blame for the disaster: 'he spent vainly so much of his ordnance, bows and arrows and other munitions that at the last he lacked, and so was, on the sixth day, compelled to yield upon the King's mercy'.[48] The defeated castellan found himself a prisoner of war, packed off to Falkland Palace in Fife whilst the victorious Scots stripped his former charge with all of their customary zeal and thoroughness. Furniture, tapestries and liquor; all spoils went to the victors.[49]

This, for the Scots, was a signal success. Norham was a long sought-after prize and its fall exposed the whole eastern flank of North Northumberland. There is a tale, again probably a later invention, which credits an English traitor who, once suborned, advised the Scots where best to lay their ordnance, moving the guns from Ladykirk to the east of the fortress. The king rewarded such duplicity with a rope's end. Appropriately, the supposed second site for the batteries is known as 'hangman's land'. The fortress was stripped and sacked but not slighted. For Surrey, this was both a disaster and humiliation. Norham was the key to the marches, its fall left the door wide open and its fall enabled James to ravage North Northumberland at will 'this chance was more sorrowful to the Earl [of Surrey] than to the Bishop [of Durham], owner of the same'.[50] The bishop did write to Wolsey, however, averring that his grief was inconsolable.[51]

Taking Norham changed the strategic picture. In 1497 James had prudently withdrawn having failed to capture the castle. And indeed why not, what gains were there to fight for? Now it was different, a significant prize had been won and this rendered the hazard of battle more logical. Having secured and slighted Norham (gatehouses and walls were demolished to render the fortress useless), Wark may have fallen without a fight soon after. Next, the Scots advanced along the east bank of the Till taking up those lesser holds of firstly Etal and then Ford, both of which were eventually also slighted.

Given that mighty Norham had proved so vulnerable, these lesser border and manorial castles likely fell like ripe fruit. James remained encamped around the latter from 1–5 September. Yet another apocryphal tale attaches to an alleged liaison with the beautiful Lady Heron whose home the Scots were about to despoil. Her unfortunate husband was a miserable hostage in the grim, sea-girt tower of Fast Castle, a surety for the unruly behaviour of his half-brother, the notorious Bastard, whose numerous outrages included the un-avenged killing of the Scottish warden.

Although it was now high summer the weather was damply autumnal, a spur to sickness and desertion; 'for there had been not one fair day, nor scarce an hour of fair weather all the time the Scots army had lain within England but great cold, wind and rain'.[52] Numbers of clansmen and likely more than a few Lowland levies, having garnered sufficient loot or insufficiently fired by patriotic zeal, were slipping away. Dysentery and plague stalked the lines, almost inevitable companions of armies on campaign.

Prior to the fall of Ford, the lady had appealed to Surrey for relief. As the earl was not yet in a position to offer material assistance he wrote to James undertaking to waive ransoms on a number of captive Scottish gentry (see below) if Ford was left intact. No compromise was entertained and the castle was slighted. The Scottish chronicler Robert Lindsay of Pitscottie, a dour Calvinist writing with the austerity of the reformed church and no fan of James, spreads the tale of the king's dalliance with Lady Heron, a bout of 'stinking adultery and fornication'.[53]

There is no real basis at this time for any criticism of James' conduct. His primary mission was to force a large body of English troops to concentrate in the north and this was already in train. Whether Henry might have wished these men with him in France is, in part irrelevant; the presence of a large, unchecked Scottish army on the loose in North Northumberland was sufficient to detain them. To achieve his objective of tying down big numbers of English soldiery did not require James to advance further into England. For the moment he had reduced several key castles and his line of retreat remained clear. The longer he stayed, the longer the English must keep the field, a substantive drain on the Treasury. By the time his men's forty-day enlistment was up, the campaigning season would be over. His French allies may yet have cause to be grateful.

## The English army marches north

Surrey, still at Pontefract, received intelligence of the Scottish invasion on 25 August. Having fixed the muster date as 1 September at Newcastle-upon-Tyne, teams of gallopers were dispatched to raise the country. Next day the earl rode northward to lodge at York where he requisitioned his war chest in the amount of £10,800 from the funds held by the Abbot of St Mary's. By 29 September he was in Durham where he collected the sacred banner of St Cuthbert, patron of the north and scourge of invaders, whose defiant pennon had flown over momentous past victories.

Northerners were no strangers to a call to arms. Soon the miry lanes and highways of Lancashire, Cheshire and the Dales were filled with the tramp of marching men. Sir Edward Stanley, raised some 6,500 who, having mustered initially at Hornby and Lancaster, advancing beneath the banners of St Audrey and that of the absent Earl of Derby, moved to Skipton in Craven. Here they were joined by 2,000 more under the colours of James Stanley, Bishop of Ely and commanded by his natural son John. A further 1,200 were on the move from south Lancashire and Cheshire.[54]

> All Lancashire, for the most part,
> The lusty Stanley stout did lead,
> A flock of striplings strong of heart,
> Brought up from babes with beef and bread.

Bowmen and bill-men thronged the roads from Wensleydale and Swaledale, mustered by Lord Scrope of Bolton. The North Riding responded to Lord Conyers whilst Lord Clifford mustered the flower of Craven. Old enemies too some of these, Stanley and Scrope had been Yorkists, Cliffords diehard Lancastrians. John, Lord Clifford, 'the Butcher' had perished with most of an earlier generation from Craven at Dintingdale during the Towton campaign. The northern burgesses sent their quotas, men from Hull and a company of 110 from York, led by the sword-bearer and carrying the City's standard of a red cross with five golden lions.[55]

By 30 August, Surrey had arrived at Newcastle,[56] despite a near-death experience in vile weather. The medieval city with its great frowning keep was soon hopelessly thronged with thousands of troops. Here he was joined by Lord Dacre with his ever-ready border lances, Sir William Bulmer, he who had earlier thrashed Home's riders, Sir Marmaduke Constable and the English artillery train. Having completed his list of appointments the earl's council of war comprised some eighteen members, cream of the northern gentry, none of whom would be likely to show any aversion to crossing swords with the oldest of old enemies.

It was soon obvious that Newcastle did not offer the best location to marshal the great host that was swelling daily. The earl therefore issued orders that the army should move north, a distance of some 30-odd miles, firstly to Alnwick and then towards Bolton in Glendale, just west of the Percy seat. By the morning of 5 September the English were arrived at Bolton. The force which Surrey commanded at this juncture might have comprised as many as 26,000. Here the captains set to work drilling men in their companies. With his great Tudor Dragon banner, resplendent in scarlet, unfurled, the earl formally took the field. On the 4th, Thomas Howard with several ships' companies had joined his father, clearly a major relief to the older man 'able soldiers and mariners which all came from the sea, the coming of him much rejoiced his father, for he [Thomas Howard] was very wise, hardy, and of great credence and experience'.[57]

Precise intelligence as to the exact whereabouts of the Scots was lacking. It was thought James most likely remained at Ford and it was there that the English Herald Rouge Croix was dispatched to bear Surrey's challenge. The latter accused James of having invaded his brother-in-law's realm of England, 'contrary to his oath and league and unnaturally against all reason and conscience, burning, spoiling and destroying … and cruelly murdering the King of England's subjects'.[58] Despite this tough talking there was room for negotiation. Lady Heron reported that the king would spare Ford if Alexander Home and Lord Johnston, both captives were freed together with George Home and William Ker.[59] Part of the proposed deal would include the release of her luckless husband, a surety for his wilder sibling. This initiative did not save her property.

To goad James, whose fiery temper the Howards knew well, the Lord Admiral enclosed some correspondence of his own reminding the king of Howard's role in the death of Andrew Barton and 'he nor none of his company should take no Scottish nobleman prisoner, nor any other, but they should die if they came into his danger, unless it were the King's own person, for he said that he trusted to no other courtesy at the hands of the Scots'.[60] Significantly, Surrey challenged James to settle the issue by combat, 'by Friday next' (9 September).[61] Thomas Howard stressed that he, as Lord Admiral, would have fought the Scots navy but could not 'because they had fled to France'.[62] The English, mindful of a herald's role as scout, forbad any Scottish emissary to approach within a couple of miles of their camp.


## Flodden Edge

Surrey had required James to linger and give battle not later than 9 September. Rouge Croix, however, was disappointed at Ford for the Scots had decamped and moved to a new position on Flodden Edge (*Plates 15 & 16*). It was part of a herald's intelligence role to glean whatever details he could of the enemy's position and strength of numbers. James, having received Rouge Croix, ordered him to be detained awhile and his formal reply taken by his Scottish counterpart. Islay Herald rode up to the English outposts where he was, in turn, detained. Next morning Surrey and his officers rode out to hear King James' reply. This was delivered 'bluntly' by the Scot. His monarch would be pleased to accept battle on or before the 9th. Leaving Islay in temporary custody the earl gave orders for a further advance to Wooler where the army encamped looking northward over the level ground of Millfield Plain.

It was only when the heralds were exchanged that the English were made to appreciate the true strength of the Scots' position. Gloomily, Rouge Croix described how their forces were deployed along the crest of the low, saddle-backed hill, an outrider of the Cheviots that, from a vantage of 500ft (150m), completely dominates the plain below. At that time treeless, it was ideal defensive ground, over a mile long and protected from the north by Marylaws and Branxton Hills. A possible approach from the east rising above the marshy vale of the Till was covered by the Scottish ordnance, dug into gun-pits, 'enclosed in three parts with three great mountains so that there was no passage or entry but one way ... one narrow field to ascend'.[63]

The Scots' army, whose camp may be marked by the farm named Encampment, was a great sprawl of brightly coloured pavilions, hundreds of horses, wagons, baggage and loot. The bare canvas of the levies, crude bothies of the Highlanders and a shifting mass of families, servants and camp followers filled the shallow valley on the northern flank, screened by the bulk of the ridge behind and mire in the hollow to front. It was an inexpugnable position. The English, damp and miserable on the plain to the south, could hear the crack and bellow of the great guns as the gunners practised their range. To add to their woes English marchers had cheerfully pillaged all food supplies being sent up from Newcastle. The Bishop of Durham, writing in the immediate aftermath of the battle and commenting on the general conduct of the dalesmen, undoubtedly summed up the prevailing view when he claimed the English borderers were as big a menace as the Scots, intent upon nothing more than booty, regardless of which nation they plundered!

Whilst the chronicles are largely silent as to how precisely James' army was deployed we can assume that the strategic corridor referred to previously was not left unguarded. Detachments would be stationed at key points with border horse riding as scouts and couriers. It would be logical to assume that the various crossing points on the Till were covered and yet no suggestion of this arises in connection with the subsequent English flank march.

However much James might relish the prospect of a fight, he was not to be tempted from his vantage. If the English meant to attack then their only apparent option was to fight their way up the southern slope in the teeth of the Scottish guns and with pike formations poised for a decisive blow. This position could not be easily outflanked and possible access from the east was dominated by cannon. Surrey was in serious difficulties. In these careful Scots dispositions we may discern the experienced hands of James' French advisers. Did they encourage James to fight? In part there was no reason for the Scots to remain, their immediate tactical objectives had been secured. There was no possibility of

an attack on Berwick with an end to the campaigning season in sight. Even if
the Scots now quietly slipped away over the border Surrey had not the time, the
means or the mandate to mount a counter invasion. In terms of succouring his
allies, James had achieved all that could reasonably be hoped for.

The form of chivalric challenges issued, in this instance, by the English,
seemingly archaic, almost Homeric in their appeal to arms, nonetheless had
ample precedent. In the course of recurrent magnatial thuggery during the
1470s Viscount Lisle penned a singularly provocative challenge to his local
rival William, Lord Berkeley:

William, called Lord Berkeley,

I marvel you come not forth with all your carts of guns, bows, with other ordinance, that you set forward to come to my manor of Wotton to beat it down
upon my head. I tell you, you shall not need to come so near, for I trust to God
to meet near home with Englishmen of my own nation and neighbour whereas
you by subtle craft have blown apart in divers places of England, that I should
intend to bring in Welshmen for to destroy and hurt my own nation and country. I was never so disposed, nor never will be; and to the proof hereof, I require
you of knighthood and manhood to meet me half way, there to try between
God and our two hands, all our quarrel and title of right, for to eschew the
shedding of Christian men's blood, or else at the same day bring the uttermost
of your power, and I shall meet you.[64]

## NOTES

1. Hall, *King Henry VIII*, vol. 1, p. 95.
2. 'Feid' or feud was a pernicious borderer custom which could usher in generations of cross-familial violence.
3. Mons Meg survives in Edinburgh Castle (Historic Scotland).
4. 'Serpentine' is said to have been a reference to Satan and, in addition to the type of artillery also referred to a dry, compounded black powder.
5. Robert Borthwick was King James' master gunner and gun-founder credited with the casting of the celebrated 'Seven Sisters'. It is likely the five large guns in the Scottish train were amongst these. Some accounts say he was killed in the fight but this seems to be incorrect; a relative William, 3rd Lord Borthwick was, however amongst the tally of Scottish dead.
6. Pitscottie, *Historie and Cronicles of Scotland*, pp. 260–1.
7. Heralds: On the Scottish side Lyon, King at Arms was the head of the Lion Court, and an officer of state; Islay herald, first mentioned in 1493, is probably a survivor from the days of the Lordship of the Isles, see www.lyon-court.com. The English herald Rouge-Croix, bearing the Red Cross of St George, is the oldest of four pursuivants in ordinary, see www.collegeofarms.gov.uk.
8. The Burghmuir covered some 5 square miles in all, outside the city walls, see Reese, pp. 3–4.

9. Barr, p. 55.

10. *Ibid.*

11. *Ibid.*

12. The Weardale Campaign, whilst a fiasco, convinced Edward III of the need for light horsemen on the borders.

13. A 'Jakke' was simply a form of brigandine, standard hobilar protection.

14. Ridpath, Rev. G., *Border History* (Berwick-upon-Tweed, 1778), p. 334 (Hall quotes a rather higher figure).

15. *Ibid.*

16. *Ibid.*

17. Hall, *King Henry VIII*, vol. 1, p. 98.

18. *Ibid.*

19. *Ibid.*

20. Ridpath, *Border History*, p. 334.

21. Hall, *King Henry VIII*, vol. 1, p. 96.

22. *Ibid.*

23. Scarisbrick, pp. 34–5.

24. *Ibid.*

25. *Ibid.*, p. 36.

26. Hall, *King Henry VIII*, vol. 1, p. 82.

27. *Ibid.*

28. *Ibid.*, p. 76.

29. *Ibid.*

30. *Ibid.*

31. *Ibid.* p. 85.

32. Surrey's retinue comprised five captains and the same number of petty captains, an ensign, 43 demi-lances (light horse); 446 men-at-arms, equipped with bows or bills. Added to this the earl's immediate HQ staff, all bearing the Tudor livery; by 1 September Surrey had assembled a contracted affinity of 27 captains, 12 petty captains, 55 light horse and 11,406 men, see Barr p. 56.

33. Sir Nicholas is described as 'Clerk to the Ordnance' ordinarily the train would be commanded by Sir Norton Sampson, 'Master of the Ordnance' but he was presently with the king in France and Appleyard was made up accordingly with William Blakenhall, otherwise also 'Clerk to the Ordnance' as 2 i/c, see Barr, p. 53.

34. Hall, *King Henry VIII*, vol. 1, p. 97.

35. Sadler, D.J., *Border Fury* (London, 2004), p. 414.

36. *Ibid.*, p. 415.

37. *Ibid.*

38. Barr, p. 46.

39. Ellem Kirk, near Duns in Berwickshire.

40. In May 1513 the Queen of France had sent James a letter enclosing a turquoise ring, urging him, as her champion, to go 'but three feet on English ground'. This has been seen as an appeal to the king's chivalric vanity. It seems likely that the substantial cash subsidy sent with the correspondence carried greater weight!

41. Hall, *King Henry VIII*, vol. 1, p. 47.

42. Pevsner, p. 522.

43. The line of the moat is now taken up in part by the modern road.

44. A barbican was a form of outer defended gateway.

45. Hall, *King Henry VIII*, vol. 1, p. 98.

46. *Ibid.*

47. *Ibid.*, p. 99.

48. *Ibid.*

49. Barr, p. 66.

50. Hall, *King Henry VIII*, vol. 1, p. 99.

51. *Ibid.*, the bishop managed to recover from his loss.

52. Macdougall, p. 273.

53. Pitscottie is making a moral rather than an historical observation, there is no actual evidence to suggest James was distracted, which is not to say he failed to take advantage of what may have been on offer!

54. Barr, p. 56. On the matter of banners, St Cuthbert's standard probably first flew above English bills at Neville's Cross in 1346. Prior Fossour, immediately before the fight is credited with a visitation from the saint who intimated he should take the holy corporax cloth which Cuthbert had used to cover the chalice during mass and attach this to a spear or lance as war banner. In 1513, Sir John Forster was paid 16*d* to carry the standard and the further sum of 13*s* 4*d* disbursed at the conclusion of the campaign for reparation. The Lord Admiral played safe in his subsequent expedition of 1522 and again drew out the saint's banner; see *Archaeologia Aeliana* Second series, vol. II (1858), pp. 51–62.

55. Kightly, p. 35.

56. Hall, *King Henry VIII*, vol. 1, p. 99.

57. *Ibid.*, p. 100.

58. *Ibid.*, p. 101.

59. *Ibid.*

60. *Ibid.*, p. 101.

61. *Ibid.*

62. *Ibid.*

63. *Ibid.*, p. 105.

64. Quoted in Boardman, A.W., *The Medieval Soldier in the Wars of the Roses* (Gloucs., 1998) p. 63. In fact the upshot of this stirring rebuke was the skirmish at Nibley Green where the two factions clashed. Lisle was the losing party, he died along with perhaps 150 others and his manor was indeed sacked!

# 6

# FULL BOLDLY ON THE BROAD HILLS:

## APPROACH TO CONTACT

The rearward marched in array ever after
as long as the light day lasted on the ground
then the sun full soon shot under the clouds
and it darkened full dimly and drew toward the night
every man to his rest readily him dressed
beaten fires full fast, and fettled them to sleep
besides Barmoor in a bank within a broad wood.[1]

On 8 September, Rouge Croix was dispatched on a second mission, bearing further correspondence signed by all eighteen members of the English council. The northerners reproached James for having firstly agreed to fight and then retreating into a virtual fortress. They demanded the king, between noon and three next day, bring his army down onto the plain where an equal trial of arms might properly ensue. The herald was to add a further verbal message from Surrey should James be seen to prevaricate, the earl 'would look for no more of his delays'.[2] Predictably the king flew into a real or staged tantrum on receiving such affronts to his honour. Nonetheless, he would not be drawn, replying that the herald (whom he at first refused to see) should 'show to the Earl of Surrey that it beseemeth him not, being an earl, so largely to attempt a great prince. His grace will take and hold his ground at his own pleasure and not at the assigning of the Earl of Surrey'.[3]

The chivalric gambit had failed. Surrey had somehow to bring the Scots to a decisive encounter by 9 September, or James might rightly consider he had come off best in the pursuit of honour. As the English had sat, wet and hungry, around their spluttering fires during the previous night, they were joined by Bastard Heron and his company of ruffians. It is he whom legend asserts planted the idea that the English army could, in a grand flanking movement, come around behind the Scots and ascend Branxton Hill immediately to the north of their present position, separated only by a gentle if very wet decline. This was a high-risk strategy by any estimation but it offered a glimmer of hope for breaking the current stalemate.

To attempt to turn the enemy's flank over uncertain ground virtually within reach of his guns was to invite attack. What other options were open to Surrey however? Put quite simply, there were none. He could not afford to keep his men in the field beyond 9 September and any attack on the present Scots position was bound to fail. James would clearly not oblige and abandon good ground to fight on the plain. Why should he, for he would know that the strong defences offered by Flodden Edge might make up for some of the deficiencies in training and morale which he recognised affected many of his less enthusiastic subjects. Cosseted by the great weight of shot the Scots guns could dispose, and with a gentle slope over which to deploy in perfect order, James' levies might yet perform as well as their Swiss exemplars.

James' supposed ire against Rouge Croix might have been largely theatre. That the English would resort to insults to draw the king onto more favourable ground where their greater experience and missile power might win them the day cannot have come as any surprise. The old taint that James was reckless and fixated upon having his battle regardless appears groundless. Quite the reverse, he was displaying prudence and extreme caution. His army might be affected by disease and desertion but his men's bellies were fuller and their condition less acute than the English. Both he and Surrey were aware that James had specifically avoided a fight in 1497 and had simply slipped back northwards leaving Surrey in possession of an empty field. A tactical victory won by guile was as useful as one wrested by force of arms and a sight less risky. James' strategic objectives were to seize Norham and pin English forces in the north. In both of these he had succeeded.

## The English flank march

On a grey afternoon on 8 September the whole English army began to move, crossing the sluggish waters of the Till and marching north-east towards Doddington 'in cloggy mire and foule filthy waies'. For some miles the Scots would have been able to keep Surrey's host in sight before they were swallowed up by the empty moorland and screened by rising ground; 'then the Englishmen removed their field on the water of Till, and so forth over many hills and streets, marching towards the Scots on another side and in their sight the Scots burned certain poor villages on the other side of the marsh'.[4] Whether James had prickers follow the English, as prudence would dictate, is unsure. If so, Dacre's screen kept them at a safe distance.

Once over the brown waters of the Till, the host was marching north towards the village of Doddington, skirting the high ground of Dod Law. Quite possibly however, they followed the parallel line of the old Roman road, the Devil's Causeway which would leave Dod Law on their left and fully screen the movement from the Scots on Flodden Edge. Above them were an ancient Iron Age hillfort and even earlier enigmatic cup-and-ring marks. Whether these dour northerners felt any comfort from the shades of their distant ancestors looking down is unrecorded. Likely, they were more aware of empty bellies and chafing harness.[5] The present impressive bastle house is rather later, though the parish church of St Mary and St Michael dates from the thirteenth century.[6]

Strung out in column, the army would have looked the very opposite of the chivalric ideal, mere 'warriors for the working day' indeed, unkempt, for the most part unwashed, now very much underfed but by no means downtrodden. Banners and colours furled, odours of wet wool, leather and humanity, women and camp followers in a great, sprawling tail. Tradesmen, tapsters, sutlers, whores and farriers were all needed to service this great beast in the field; gunners, sweating matrosses and begrimed pioneers labouring together, for moving even the lighter field guns was a tough assignment over such ground in such dismal conditions. (For the line of march taken by the English army refer to *Map 2*).

The rutted road would have quickly been churned into a quagmire by the passage of men and animals. Leading almost due north towards Barmoor and once clear of the moor it now runs through tranquil fields more reminiscent of a nostalgic view of 1950s Britain than the early sixteenth century. Then, it would have been very different for this was all frontier, the threap or wasteland between two warring states whose bitter enmity now stretched back over two centuries. Crude and nervous settlements clung to a precarious existence, fearful of armies of both nations.

The Scots were now at a loss as to their enemy's intentions. Was Surrey falling back on Berwick from whence he could be resupplied? Did he intend to cut off the Scots line of withdrawal? Home and the other marchers must have felt a prick of alarm. His and their estates in the Merse were exposed to any attack from Berwick. The Scottish prickers do not appear to have been overly active, contenting themselves, as Hall tells us, with torching the small hamlet of Fishes Steads which had stood on the rim of alluvial marsh below the eastern flank of their position.

Guided by local scouts, Surrey pitched tents that afternoon in the lee of Barmoor Wood some 5.5 miles east of the Scots position on Flodden Edge. As the light waned, the Lord Admiral and a party of his officers trekked to the summit of Watch Law to view the enemy's positions from this new vantage. They were greeted with a salvo from the Scottish guns, more symbolic than threatening given the extreme range. From the swell of the hill which rises 500ft (150m) from the plain Howard could see that the Scots were protected on all sides. The only possible approach was from the north up the moderate slope of Branxton Hill. An approach from here and an advance over the intervening dip would place the English almost within bowshot and screened from the Scottish guns. Some hard marching would be needed on 9 September, but the council of war, dominated as it was by Howards and their affinity, was unanimous in the decision to offer battle.

The northern lords probably required little persuasion. The Scots were their traditional enemies, holding ground in Northumberland with apparent impunity. English war bows and English bills had won hard-fought battles in the past and could do so again. Surrey was likely aware that the Scots had been practising new drills, he would be all too aware of the size of their artillery train. No English army had encountered the Swiss or their methods but the earl knew King James and he understood the Scots. He would know how little time his enemies had had for training in new tactics.

This was still a risky proposition, involving a long and exhausting approach march, difficult in places for the guns and dependent upon the hope the Scots would remain inert in their present positions. They must remain largely supine to allow the English to reach then ascend Branxton Edge, to give battle in the hollow of that intervening saddle. It would have been obvious the Scots should simply to about face, march over the easy ground and take up a fresh northward facing position on Branxton Edge their overall position could be equally advantageous. The English would, crucially, be between their enemy and his homeland.

A fight would thus be inevitable. Had Surrey not emerged victorious then allegations of recklessness would have been hurled at him, the capacity to win mends any defects. It was said of Captain Lewis Edward Nolan, who fell in the Charge of the Light Brigade at Balaklava in the Crimea several centuries later and upon whom much of the blame for the catastrophe fell, that dead men carry a heavy burden. In war generally this is very often the case as James IV of Scotland would discover.

Hall tells us of the English camp that night that it was 'under a wood side, called Barmoor Wood, 2 miles from the Scots, and between the two armies was the River Till'.[7] Barmoor Wood forms part of the Barmoor Estate, historically a noted source of timber and, at that time, a hold of the Muschampes.[8] The present picturesque remains of Barmoor House date from the early nineteenth century, constructed for the distinguished Sitwell family.[9] The Adam-style country house stands on the site of a much earlier tower which is described in 1509 as being capable of holding a garrison of thirty lances.[10] It would be here with accommodation, albeit rather cramped, for his staff, that Surrey would set up his HQ. We know that Thomas Howard, by then Earl of Surrey, used Barmoor as his base when preparing to relieve the siege of Wark in 1523.[11]

It was not only the English who held urgent councils that evening. The Scots too were debating their strategy. As yet unsure as to the intentions of the English it seemed likely that they might be seeking to cut off the line of retreat via the Tweed and the fords at Coldstream. Buchanan takes the view that the Scots saw the English manoeuvre as a precursor to a strike against the Merse, thus hoping to draw the Scots off by wasting lands in the East March. This is by no means an illogical assumption as the Scottish army was confident of its present position. There is further some suggestion that Surrey had caused rumours to this effect to mask his true intention. Again, this would not be unexpected. It seems likely that the Scots had taken the precaution of garrisoning certainly Ford and most likely Etal bridges. Whether they had left a garrison in the medieval predecessor of Twizel remains uncertain.

Ridpath tells us that:

The Scots had thought themselves secured against the approach of their enemies from the opposite side of the Till, by the depth and bad fords of that river,
through a long tract of its course on each hand of them, and by a battery of

cannon they had erected near the foot of the eastern declivity of Flodden Hill bearing full on the bridge of Ford.[12]

It seems entirely logical that the crossing at Etal would be similarly covered. Whilst the Scottish magnates did not fear a fight, they were loath to witness their king hazard his own person in the melee. Pitscottie portrays their chief spokesman as being Lord Lindsay of the Byres (his own grandfather). Lindsay, with smooth eloquence, summed up the case for the king avoiding the field: 'So my lords, ye may understand by this you shall be called the merchant, and your king a "rose nobill", and England a common hazarder that has nothing to jeopard but a bad halfpenny in comparison of our noble king and an auld crooked earl lying in a chariot.'[13]

This homely analogy pointed to an essential truth. Scotland had far more to lose than England. James, predictably, would have none of it, even threatening to hang Lindsay for his temerity.[14] His whole character and ambition inclined him to the hazard. It is possible this exchange was largely the work of Pitscottie who was on something of a mission to lambaste James for his shortcomings. Though James had an understandable yearning to prove himself as a general, he was not some reckless Custer figure willing to chance all on do or die. He took his responsibilities as sovereign most seriously and had previously, as in 1497, demonstrated a canny intuition for *realpolitik*. It is more likely that, if it came to a fight James was confident in the ability of his army, despite the visible cracks, to hold its own. Precisely because the Scottish army's morale was uncertain, he felt the need to lead in person. Whilst this added immeasurably to the risk it was, in the circumstances, also entirely understandable.

Therefore this was not mere impetuosity. James knew the value to his army of personal leadership, the paladin at the head of his disparate force, welding them into a cohesive whole by the force and charisma of his example. In this he was perhaps wiser than his councillors understood. The Renaissance prince was a different type of ruler. His power was becoming more absolute than that his medieval predecessors had wielded but the burden of policy consequentially sat more heavily. Military triumph, glory and renown, were the hallmarks of success, the measure of his fitness to be admitted into the wider counsels of his fellow monarchs. Such triumphs and the attendant risks could not be delegated or the lustre would vanish. Those meagre rewards doled out to the victorious English peers by a grudging monarch reflected this same consideration. Henry might offer thanksgiving and fulsome praise but in reality he was jealous of Surrey's achievement. Any campaign wherein a mere subordinate won renown was a poor investment for the prince.

What was happening on that dank evening of 8 September was that the tactical initiative was passing to the English. Many difficulties awaited the

Howards but their boldness would pay huge dividends. This gambit would prove the key to success. It is highly doubtful if the English army felt any particular elation that damp and dismal night in late summer. It would have been dark around 8 p.m. and they would huddle in sodden wool beneath dripping trees around meagre fires, grousing. There was ample scope for complaint. The weather was foul, supplies were running out, the Scots appeared to have the better of them, largely without effort and their own border auxiliaries were as much support as a hornets' nest. They were a very long way from most places and the next day could offer only further toil and frustration with the added potential bonus of an agonising death.

## The morning of 9 September

> From Flodden ridge
> The Scots beheld the English host
> Leave Barmoor Wood, their evening post,
> And heedful watched them as they crossed
> The Till by Twizel Bridge.

Scott, *Marmion*

September 9th: reveille in the English camp was early, around 4 a.m., before the first filtering of another grey dawn. The army would first need to march 7 miles west to Twizel where the bridge crossed the Till. Some brigades were to cross downstream by the fords at Heaton Mill. Both crossing points were invisible to the Scots atop Flodden Edge. It was Friday and the English carried only their personal weapons and gear, the rest was left in camp. To here, they would return victorious or not at all.

The vanguard, led by the Lord Admiral, passed an ancient ring of stones at Duddo (*Plate 6*) and probably reached the bridge at Twizel around eleven (*Plate 8*). Today the gaunt spire of a surviving gable is all that remains of Duddo tower, dating from the late sixteenth century. In 1513, the original was most likely still ruinous having been slighted by the Scots during the raids of 1496. The prehistoric ring stands ¾ of a mile north-west of the settlement.[15] Twizel Bridge survives. The old crossing, now bypassed by the new, is said to have been that which stood in the fifteenth century.[16] A most elegant and impressive structure with a soaring span of 90ft (27m) and beautifully located with the somnolent waters of the Till sweeping around, and spectacular bluffs to the north crowned by the ruins of Twizel Castle, an eighteenth-century construction on medieval foundations.

It would take at least an hour to get both men and guns over the narrow span, a matter of debate as to whether (a) there was an earlier medieval fort on the site of Twizel Castle and (b) whether the Scots had left an outpost here. It is clear there is a much earlier and thick-walled medieval building shrouded in the core of the later accretions. The massive nature of the construction would certainly suggest defensible intent. Whether there were any Scots stationed there is entirely a matter of conjecture.

The main body, under Surrey, might have begun splashing through the fords somewhat later, with Dacre's marchers employed as a light-cavalry screen. For the earl, the Till was his Rubicon, once across there was no going back, the lives and fortunes of his line and affinity were now in the ring. As his soldiers crossed, Surrey exhorted them to fight 'like Englishmen, this day take my part like men, which part is the King's part'.[17] Wet, cold, hungry and weary the men responded with élan shouting 'they would serve the King and him truly that day'.[18] Surrey was no master of eloquence, nor one for finesse. He spoke bluff, soldierly talk and his men responded. Nobody who knew of the Howards could ever doubt they would be anywhere other than in the thick of the fighting.

Now marshalled into battle formations, the army comprised two large divisions, van and centre each flanked by a brace of smaller brigades; Edmund Howard led the right wing of the former, perhaps 3,000 strong. This comprised 1,000 or more Cheshire men including the Macclesfield contingent under Christopher Savage, 300 tenants from the mesnie lands of the Abbey of Vale Royal led by the Abbot and two of his esquires. Half a thousand from Lancashire, more from South Yorkshire, Hull and Doncaster and, lastly, a stiffening of 200 marines under Maurice Berkeley, master of the *Mary George* (these were detached from the total complement of 1,200 brought by the Lord Admiral).[19] There were rumblings of discontent from some of Stanley's affinity who expected to be brigaded with their fellows.

The central division of the vanguard, led by Thomas Howard, fielded perhaps 9,000, including the remaining 1,000 crack marines. These, wearing the Tudor livery, served under their usual captains, Sir William Sidney of the *Great Barque*, Edward Edyngham of *Spaniard*, James King, *Julian of Dartmouth* and a dozen others. In the centre of their division would stand 2,000 men from the Palatinate, clustered beneath the talisman of St Cuthbert, commanded by Bulmer and Lord Lumley. With them was the Northumbrian contingent under Lords Ogle and Gascoigne.[20]

For the rest, these were mainly from the Ridings. Clifford brought 207 bows and 116 bills, liveried in the famed Red Wyvern. Lord Conyers, Lord Scrope of Uppsall, the Sheriff, Sir John Everingham with a score of minor gentry led the rest and, with them the guns. Sir Marmaduke Constable, another septuagenarian, commanded on the other flank. This was very much a family affair. He was joined by his brother William, three of his sons, two cousins and a son-in-law. Sir William Percy. His retainers and 1,000 of the Lancashire men brought this brigade up to strength, perhaps 2,000 men in all.[21]

At Heaton Fords, Dacre held the right flank of the rear or main body. His Cumbrian marchers were stiffened by Kendal archers, Heron's reivers and a detached body of riders from Bamboroughshire and Tynemouth. An unhappy pairing as these were both at feud with the warden! It is possible; perhaps even likely, that Dacre was assigned a battalion of 1,800 foot under Bishop Stanley. These men wore the family livery (an eagle's claw surmounted by the three gold crowns of the bishopric) and they would fight beneath the sacred banner of St Audrey. Dacre's brigade numbered some 3,500 in total. Surrey's personal retinue and staff clustered under the earl's colours in the central division, 5,000 strong in all and mainly from South Yorkshire. Scrope of Bolton was there with his dalesmen, citizen soldiers from York, tenantry of the Abbey of Whitby under their captain Lionel Perry; East Riding men led by the Archdeacon. Gentry such as Richard Tempest, Sir Christopher Pickering, Sir Ninian Markenfield and Sir Bryan Stapleton brought their own companies.

With the earl was redoubtable George Darcy, a seasoned soldier destined to become one of the leaders of the Pilgrimage of Grace, an exercise in faith that would cost him his life. On the extreme left was stationed Sir Edward Stanley, fifth son of the Earl of Derby, whose division appears to have rather lost contact with the main body ahead shortly after the crossing and was consequentially late onto the field. Although delayed, Sir Edward's deployment would be both skilful and timely. This was very much a Stanley command, some 3,500 liveried retainers, officered by Stanley kin and affinity. Sir Edward was a mature and seasoned campaigner. His family, as hereditary keepers of Man, had clashed with the Scots on numerous occasions.[22]

## Rubicon

By rock, by oak, by hawthorn tree,
Troop after troop are disappearing;
Troop after troop their banners rearing,
Upon the eastern bank you see
Still pouring down the rocky den,
Where flows the sullen Till …

Scott, *Marmion*

Most modern writers agree that the *Mylforde* mentioned by Hall[23] is indeed Heaton Mill Ford which lies only a mile or so south of Twizel Bridge though some earlier accounts, notably Jones, dispute this.[24] The logic which supports the more recent contention, with which we concur, is that the two crossings, Twizel and Heaton, are within sight of each other. This would surely be relevant in Surrey's thinking.

Despite repeated soakings and empty bellies, the English army would now have provided a finer spectacle than the day before, proud banners floating in the steady breeze, still laden with drizzle. Such light as filtered through the fat bellied, grey clouds would have glinted on burnished harness and the business end of bills. Many would wear Stanley's badge, marines stepping out smartly in their *almain rivet* (mass produced) harness with the white-and-green Tudor livery. Surrey and his knights, mounted and resplendent in full plate, enjoyed an easier passage than the heaving, sweating gunners and matrosses, battling with wet ground and the onerous weight of their charges.

> Then full boldly on the broad hills we pushed our standards
> and on a hill us beside there seen we our enemies
> were moving over the mountains to match us they thought.[25]

Their line of march would easily stretch back several miles. In 1914 an infantry brigade, comprising four battalions of 1,000 men, needed a 3-mile stretch of road. Surrey had at least the equivalent of five full brigades. Keeping the host moving was a major logistical exercise and the responsibility of Edmund Howard as Marshal, sergeants cursing as men slipped, slithered and stumbled. For ordinary folk of the sixteenth century as in preceding centuries, the passage of armies was a terrifying event. People, particularly in the upland areas of bleak Northumberland, lived in scattered villages and hamlets. The sheer scale of such an intrusion, the devilish racket of 20,000 and more armoured men, was alien and unnerving. Newcastle in 1513 might have held 10,000 citizens; Surrey's host was over twice as many. For the rural populace the tramp of soldiers' boots promised little comfort, be they nominally friend or foe; robbery, despoliation and worse could confidently be expected of either.

From the banks of the Till, the English faced a 4-mile march to Branxton Ridge, over fairly level, gently undulating ground. After 3 of those miles they would descend into the shallow valley of the Pallinsburn, a minor obstacle 'but a man's step over' now swollen by heavy rain, spongy mire spreading around. Branxton Edge swells some 300ft (90m) with a reverse slope up toward the lower crest of Piper's Hill, where the present monument stands[26] (*Plate 17*). Beyond this and to the north, the ground declines some 60ft (20m) into the dip of the Pallinsburn. The climb to the top of Branxton is quite steep though nowhere is the gradient more severe than 15>1.

The present village is a cluster of orderly dwellings which clings to the valley floor, most of which are nineteenth century or even more recent. St Paul's, to feature in the aftermath of the battle, mainly dates from *c.* 1850 with some medieval traces.[27] Branxton features in a later skirmish on 21 June 1524 when a party of Scottish raiders, perhaps 500 strong who'd plundered English traders aiming for Berwick Fair, were challenged by an inferior force led by the Lord of Fowberry. Despite the odds, the English came off best and took 200 prisoners. Scots never had any luck by Branxton.

In its flooded state the burn could best be crossed either at the westerly Branx Brig or further east at Sandyford. The old causeway can still be seen from the track which passes through the wooded ribbon of Inch plantation. We can see, even today, with several centuries of field drainage, the stream, whilst indeed narrow, still presents quite an obstacle. In the sixteenth century the marshy bottom would have been more difficult still. At Sandyford, the ford was obscured by low trees and encroaching bushes but either Heron or one of the other local guides pinpointed its location and the rear would be able to cross. This was a nervous time, for the swell of Piper's Hill spoils the view of Branxton beyond and the English, once in the dip of the Pallinsburn, were effectively marching blind. Whilst the van filed over the narrow causeway the guns had to be left with Surrey's division crossing by the ford as the planks were felt to be incapable of bearing their considerable weight.

*Alea iacta est*: the die is cast. The English were committed for they would fight with the Pallinsburn to their rear and Till on their left. Retreat would be virtually impossible, defeat would imply annihilation. There would still be ample grousing but no evidence of faltering, even when the Scottish great guns began to speak and their vast thundering would very soon be heard.

Reverend Jones, in his account, suggests that the populace of Coldstream sallied out to watch the battle.[28] Whilst bloodletting was often a spectator sport, there is no mention of onlookers in the contemporary accounts which is not to say they were not there. Locals, particularly on the border, had a well-attuned sense for plundering opportunities, though it is questionable if they would have been aware of the English approach. Certainly, after the battle, many locals would flit over the field like hungry jackals, despoiling dead and wounded alike. Many an injured combatant was ushered from this world towards the next by a practised thrust from the scavenger's knife.

And this field would soon be amply stocked with victims. Surrey's army would have been instantly recognisable to their fathers and indeed grandfathers who had mustered to fight for Lancaster or York. Despite their handy train of light guns, bows and bills predominated and, though the legendary war bow was beginning to decline in use, its potency was undoubted. Decline there was, however. Within a generation, hand-held firearms would come to dominate the field. For some time there had been concern, even as far back as the reign of Edward IV that practice at the butts was slipping:

> By law every man should be compelled
> To use the bow and shooting for his sport,
> And all insolent plat repelled,
> And each town to have butts for resort
> Of every creature for their comfort,
> Especially for all our defence
> Established before of great prudence[29]

## The alternative view

There exists a rather different interpretation of the events of 8 September and a wholly different analysis as to how the battle then came about. This was put forward by the then president of the Berwickshire Naturalists' Club in 1937, Gerard F.T. Leather in *New Light on Flodden*.[30] His view is that the flanking march took an altogether different route and that, on the 9th, James was attempting an orderly withdrawal – the battle thus came about as a series of largely unexpected encounters. This is contrary to the majority of commentators but nonetheless commands some consideration.

Leather argues that Surrey's strategy was for a grand envelopment by the van under his older son whilst he with the main body took a shorter route. This division of forces was needed to ensure the Scots were unaware of the hostile intent and would be lured into thinking the English were headed towards Berwick.[31] This was a Napoleonic gambit, the strategy of envelopment, and would represent a very sophisticated and extended manoeuvre for Renaissance forces. Furthermore, he alleges the Lord Admiral was unaware of the wider plan as his father kept him somewhat in the dark. Failing to brief divisional commanders thoroughly is a cardinal sin of command and control at any time and we cannot discern any evidence for this.[32]

Colonel Leather bases his as assertion on an interpretation of the 'trewe encountre'. Surrey's declared objective was to tie James to his Flodden position and prevent him decamping, thus slipping the net. It is, however, easy to agree that Scottish scouts or prickers would be tracking every move made by the English and that James was not simply supine and blind. Leather is of the view that most scouting was done by Highlanders. But Home's borderers, familiar with the ground and well mounted, would be the obvious choice for reconnaissance.

Once James was appraised by his prickers that the English were march-ing north-east he would naturally assume Berwick as their destination. On 9 September therefore, he began a fairly leisurely muster prior to march-ing back via Coldstream. This manoeuvre would require some six hours to complete overall.[33] At this juncture, time did not appear to be of the essence. Men could gather their kit, enjoy a leisurely meal before mustering by com-panies, scouts and rearguard were withdrawn, guns harnessed and made ready to move. Even when some sign of Surrey's approach was detected, no greater sense of urgency arose as it was thought the army could easily circumvent the English and slip over the Tweed unmolested.[34] Leather places Home and Huntly in the vanguard of the Scots army on the march, followed by the earls, the main body under James and finally the Highlanders as rearguard.

With this interpretation, Leather is absolving James from any accusation of recklessness, behaving with circumspection as he'd done in 1497. This notion (that the Scots were withdrawing) has considerable attraction. Having viewed the Scots as supine from Watch Law the previous evening, the Lord Admiral with his younger brother's division and his own, set off on their exhausting march before first light. Colonel Leather is confident James did not have an outpost at Twizel. We are not as easily persuaded. Given that we are confident a minor stronghold did command the bridge it would be most unlikely the Scottish king would leave this flank of his strategic corridor unguarded.

The colonel believed that Thomas Howard's strong division passed through Duddo and over the bridge as most authorities agree but that their com-bined line of march now swung towards Cornhill, a wide circling movement that would interdict any proposed Scottish withdrawal to the Tweed. Guns and carts remained with Edmund Howard and his smaller force. This parted company with the rest just before Melkington, swept around by Cornhill and approached the field from the west, past East Learmouth.[35]

Howard took a more direct line, due south to ford the Pallinsburn, north of Piper's Hill to take station there. He was, it is alleged, still ignorant of his father's shorter and more direct deployment. This would, to say the least, be a high-risk strategy, dependent upon excellent communications and perfect timing. If James, as he retreated, simply sidestepped Surrey and encountered the unsupported English vanguard then defeat in detail must surely ensue. It would also be uncertain as to whether the Scots were intending to cross the Tweed near Coldstream or further west, via 'the dry marches' at Kelso.

Surrey's march began around midday and proceeded north in the tracks of his sons but turning left at Bowsden, through Brakenside and Winterburn, north of Watch Law. Deception was the key to Surrey's plan; the Scots, dis-tracted by the vanguard's earlier departure must not suspect the nature of the earl's deployment. Surrey now proceeded over Slainsfield Moor toward the bends in the Till by West Haugh and the fords. The earl was naturally aware how dangerous his strategy was and, once his men were safely over the fords, sent Dacre ahead with the cavalry ride westwards in search of the Lord Admiral and his brother.[36] This would be none too soon, for Sir Edmund Howard's division had sighted and been sighted by Home and Huntly's joint command, to the apparent surprise of both.

The Scots very soon recovered and launched an immediate attack. Thus battle was joined by chance. Edmund Howard's men had already marched 13 miles (by Colonel Leather's calculation) and the rout of his division followed contact with Home and Huntly (see Chapters 7 & 8). Overall, and whilst we respect Colonel Leather's well-considered hypothesis, we are unable to agree. It is possible that the 'trewe encountre' could be interpreted to suggest that the Scots were in the act of withdrawing at the time when the battle opened, but Howard's view appears to state quite categorically that this was not the case and that they were fully deployed inline along the ridge. On the balance of probabilities we must concur that this appears most likely.

NOTES

1. Baird, Scottish, *Feilde and Flodden Feilde*, p. 10.
2. Hall, *King Henry VIII*, vol. 1, p. 105.
3. Laing, *Trewe Encountre*, p. 146.
4. Hall, *King Henry VIII*, voı. 1, p. 106.
5. Now the home of Wooler Golf Course.
6. Pevsner, p. 254.
7. Hall, *King Henry VIII*, vol. 1, p. 106.
8. Ferguson J. & Ferguson A., *The Encampment of the English Army at Barmoor, 8th September 1513 before the Battle of Flodden* (Cold Harbour Press, 2011), p. 3.
9. Pevsner, p. 158.
10. Ferguson & Ferguson, p. 4.
11. *Ibid.*, pp. 4–5.
12. Ridpath, p. 338.
13. Pitscottie, *Historie and Cronicles of Scotland*, p. 270.
14. *Ibid.*
15. Pevsner, p. 256.
16. *Ibid.*, p. 586.
17. Hall *King Henry VIII*, vol. 1, p. 106.
18. *Ibid.*
19. *Ibid.*, p. 100.
20. *Ibid.*, pp. 100–1.
21. *Ibid.*
22. *Ibid.*
23. *Ibid.*, p. 106.
24. Jones, p. 23.
25. Baird, *Scottish Feilde and Flodden Feilde,* p. 12.
26. Erected by Berwickshire Naturalists in 1910.
27. Pevsner, p. 200.

28. Jones, p. 22.
29. Quoted in Boardman, p. 147.
30. Leather, G.F.T., *New Light on Flodden* (Berwick-upon-Tweed, 1938). The author was a soldier who had served in the Great War, where he attained his colonelcy. Thus his views are backed by actual military experience.
31. *Ibid.*, p. 35.
32. *Ibid.*
33. *Ibid.*, p. 38.
34. *Ibid.*, p. 39.
35. *Ibid.*, pp. 42–5.
36. *Ibid.*, pp. 46–7.

# 7

# ALL BEFORE ME ON A PLAIN FIELD:
## TRIAL BY BATTLE I

At Flodden Field the Scots came in,
Which made our English men fain
At Bramston [Branxton] Green this battle was seen,
There was King James slain.[1]
It was now early afternoon on 9 September, a wet, cool day, certainly familiar
to those of us who live in North Northumberland.

King James is made aware of the English approach.

And what of the Scots: until noon James seems to have been unaware of his enemy's intentions. As English forces were nowhere to be seen, it appeared to the king that the honours might yet be his. It was now the 9th and Surrey had failed to give battle. By early afternoon, however, scouts were reporting movement west of the Till and, though at first he refused to believe it, the realisation was being forced upon James that he had been outflanked. Calling for his horse, the king rode out to see for himself. There could be no doubt. The English were coming. The tactical problem which now confronted the Scots was how best to counter the move. To stay where they were currently deployed was out of the question. Their fastness could as easily become a trap, an untenable salient that the English were about to pinch. To seek another vantage meant swinging the entire army around from its leaguer and marching northwards to take up a new position lining Branxton Edge.

Behind him streamed the Scottish encampment; this sudden city would teem with a mess of domesticity, women peeling, skinning, cooking, complaining and grousing as camp followers have done through every age of warfare, children shrieking and skirling naked in the mire. And there would be filth, acres of it, the dismal wet summer and congress of man and beast would churn the plateau into a reeking quagmire. Few cities of the day in England could boast such a dense population, sweat, ordure, stink of man and animal, of horse and cattle, sheep, pigs, goats, chickens rising like a rich miasma.

Soon trumpets were sounding, sergeants hoarse with bellowing as the host began to stream north, over the narrow saddle toward Branxton. The ordnance had to be dragged from gun pits and manhandled into line. The lie of the land obscured any sight the English may have gained and, to the natural topography, was soon added a vast pall of greasy smoke. The camp followers burnt wet straw, bothies and the general accretion of rubbish that 30,000 men and more will soon accumulate. A handy smoke screen was a tactic previously employed by Scots armies (Mytton in 1319 is a particular example) though, in this case, it would appear that the fires owed more to housekeeping than deception.

Hurried councils were again held amongst the magnates, concerned the king would persist in giving battle when it might be best to use the respite to withdraw safely. These cautious advices met with the usual blast from the king who, typically, flew into 'ane furieous rage'. Lord Lindsay of the Byres had artfully put the argument to his touchy monarch, likening the king to a reputable businessman risking his gold piece in a chance game with a mere vagabond who risked only a bent halfpenny. England, he argued was the party hazarding but little, 'an old crooked earl lying in a chariot, and a company of tailors and shoemakers with him'. Lindsay pointed out that Scotland risked the person of her king and all his great lords, possibly her very nationhood.[2]

He proposed that a staff of magnates should fight the battle at James' direction, keeping the king safe. Good advice but it liked not. The king had threatened to string Lindsay up for his temerity and whilst his lords might bring shame on themselves, he himself would never flee the hazard.[3] Noble words indeed but the doubters were right. The tactical position, though changed, was by no means critical. Provided they could attain the north-facing vantage of Branxton, the Scots remained strongly placed. Surrey would be obliged to mount an attack uphill onto the points of Scottish pikes. The king had every confidence that his guns, with their weight of shot, could silence those of the English.

## The King of Scots begins to deploy

In the vital sphere of reconnaissance the king was advised by a west March reiver named Giles Musgrave. Borderers tended to weigh the purse above national interest and James needed good local knowledge. Hall[4] rather muddles the situation by asserting Musgrave lured the king into battle. Leslie[5] expresses the likely realities more clearly. Musgrave realised the purpose of the flank manoeuvre was to come around behind the Scots and gain the vantage of Branxton Hill, obliging James to re-deploy and fight a battle between the two ridges.[6] This analysis was of course correct and the Scottish king divined his best course was to swing around through 180 degrees and take up position on Branxton Edge, here he would still have the advantage of ground, he could oblige the English to storm the slope or take the initiative as circumstances offered.

Shifting this great train of ordnance was, of course, another matter entirely. These weighty iron monsters had been laboriously sited in pits overlooking Millfield plain, protected against counter-battery fire by earth ramparts and stacked gabions. Moving them required a vast outpouring of sweat from man and beast, wet grass a muddied, slippery, cursed carpet of slime. Gunners and matrosses had to harness their pieces, draw them from their temporary bastions and haul them over the intervening saddle between these two ridges. No great distance but a major task. Not just the guns themselves, but powder, shot, tools and possibly gabions. Gun captains fretted over their charges, a cracked trunnion spelled disaster and this time none would have the leisure to carefully lay and sight the guns. The gunner's art was best practised when not undertaken in undue haste.

Whilst the cannon were dragged and laid around what is now Branxton Hill Farm, the army could be marshalled in the dead ground of the dip. It has been suggested as part of the research undertaken by *Remembering Flodden* that the guns were re-located by a more circuitous route, 'contouring' westwards from Flodden Hill and circling around to their second position. The lie of the ground is favourable and such a manoeuvre might make a deal of sense rather than hauling uphill over wet ground. We are looking at a distance of, say 2.5–3 miles, it would likely take a good two hours per mile and this would fit with the guns coming into action late afternoon.

The left-wing foot would be led by Home and Alexander Gordon, Earl of Huntly; a muster roll of perhaps 10,000 men in all, less those who were sick or had simply deserted. With the Scots formations there is the recurrent problem that numbers on the field would be subject to considerable shrinkage, perhaps as much as ten to twenty-five per cent. The borderers had been drilled in new pike tactics whilst the Highlanders, from Aberdeenshire and Moray and wielding their *twahanditswerds* (double-handed swords),[7] could act as flankers (for detail on the initial deployment of the armies refer to *Map 3*).

To their right would stand the division jointly commanded by a trio of peers, William Hay, Earl of Errol, John Lindsay, Earl of Crawford and William Graham, Earl of Montrose: beneath their banners were the levies of Perthshire, Angus, Forfar and Fife, some 7,000 strong in all. In the centre, the king would lead his own magnificent phalanx, up to 15,000 serried pikes, the defiant banners of St Andrew and St Margaret fluttering proudly, Sir Adam Forman carrying the royal standard. With the Household were the Earls of Cassilis, Morton and Rothes, Lords Herries, Maxwell, Innermeath, Borthwick and Sempill. The burgesses of Edinburgh, with their provost and those from Ayr and Haddington were swelled by those wild, unkempt Gallowegians from the south-west.

On the far right, James stationed his main reserve, 5,000 Highlanders led by Archibald Campbell, Earl of Argyll, and Matthew Stuart, the Earl of Lennox. There were Campbells from Glenorchy and Loudon, MacLean of Duart, Mackenzies, Grants, MacDonalds, their chief MacIan of Ardnamurchan, the levies of Sutherland, Caithness and Orkney, liveried in their fatal green and beneath the banner of William Sinclair, Earl of Caithness. As a stiffener, James placed the Frenchman D'Aussi and his cadre on this flank. With the Highlanders notorious for internecine squabbles, he perhaps hoped the presence of a hard core of continental professionals might facilitate an element of cohesion.

Adam Hepburn, Earl of Bothwell, commanded the final reserve, a picked body of 5,000 Lowlanders, men from the Lothians, the Forest of Ettrick, Galashiels and Selkirk. The three main attack formations; Home and Huntly, Errol, Crawford, Montrose and the king's division would thus be placed to deliver an attack in echelon, in the preferred Swiss manner; textbook perfect. Reserves would be on hand to exploit success; Highlanders securing the exposed flank. It is one thing to plan the deployment of the army in this manner of textbook practicalities on the day would be rather less neat.

Marshalling this great horde of perhaps not entirely willing warriors into columns for the march, albeit short, then shaking out into line on unfamiliar ground was no easy undertaking. Lowering grey-bellied clouds whipped by a fitful wind that gusted over the bare upland of sodden green and mire tore away the furious shouts and imprecations of officers and NCOs.

The men would grouse and moan, they would have practised their drills continually during their sojourn on the hill but then there had been no real enemy, the strength of their position affording ample comfort. But this afternoon it was altogether different, rumour would spread through the ranks like wildfire, men might find themselves dry mouthed, worms of fear gnawing at their intestines. These were, for the better part, conscripts and they'd had a pretty decent war thus far. Most had probably thought they'd withdraw into Scotland at some point, each man's knapsack rather heavier than when he'd come. As wars go, not a bad show. There had not been a major trial of arms between the two kingdoms for over a century, the last being at Homildon, quite close by and not a reassuring precedent.


## The Lord Admiral makes his dispositions

Englishmen, labouring through the dank Pallinsburn valley, could not see the mass of their opponents forming along the crest beyond. The admiral ascended Piper's Hill to gain a clearer view. The sight can hardly have been comforting. Worse, he was most uncomfortably aware that a gap had opened up between his division and that of his father. If the Scots were now to initiate an attack he was horribly exposed. Howard sent an urgent galloper toward the earl: 'for the forward battle alone was not able to encounter the whole battle of the Scots.'[8]

To reinforce the need for haste Howard chucked the rider his medallion featuring the charm of *Agnus Dei* (Lamb of God). By this Surrey would better understand the imperative. In this Renaissance battle, the admiral's division would fight beneath the ancient talisman of St Cuthbert's banner[9] and the Northern Saint had never failed to augur well. As Scottish camp followers had begun burning the straw and detritus from their tents (the question of whether any such mass burning occurred remains undecided), a pall of smoke was curling over the ridge obscuring Howard's view. As Sir Charles Oman points out, this shroud would also have enveloped the Scots and hindered their deployment and so surely this lighting of fires, if it took place, was more habit than policy.[10] Meanwhile, the Scottish foot discarded their leather-soled shoes; these simply wouldn't grip on wet grass so they 'faught in the vampis of their hoses'.[11]

James had already decided that he must exercise personal leadership of the main body. He has, of course, been roundly and constantly criticised for this and yet such action was entirely consistent with prevailing Swiss doctrine. His nobles, however, distinguished between the role of a brigade commander, even a general, and the person of the king. The Swiss did not have kings. This is echoed by Holinshed:

> His captains did what they could by words to remove him from his purpose, declaring to him the dutie of a prince; which is not rashlie to enter the fight, but to provide and see that evreie thing be done in order: and whereas coming to trie the matter by hand blowes, he can doo no more than another man; yet keeping his place as apperteineth to his person, he may be worthe manie thousands of others.[12]

Pedro de Ayala had commented on James' character sixteen years earlier; 'He is courageous, even more than a king should be. I have often seen him undertake most dangerous things in the last wars ... He is not a good captain, because he begins to fight before he has given his orders.' James' reply to these cautious entreaties had been that, as it was he who brought his subjects to war, it was only right he should be first to share the hazard.[13] The truth lies between the two extremes. James was following accepted Swiss tactics by leading in person and it is commendable that he felt an obligation to share the risk of battle with his men. At the same time this, on a policy level, was rank folly. He was not a captain but a king and it was his greater obligation to the Crown and to the realm of Scotland which mattered here.

Hall tells us that Henry VIII was equally impetuous. At the so-called 'Battle' of the Spurs, the king was keen to charge with the cavalry but accepted the advice that he was wiser to remain safe with his infantry: galling perhaps but sound.[14] It was Hall who admired James' Homeric valour, fighting as a 'meane souldier'. Sir Philip Sydney, later Tudor paladin observed 'a brave captain is as a root, out of which, as branches, the courage of his soldiers doth spring'.[15] This is unquestionably true of captains and leaders of formations, as for James, the king who would be captain, someone might have said '*c'est magnifique mais ce n'ait pas la Guerre*'.

Surrey, receiving the urgent message from his son, promptly urged his men forward. The space between his division and the Lord Admiral's amounted to nearly a mile and a half. The Scots were in fact considerably closer to the English van. It is perhaps at this point that James' master gunner may have approached the king, seeking permission to commence firing. Several ranging shots had already dropped harmlessly, if alarmingly, into the wet ground of the Pallinsburn. The king is said to have refused his consent on the basis that he wished 'to have them all before me on a plain field, and try what they can all do against me'.[16] This might appear to be nothing more than chivalric posturing but James, if he wished to fully exploit the Swiss model, actually required his enemies to be concentrated and in line facing him so the great weight of the blow he would deliver might tell to best effect. Most Swiss captains would very likely have agreed with him, even if his choice of ground would send frissons of alarm down their spines.

Sir Charles Oman takes a contrary view. He asserts that James did indeed take advantage of the admiral's difficulties and began the fight before Surrey was fully come up.[17] This argues that the opening exchange of artillery fire was clearly both brief and indecisive. There is indeed some further confusion as to the exact nature of the Scots deployment. James had allowed his French advisers to draw his divisions up in pike columns, indeed this would have been both sound and fully in conformity with continental practice. Howard reports that the Scots mustered with five such columns, each of two brigades and the length of a bowshot between each main formation. Hall suggests there were only four columns which subsequently engaged and a further two 'battles' which remained supine.[18] Oman interprets this to suggest Hall is referring to Home and Huntly and their subsequent inactivity after the first clash.[19]

Despite the parlous nature of his position, Thomas Howard was not a man to lose his head. As he waited for the rear to catch up he ordered his brigades to echelon to their right along the south-facing slope. There was sufficient ground between Branx Brig and Branxton Church for them to form up out of sight. It was perhaps now mid-afternoon and it would be nearer four by the time Surrey had made good the gap and the English could fully deploy. Above them great masses of Scots infantry crowded the skyline:

> four great battles all on foot with long spears like Moorish pikes ... The king of Scots army was divided into five battles, and every battle an arrow shot from the other, and all like furnished from the English army in great plumps, part of them quadrant and some pike wise, and were on the top of the hill, being a quarter of a mile from the foot thereof.[20]

'Quadrant' (*en quadrans*), in this case, implies a square shaped formation whilst 'pike-shaped' (*en maniere de pointe*), implies a more rectangular deployment with its narrower face to the enemy. The Scots descended the slope in, as the English described it the *Almayne* [German] *fashion*, silent, very orderly and purposefully.[21] As to the meaning of bowshot, Oman suggests 200yds (180m),[22] Lt. Col. Elliot notes that normal distances set for the butts were between 200–300yds (180–275m). Contemporary English ordinances provided that 'no person above the age of 24 should shoot at any mark that was not above eleven score yards distance, under pain of forfeiting for every shot 6s 8d' (38p).[23] If we take 200–250yds (180–230m) as the distance, this will very likely be correct.

And there they stand; the largest, arguably best-equipped national army that Scotland had ever mustered:

> with this beautiful landscape before them to the far west and north-west, and the English army below them steadily forming in position, and preparing for the battle that was on the eve of commencement, thousands of the bravest men in Scotland, together with their beloved king, viewed for the last time the country that gave them birth, and which was shortly to weep and mourn over the death of so many of her great and heroic sons.[24]

Grossman, in his study of soldiers and killing, speaks of 'the well of fortitude'; essentially the ability of the individual, and thus of the unit, which is nothing more than a collection of individuals, to resist the horrors and privations of combat. He argues, and most authorities would concur, that this resource of individual courage is finite, like a bank account and once overdrawn, begins to lose currency; 'heroism … is endurance for one moment more'.[25] During both world wars, it was often those hardened veteran units which performed less well in a fresh challenge than raw recruits whose resources had not been so abused. Thus James is perhaps better placed than might at first be considered the case. His men were, for the most part raw, but their very inexperience ensured their reserves had not been previously depleted. And, in reality, for the most part, they did not fail the test to come.

It would be a sanguine man indeed amongst the English who did not find this great Scottish host a daunting sight. That vast array of pikes seeming like a forest of staves, 'Birnam Wood come to high Dunsinane', great guns belching smoke and fire, whistle of round shot and the knowledge these could scythe a file of men into bloody, limbless pulp. Surrey, better to conform to the Scots deployment, adjusted his formations – his six divisions freshly consolidated into three. Dacre, whose riders 'stood apart by themselves to succour where most need was',[26] maintaining the only mounted reserve. Edmund Howard now commanded the right, next to him his brother, with their father taking the left.

And Stanley was still trailing. Surrey, in the heat of the moment, had apparently forgotten to send back guides to bring Stanley's brigade forward so he was obliged to feel his way by a more circuitous route. He and his Lancashire-men would nonetheless do their part. It would not be true to say that the Scots were on top of the hill, the English at the base. A small stream, sluggish and swelled by marsh, filled the valley bottom. From there, northwards the ground rose to the line upon which the English centre and left now stood. Should the Scots descend the hill to attack they would be obliged to negotiate both the wet and the slope. From their present vantage these difficulties were by no means obvious. The speed of their re-deployment had meant the Scots did not have time to fully acquaint themselves with the ground. This significant deficiency would yield dire consequences.

One unanswered question is why were the Scots apparently unaware? We know James had at least one renegade marcher in his pay, most likely others besides. Herein, we think, lies a clue which helps us answer the apparent disagreement between the Oman school which favours an immediate Scots attack and Barr's view which prefers an opening gun duel precipitating an advance compelled by necessity, a view to which we subscribe. Had James been planning an attack downhill, he had leisure to scout the base of the hill most thoroughly; that he appears not to have done so would imply he did not plan to descend at all.

It was now apparent that the Scots were in four main divisions and Surrey realised he had to amend his deployment to conform at least in part, as the smaller wings of his own two larger contingents would be inadequate to meet any attack on their own:

> Therefore my Lord Surrey and Lord Howard suddenly were constrained and enforced to divide their army in another four battles, or else it was thought it should have been to their great danger and jeopardy.[27]

Dacre's wing was thus robbed of all his foot which were brigaded with Surrey's division, his cavalry kept intact as a reserve. Sir Marmaduke Constable likewise, his men were pushed into the ranks of Howard's. Thus Surrey now had five distinct divisions, his own, the admiral's, his younger son's, Dacre's and the laggard Stanley. His position was overall, far from ideal, his men were at a disadvantage, strung out after an exhausting march and outnumbered.

Edmund Howard was leading the smallest of the English units; the right flank or wing of his brother's division. He had perhaps 1,000 men from Cheshire, with the Macclesfield men, and half as many from Lancashire. They were not happy, expecting to fight beneath their traditional Stanley colours, not those of the untried Howard. His officers, Sir John Booth and Sir Richard Cholmondely, were proven men. Burghers of Hull, royal tenants from the Abbey of Vale Royal, captained by the abbot in person and a parcel of gentry affinities Fitzwilliams, Warcops, Savages, Stapletons, Harbottles, Tunstalls mustered beneath his banner.[28] A stiffening of 200 additional marines under Maurice Berkeley, master of the *Mary George* completed his muster.[29] Surrey's English deployment offered a very different aspect to that of their adversaries ranged above. Here were bows and bills, standing by companies in a manner their grandfathers would have readily recognised.

The admiral commanded his own crack mariners, the kernel of his contingent. In their Tudor green,[30] these marines formed up in ships' companies, captained by their skippers; Sir William Sidney of the *Great Barque*, Edward Echyngham of the *Spaniard*, James King of *Julian of Dartmouth* and a dozen others.[31] With these hardy seadogs, stood the Durham men under Sir William Bulmer, Lord Clifford's affinity of 207 bows and 116 bills from the 'Flower of Craven' flaunting the red wyvern,[32] with the followers of those hardened northern knights, Conyers, Latimer, Scrope of Upsall, Lords Ogle and Lumley. These men had fought the Scots for generations; to Sir John Forster fell the honour of bearing St Cuthbert's standard.[33] 'Little' Sir Marmaduke Constable led the left flanking unit, within his contingent a Northumbrian company under Sir William Percy, the earl's cousin with another thousand bows and bills from Lancashire.[34]

Surrey's battle, described as both 'main' and 'rearward',[35] comprised his personal staff and affinity. The Norfolk men mustered beneath their own sacred banner, that of St Audrey, the Abbot of Whitby's people, men from the York Levy, Scrope of Bolton, George Darcy[36] and companies of Yorkshire gentry; Barkeley, Pickering, Tempest, Dawnay, Clapham, Gascoigne, Willoughby, Tilney and Radcliffe. Initially, Dacre's Border Horse had formed the right-hand contingent, mostly Cumbrians but with rowdies from Tynedale[37] and east marchers, who were brigaded with him to make up numbers if, as it turned out, they added little value. Stanley's men, still not yet on the field, comprised a rump of the Cheshire and Lancashire men, officered by Sir William Molyneux and Sir Henry Kickley. But these men marched beneath the Eagle's Claw of the Stanleys, where they knew they belonged!

As the first shots were fired, all three English divisions stood on the field were commanded by Howards, father and two sons. A complex family, fully and ruthlessly entwined in the dangerous weft of court politics, Thomas Howard would be the *eminence grise* behind two doomed queens and his younger brother the father of one. Relentlessly ambitious and utterly venal, the Howards never lacked courage. By now the admiral had briefed his own officers, northern men all and seasoned. These might have been a rough-and-ready army by Renaissance standards, old fashioned, even archaic but all the pride of their very Englishness and the ghosts of generations of forbears who had successfully defied the Scottish nation stood behind, casting long shadows. Above their heads fluttered the great banner of St Cuthbert whose divine protection had flown over victorious fields for nearly four centuries.

## The guns speak out

The fight began with an artillery duel, the first British battle to open in this way (Warwick's cannonade at Barnet excepted), at a range of about 600yds (550m). It might be anticipated that the Scots, having the benefit of a greater weight of shot and of higher ground, should enjoy a marked advantage. However, their great guns were siege pieces which could perhaps and at best fire one round a minute. The English field guns could fire twice or even three times that. As the guns recoiled after each shot they had to be laboriously manhandled back into place. The English gun crews were more experienced and this quickly began to tell. It has been suggested that the downward angle was too acute for the Scottish gunners and the barrels could not be sufficiently depressed. This is untrue, as the pieces of the day could be wedged sufficiently at the breech to allow for the depression but the angle would affect the fall of shot.

> Then ordnance great anon out brast [blast]
> On either side with thundering thumps,
> And roaring guns, with fire fast,
> The levelled out great leaden lumps.[38]

Solid balls, round shot, are intended to bounce on striking ground, 'grazing' the surface so they then bound into an enemy formation, doing fearful damage. It is likely that the Scottish shot smacked harmlessly into the wet ground, 'they did no harm to the English army', whilst the English rounds took effect, killing men and disabling guns. Already topography was working for the English. Whilst Robert Borthwick, the king's master gunner, survived (contrary to Hall's assertion), at least one of the Scottish gun captains was killed and the rest so disheartened they ran away. 'The English Ordnance … shot fast and did great skaithe [damage] and slew his principal gunners; but the king's ordnance did small skaithe by reason of the height where they stood they shot over the English army.'[39]

Reverend Jones, in his account of 1864, refers to round shot picked up from the site[40] and that the Scots were firing lead shot, the English iron. Hall tells us that 'oute brast the ordinaunce on both sides with fyre flame and hydeous noise'.[41] There seems to be consensus that the Scottish gunners simply overshot and that the gun duel was fairly short for it is clear the English gunners played upon the pike columns as they descended the hill, inflicting loss. Leslie concedes 'our bullets … did thame na hurt, bot flewe ouer thair heidis'.[42] The *Trewe Encountre*[43] boasts, however, that the English fire took deadly effect 'to breke and constreyn the Scottissshe great army'. If we consider Grossman's view that most killing on modern battlefields is done by gunners as opposed to 'grunts'. Artillerymen, working in the open and trained to function as a team, as a well-oiled machine, and not subject to the sight of the immediate consequences of their fire, are the most efficient killers on the battlefield. James IV, had he survived, would have heartily concurred.

James would reasonably have expected that odds in the gun duel would have been heavily weighted. Peter Reese has very properly observed that the king rejected Borthwick's suggestion he open fire as the English crowded the narrow path of the Branx Brig most probably because he did not wish to waste precious powder on long-range shooting. He trusted that, as the English were forced to advance, his guns could flense their files with impunity. Whilst we cannot exactly ascertain what was going on in James' mind, this seems highly plausible. At this point, the Scots appeared to hold all the aces. They retained high ground, were fully deployed and had just been offered an ostensibly perfect target.

Some of the Scottish rounds, throwing up fountains of wet clods, smashed into the turf by Dacre's reserve and panicked the east coast riders into rout. The rest held firm and the contagion, so easily infectious, did not spread. Dacre's own report[44] suggests the Scots did not commence their cannonade until Howard's men were engaged by Home and Huntly and routed. The warden seems to suggest the guns began to speak only as he hurried his riders to plug the yawning chasm on the English right. It was the first crashing volley that persuaded the middle and east marchers they urgently needed to be elsewhere, though not until they'd profited from the day by lifting horses from their own central division![45] One troop which did not bolt was Bastard Heron's: 'None was more formidable on the field, and none more willing for the battle-encounter.'[46] This sequencing, from as telling a witness as Dacre, could be interpreted as lending weight to Colonel Leather's version of a developing encounter battle.

Happily for the English, neither of the senior Howards lost his nerve. Peter Reese suggests that the admiral, like Wellington, had his men shelter on the reverse slope above the Pallinsburn, whilst these huge rounds either flew harmlessly overhead or splattered alarmingly if uselessly. It was Edmund Howard's misfortune that the horsemen bolted next to his small division and his own men, already unsettled, suffered another blow to their shaky morale. We should not underestimate the psychological effect of this vast, satanic roaring in the otherwise quiet world of that era. 'Infernal' is a term often applied to the guns' bellow and accompanying dark clouds of vile smoke with hints of brimstone, added considerably to the effect. Nonetheless, it's a tribute to the English commander and his officers that their troops did not lose heart. Very soon, the English guns came into play.

Assuming (as we think we must) that the Scots had remained stationary whilst artillerymen slogged it out, the English had convincingly won the first round and Appleyard's gunners could now switch their aim to the massed files of the two central divisions. These raw levies were not ready for the great roar and bellow of the guns. Still less were they prepared to stand as their comrades were mangled by shot. It could be argued that damage wrought by the English artillery was mainly psychological and yet the chroniclers confirm that 'the English artillery shot into the middle of the king's battle and slew many persons'.[47]

These Scots, young men dragged from the plough or an apprentice's bench, had not been taught how to withstand bombardment, that nerve wrenching terror of flying, random shot that takes off limbs and bowls a file of men like ninepins. Only bitter experience or deep resolve could stiffen men against such horrors; they possessed neither. There was thus no need for the English to attack with their infantry. Guns could do the killing. James now had to decide what best to do. In previous encounters the Scots had sought to advance to contact as quickly as possible to close the 'killing gap' between them and the English who, with their longbows, had traditionally had superiority in the missile arm. Now it was their guns that enjoyed fire superiority, the range still being too long for bows. An artillery duel had replaced the arrow storm as arbiter. Whoever fared worst would be compelled to advance. In one sense it could be said the outcome was already decided. On the other hand, those fearsome Swiss mercenaries had not earned their reputation by standing on the defensive.

Neill Barr emphatically takes the view, contrary to Oman (who is followed by Phillips), that the artillery duel preceded any move by the Scots and that it was losing this initial exchange which forced James onto the offensive.[48] Peter Reese supports Barr as do we. From James' initial perspective and however compelling Swiss offensive tactics might be, there was no imperative to attack. His position on Branxton Edge was very nearly as strong as the army's previous stance. It would be preferable to allow the English to struggle forward in an uphill assault. Once his divisions were exposed to the full fury of the English fire, with the Scottish guns silent and out of action, options were limited. Had he ordered a withdrawal, this would have been tantamount to defeat and the army might well have begun to disintegrate.[49]

We have to reconcile this with Dacre's account which seems to clearly state that the guns fired only as the Scots advanced. Our view is that the sequence of events may have been that the artillery opened up on the Scottish side but that it was immediately apparent to the English that the enemy gunners were way off. Appleyard and his assistant Blakenall may have directed some of their guns to counter-battery fire whilst turning the rest on the wonderful target the massed Scottish formations presented. It is impossible to assess how many casualties this English cannonade inflicted. These were light pieces throwing balls of 1–2lbs weight but which could inflict significant damage on men so crammed together. In all probability, however, the losses were not great. More telling was the psychological effect of the bombardment upon untried troops.

Despite the emphasis prevailing doctrine placed upon shock action, James was not obliged to throw away the advantages of ground. Clearly, he had refused to do so earlier when his army was so strongly posted on Flodden Edge. In one way the situation had not significantly changed, except that the English stood between him and home. But it was they who *needed* to fight, he did not. All of his strategic objectives had been secured – the mere presence of Surrey's force below proved that. He had led the English earl a merry dance thus far and risked nothing. Throughout he had displayed cleverness and resolve. Only now had he been humbugged by the English flank march but that need not be fatal.

Once his guns had been silenced and screaming round shot began flensing his shuddering files, attack, for James, was the only option remaining.

NOTES

1. Ancient ballad, quoted in Jones, p. 67.
2. Kightly, p. 38.
3. *Ibid.*
4. Oman, p. 308; It is thought Giles Musgrave may have been the husband of one of those ladies who'd accompanied Margaret Tudor into Scotland: *Giles Musgrave was a guileful Greek / And friend familiar with the king Who said, Sir King, if you do seek / To know the Englishman's meaning / Your marches they mean to sack / And borders fair to harry and burn / Wherefore it's best that we go back / From such intent them for to turn / This Musgrave was a man of skill/ And spake thus for a policy / To cause the king come down the hill / That so the battle tried might be*; see Ferguson, *Lords to Labourers*, p. 21.
5. Leslie, *Historie of Scotland*, p. 348.
6. Oman, p. 308.
7. Highlanders with claymores would perform the same role as double-handed swordsmen for the Swiss.
8. Hall, *King Henry VIII*, vol. 1, p. 85.
9. St Cuthbert's banner, as previously noted, had flown above English armies at the Battle of the Standard 1138, Falkirk 1298 and Neville's Cross 1346.
10. Oman, p. 310.
11. Laing, *Trewe Encountre*, p. 150.
12. Holinshed, *Historie of Scotland*, p. 481.
13. Mackie, R.L., *King James IV of Scotland* (Edinburgh, 1958), p. 84.
14. Hall, *King Henry VIII*, vol. 1, p. 85.
15. Quoted in Grossman, Lt. Col. D., *On Killing* (New York, 2009), p. 84.
16. Pitscottie, *Historie and Chronicles of Scotland*, p. 270.
17. Oman, p. 311.
18. *Ibid.*
19. *Ibid.*
20. Hall, *King Henry VIII*, vol. 1, p. 85.
21. Oman, p. 311.

22. *Ibid.*, p. 312.
23. Elliot, n. p. 71.
24. Jones, p. 28.
25. Grossman, p. 82.
26. Hall, *King Henry VIII*, vol. 1, p. 86.
27. Laing, *Trewe Encountre*, p. 148.
28. Oman, p. 305.
29. Kightly, p. 35.
30. *Ibid.*
31. *Ibid.*
32. *Ibid.*
33. Jones, p. 26.
34. Oman, p. 305.
35. *Ibid.*
36. George Darcy rebelled against Henry VIII during the period of the Pilgrimage of Grace; his many past services earned no clemency.
37. Oman, p. 305.
38. Ballad, quoted in Jones, p. 31.
39. Hall, *King Henry VIII*, vol. 1, p. 86.
40. Jones, p. 30.
41. Hall, *King Henry VIII*, vol. 1, p. 108.
42. Leslie, *Historie of Scotland*, p. 145.
43. *Ibid.*, pp. 147–48.
44. Oman, p. 313.
45. *Ibid.*
46. Jones, p. 26.
47. Hall, *King Henry VIII*, vol. 1, p. 108.
48. Barr, pp. 95–6.
49. *Ibid.*

# 8

# THE KING OF SCOTS IS KILLED, WITH ALL HIS CURSED LORDS:
## TRIAL BY BATTLE 2

The stubborn spearmen still made good
Their dark impenetrable wood,
Each stepping where his comrade stood,
The instant that he fell,
No thought was there of dastard flight;
Linked in the serried phalanx tight,
Groom fought like noble, squire like knight,
As fearlessly as well.

Scott, *Marmion*

If I had time and anything like your ability to study war, I think I should concentrate almost entirely on the 'actualities of war' – the effects of tiredness,
hunger, fear, lack of sleep, weather ... The principles of strategy and tactics, and
the logistics of war are really absurdly simple: it is the actualities that make war
so complicated and so difficult, and are usually so neglected by historians.

Field Marshal Lord Wavell writing to Basil Liddell Hart

Once committed, late medieval/Renaissance forces were difficult if not
impossible to rally; to strike decisively was imperative. The weight and force
of the blow must smash an enemy or fail. Whichever side broke would suffer
consequentially much higher loss. To the English, this great ocean of pikes,
deluging like a steel-tipped avalanche from the ridge, must have appeared as
a vision of the apocalypse. Even though Appleyard's guns were still banging
furiously, screaming round shot punching holes in this bristling mob, a very
great mass remained.

Grossman quotes the pioneering work of his predecessor, S.L.A. Marshall,
whose studies of battle from the Second World War suggested that only perhaps 15–20 per cent of US soldiers actually fired their rifles in action.[1] We
have no comparable data for the sixteenth century of course. In such battles as
Flodden, fighting was very much 'up close and personal'. Grossman suggests
that part of the allure of the pike as a weapon and a key to its success was that
the act of killing was carried out at a moderate distance.

We are not entirely persuaded this was the case. Life in the sixteenth century was harsher by an immeasurable degree. Companies were commanded
by officers their men were accustomed to both respect and obey, bound by
long generations of feudal ties. English and Scots had been at each other's
throats for the last two centuries and this bitter legacy of ethnic hate was
palpable. MacDonald Fraser quotes incidents from later conflict in the mid-
sixteenth century, era of 'the Rough Wooing': 'the Scots paying back the rav-
ages of years, were pitiless, and one hears of their buying English prisoners
from the French in order to slaughter them'.[2]

Studies also suggest fighting with cold steel is now mercifully rare and,
when one side does launch a bayonet charge, the party on the receiving end
will generally break before contact. The value of edged weapons in contemporary conflict depends more upon the psychological advantage the superior
morale of the attacker confers, than the actual tally of unfortunates he spits in
the charge: 'The fixing of bayonets is more than a fixing of steel to the rifle
since it puts iron into the soul of the soldier doing the fixing.'[3] A crucial difference perhaps is that the sixteenth-century combatant *expected* the fight to
come to close quarters. Even after allowing for the winnowing effect of guns

and bows, few in the English line would have entertained any doubts that the Scots' charge would be halted short of their line.

And now it was the killing time. Now was the time of Masefield's 'the scorned, the rejected, the men hemmed in with spears'. The commanders had brought their men into the ring but the outcome would be a soldier's battle.

## King James advances his divisions

> The battlefield is the epitome of war. All else in war, when war is perfectly con-
> ducted, exists but to serve the forces of the battlefield and to assure final success
> on the field.

> S.L.A. Marshall, *Men Against Fire*

For the Renaissance prince, when faced with the critical decision of when to strike, practical advice was at hand. Machiavelli was of the view that:

> It is certain that small pieces of cannon … do more damage than heavy artillery.
> The best remedy against the latter is making a resolute attack upon it as soon as
> possible; if you lose some of your men in so doing (which must always be the
> case), surely a partial loss is not so bad as a total defeat. The Swiss are worthy of
> imitation in this respect, they never decline an engagement out of fear of artil-
> lery, but always give the death penalty to those who would stir from their ranks,
> or show the least sign of being frightened by it.[4]

This was pragmatic counsel James was inclined to heed. He ordered his left-hand division forward, the serried pikes and broadswords of Home and Huntly's division glinting in the pallid sun. It had rained earlier, squally show-ers now followed by calm. Hall relates that 'the King of Scots and his noble men, made the more haste to come to joining, and so all the four battles in manner descended the hill at once'.[5] In this, he is supported by the words of the *Trewe Encountre*, 'our guns did so break and constrain the Scottish great army that some part of them were enforced to come down toward our army'.[6] Not quite correct, the Scots plan was to attack in the 'Almayn' or Swiss manner, each division striking in echelon, pulverising the linear forma-tions of the English with a series of massive blows, dense packed columns simply rolling over their adversaries.

These tactics do appear to have temporarily confused the English. This was the first time continental methods had been tried out on English soil. Most of the men serving under Surrey related their understanding of battle to the

Wars of the Roses: 'All these four battles, in manner fought at one time, and were determined in effect, little in distance of the beginning and ending of any one of them before the other, saving that Sir Edward Stanley which was the last that fought.'[7] It was, from the English perspective, most unfortunate that the first assault should fall on their weakest division. Home outnumbered his opponent by at least two if not three to one and the ground here favoured an attacker. The marshy dip that was to so influence matters in the centre (*Plates 11 & 12*), petered out and left a level field (*Plate 10*). Worse, those Lancashire and Cheshire men on the English right were discountenanced at being brigaded with Howard's wing, an unknown and alien commander when they had expected to fight under Stanley.

There was wavering even before the charge struck home: 'The Cheshire and Lancashire men never abode stroke and few of the gentlemen of Yorkshire abode but fled.'[8] For the Scottish left, under its two captains Home and Huntly, these Swiss tactics brought dazzling success. Howard's division simply crumbled, 'they proched [pricked/stabbed] us with spears and put many over, that the blood ran out burst at their broken harness'.[9] Rout is like fire, it spreads without warning, consumes all and seizes men who might till then have fought like lions. Once this contagion strikes it can be almost impossible to halt. The Scots' advance would have been a truly terrifying spectacle for men already rattled. Home's steady phalanx in the centre, a steel-fanged monster, inhuman and relentless with Huntly's formidable swordsmen, fleet of foot, swarming from the flanks 'like troops of hungry wolves' (as one commentator described their descendants at Culloden in 1746).

It is regrettable from a historian's perspective that none of the individual combatants has left us a personal memoir. To reconstruct the effect of hand-to-hand combat, we are obliged to refer to later accounts, 'I stabbed him through the chest. He dropped his rifle and fell, and the blood shot out of his mouth. I stood over him for a few seconds and then I gave him the coup de grâce. After we had taken the enemy position, I felt giddy, my knees shook, and I was actually sick.'[10]

Killing a man is never easy. Most of those on the field would wear full or part harness or would, at least, be wearing jacks. To bring your man down was but part of the killing business for you had best ensure he did not rise again, nor still have sufficient vigour to deliver a killing stroke as he fell. Those who were laid in the mass grave discovered on the field of Towton were mainly done to death by head blows; clearly delivered in a frenzy of murderous haste. There would be no glorious deaths, no pithy oratories as men shuffled off, rather a screaming, blood-deluged slaughterhouse.

Not all fled; Sir Bryan Tunstall of Thurland,[11] kneeling to take in a last mouthful of earth as confessional, hurled himself upon the Scots, killing

Sir Malcolm Mckeen and others before himself dying beneath Scottish spears. With him fell the Cheshire knights Sir William Handforth, Thomas Venables and Robert Foulehurst. Lancashire lost Sir John Booth and John Lawrence. Robert Warcop and Sir William Fitzwilliam from Yorkshire died as did skipper Maurice Berkeley and John Bostwick, the latter cut down trying to rally the Abbot of Vale Royal's contingent. Despite such heroism from individuals and small contingents the picture, overall, was bleak. This wing had simply folded, the fight dissolving into knots and eddies of struggling, hewing men.

Edmund Howard, with his standard bearer and a core of personal retainers, made a desperate stand. Most were killed. Howard, fighting with great courage, was three times felled but rose to continue laying about him. All appeared lost. As Pitscottie relates: 'the Earl of Huntly's highland men with their bows and two handed swords fought so manfully that they defeated the Englishmen.'[12] Christopher Savage was also slain[13] and his Macclesfield contingent virtually annihilated.

We have Hall as our primary source for the opening exchange of gunfire and it is he who asserts the English gunners 'slew the master gunner of Scotland and beat all his men from the field'[14] and that the English shot fell mainly amongst the packed ranks of the 'King's Battle [division]'. The *English Gazette*, a contemporary account, refers to the first strike as being the clash between the three earls and the admiral, next Surrey against King James, then Stanley versus Lennox and Argyll's Highlanders and lastly the fight on the English right/Scottish left.

The *Gazette* claims the fight proper started at '*environ de quatre a cinq heures après diner*' (between four and five in the afternoon).[15] Hall, however, has the first clash as being that involving Home and Huntly with Edmund Howard. Hall does suggest the various stages of the battle unfolded very quickly with the only noticeable gap being the delayed arrival of Stanley and his trouncing James' Highlanders. He also gives Home's borderers full credit for the initial Scottish success on their left against Edmund Howard.

We cannot therefore say for certain that the battle did commence on the Scottish left, though this sequence of offensive action from the attacking side would tie in with defined Swiss doctrine. Pitscottie clearly avers that Home and Huntly began the action and that the fight here was rather harder and more protracted than we might have considered. He also credits the Scots success to 'the Earl of Huntly's men, with their bows and two handed swords'.[16] This seems a rather romantic gloss for it would be the serried pikes that carried the day. Huntly's Highlanders with their great two-handers would have been deployed as *dopplensolders* on the flanks. This is not to say they did not contribute to the tactical victory on this flank, they were most accomplished warriors.

Pitscottie confirms Home and Huntly's men had suffered only trifling loss, 'few of their men either hurt or slain'.[17] The chronicler then goes on to record a conversation between the two commanders. Huntly wished to intervene in the centre, to take his men to aid James. It is then Home allegedly uttered his famous rejoinder – 'we have fought our vanguards and have won the same'.[18] Huntly demurred, feeling unable to abandon his king in such dire circumstances. He then summoned his affinity to follow but by the time his men were rallied 'all was defeat on either side, so that few or none were living'.[19] Seeing the day was irrevocably lost, Huntly immediately adopted a pragmatic stance. There are limits to most loyalties.

## Now to the centre

If Home and Huntly formed the *Vorhut*, then Errol, Crawford and Montrose were the *Gewaltschaufen*. Now, they streamed down the hill to engage the Lord Admiral's division and the king, seizing a pike prepared, deaf to all entreaties, to lead his main body. Reckless as this might appear it was consistent with Swiss practice. The phalanx, in James' case, with files 450 strong and a formation twenty ranks deep,[20] once committed, could not be recalled.

The Swiss did not have alternative strategies. Theirs was, though highly effective, very much a blunt instrument. Once divisions were committed, one following on in echelon behind the other, the die was cast. There was no further scope for general-ship. Nonetheless, as had been pointed out to James, he was not just a general but king and commander-in-chief. To throw himself bodily into the fight, however noble sounding, was irresponsible. That he should share the hazard of his subjects, that he should rally his disparate forces by shining personal example is laudable in theory but lamentable in practice.

Furthermore, had the king hesitated, he might have seen that matters on the English right had now taken a rather different course and that victory there was by no means assured. Dacre's Border Horse swiftly moved up to plug the gap created by the mass defection of the Lancashire and Cheshire levies and a further, fierce fight ensued. Scottish pikes and broadswords emptied more than a few saddles, Dacre's losses were around 160, with Philip Dacre, Sir Humphrey Lisle[21] and Harry Gray all taken. Many Scots also fell, spitted on Cumbrian lances, including three of Home's cousins, one of whom was Cuddy Home, a celebrated paladin from stark Fast Castle. With them died Crichtons, Cockburns, Douglases,[22] Kers and Bromfields; four Gordon tacksmen[23] were also added to the score.

Leading his own company of hardened cut-throats, the Bastard Heron cut his way through to rescue Howard, both men soon being wounded: 'came

John Heron, Bastard sore hurt, saying there was never a nobleman's son so like to be lost as you be on this day, for all my hurts I will here lie and die with you.'[24] They fought their way clear, Howard, despite his wounds, killing Sir Davy Home of Wedderburn, the warden's brother in the fury of hand to hand. Both sides now sounded the recall and drew apart, 'convened their men again to their standards'.[25] Dacre kept the field and Home withdrew his men part way back up the slope. Though they had suffered relatively minor loss; neither marchers nor Gordons would play any further part.

It is said that when Home subsequently received a royal summons to bring his division to the relief of the centre, now sorely pressed he replied; 'He does well that does for himself; we have fought our vanguard already and beaten the same, let the rest do their part'.[26] This may or may not be true, equally the rumour that Home and Dacre had an 'understanding' may also have a factual basis. Such arrangements were by no means uncommon and the borderers of both sides, who bore the brunt of most offensives, were not noted for putting the national interest above local loyalties. The taint of treachery followed Home to his execution for treason in 1516. Nonetheless, the warden was correct in holding his ground as, were he to move, Dacre would certainly follow. Practically, the situation was a stalemate.

The three earls' division now swept down the hill and was almost immediately in difficulties. Their advance was carried out in chill silence; prevailing tactical doctrine did not favour traditional clamouring war cries. Machiavelli again:

> The opinions of ancient authors vary concerning this matter, whether those beginning the battle should rush on with furious shouts and outcries or march up to the attack with silence and composure. The latter is certainly the most proper means of preserving good order, and of hearing commands most distinctly. But I do not think a continual shout can be of any service; quite the contrary it will prevent the general's orders from being heard – this must be attended with terrible consequences.[27]

As the Scots, discarding their shoes, so their bare feet might keep a better grip on the slippery turf, descended (*Plate 14*), it was the turn of the English archers to step forward, draw and loose. James had taken care to pack his front ranks with chosen men, well harnessed and bearing heavy wooden pavises to soak up arrows, 'which were the most assuredly [best] armoured that hath been seen and the tallest and goodliest persons withal'.[28] Whilst these could come on with relative impunity the less well armoured in the rear ranks undoubtedly suffered, 'which sore them annoyed'[29] and the English guns, as one of the Scottish chroniclers admits, were continuing to fire, still causing casualties.

1  King James IV of Scotland by Charles Dawson. This early twentieth century copy shows the king with reddish hair. *Courtesy of Ford Castle*

2  Margaret Tudor, wife of James, sister of Henry VIII of England. *Courtesy of Ford Castle*

3 A view of Flodden Edge looking west from the curtain wall of Ford Castle. *Courtesy of Ford Castle*

4 An elevated view of Flodden from the roof walk of Ford. *Courtesy of Ford Castle*

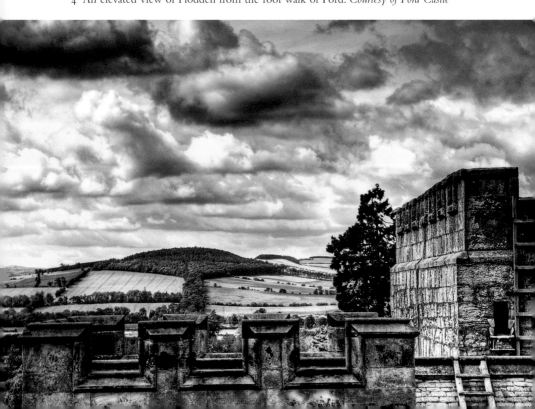

5 Norham Castle, through the west gate looking towards the great Norman keep. *Authors' collection*

6 Duddo Tower, the surviving spire of one gable looking north. *Authors' collection*

7  Etal Castle, the gateway. *Authors' collection*

8  Twizel Bridge, looking from the south, sluggish, broad waters of a somnolent Till below. *Authors' collection*

9 The field – looking south down the length of the dip stretching in front of the English centre towards the ridge. *Authors' collection*

10 Looking towards the English right with the ground covered by Home and Huntly's advance. *Authors' collection*

11 The marshy dip looking east, the obstacle that so disordered the Scots' advance in the centre and contributed significantly to their defeat. *Authors' collection*

12  The dip looking westwards as it begins to peter out towards the ground covered by the Scottish left. *Authors' collection*

13  Looking northwards from the dip towards the English centre and Piper's Hill, now crowned by the monument. *Authors' collection*

14  A Scotsman's view looking west from the higher ground of the ridge. *Authors' collection*

15 Looking towards Flodden Edge from the south, a track leading from Encampment towards the ridge. *Authors' collection*

16 A view of the area occupies by the Scottish camp, with Flodden Edge swelling behind. *Authors' collection*

17 The memorial on Piper's Hill viewed looking south-west from Branxton Church.
*Authors' collection*

18 Branxton Church, temporary mortuary for the English dead after the battle. Most of what is seen today obviously postdates 1513. *Authors' collection*

19 James' sword and dagger – copied by Charles Dawson. *Courtesy of Ford Castle*

20 Banner of William Keith, Earl Marischal: *Veritas Vincit*, 'The Truth Prevails'. This may be a copy as the original was said to have been recovered from the field by John Skirving of Plewlandhill, notwithstanding he was captured on the field. *Courtesy of Ford Castle*

21  Fit for a king – one of the authors brandishes the facsimile sword. *Courtesy of Ford Castle*

22 The King's Chamber at Ford. *Courtesy of Ford Castle*

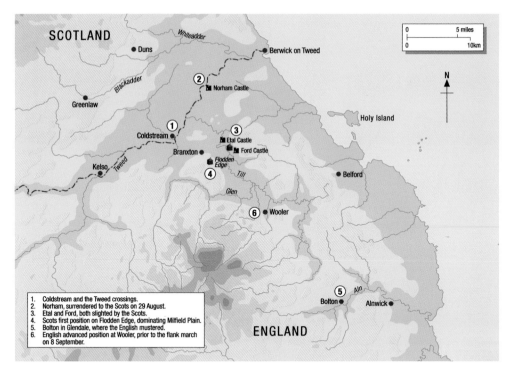

1. Coldstream and the Tweed crossings.
2. Norham, surrendered to the Scots on 29 August.
3. Etal and Ford, both slighted by the Scots.
4. Scots first position on Flodden Edge, dominating Milfield Plain.
5. Bolton in Glendale, where the English mustered.
6. English advanced position at Wooler, prior to the flank march on 8 September.

Map 1  The Scots' invasion route.

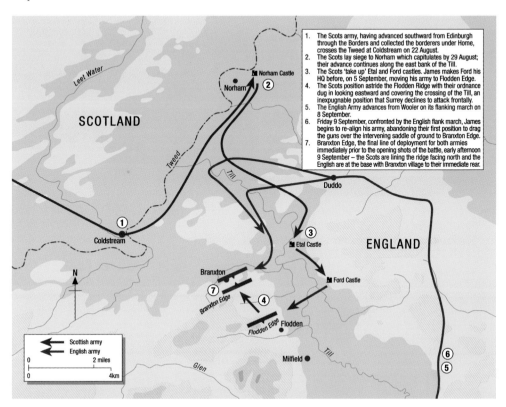

1. The Scots army, having advanced southward from Edinburgh through the Borders and collected the borderers under Home, crosses the Tweed at Coldstream on 22 August.
2. The Scots lay siege to Norham which capitulates by 29 August; their advance continues along the east bank of the Till.
3. The Scots 'take up' Etal and Ford castles. James makes Ford his HQ before, on 5 September, moving his army to Flodden Edge.
4. The Scots position astride the Flodden Ridge with their ordnance dug in looking eastward and covering the crossing of the Till, an inexpugnable position that Surrey declines to attack frontally.
5. The English Army advances from Wooler on its flanking march on 8 September.
6. Friday 9 September, confronted by the English flank march, James begins to re-align his army, abandoning their first position to drag the guns over the intervening saddle of ground to Branxton Edge.
7. Branxton Edge, the final line of deployment for both armies immediately prior to the opening shots of the battle, early afternoon 9 September – the Scots are lining the ridge facing north and the English are at the base with Branxton village to their immediate rear.

Map 2  The English flank march.

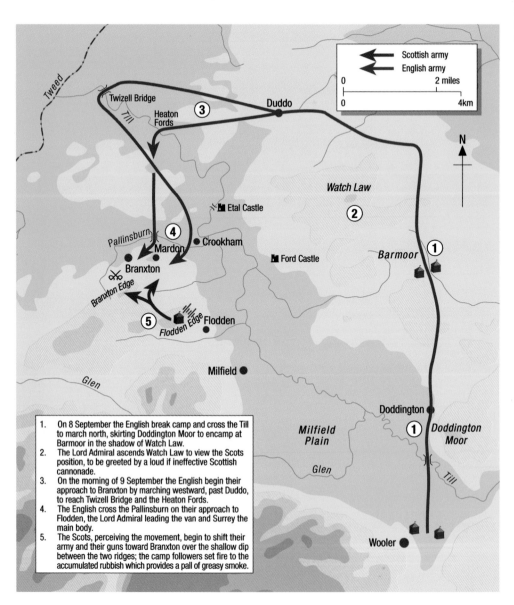

Scottish army
English army

0                    2 miles
0                                4km

N

Tweed

Twizell Bridge

Till

Heaton Fords

③

Duddo

Watch Law

②

Etal Castle

Barmoor

①

Pallinsburn

④

Mardon

Crookham

Ford Castle

Branxton

Branxton Edge

⑤

Flodden Edge

Flodden

Milfield

Glen

Doddington

①

Doddington Moor

Till

Milfield Plain

Glen

Wooler

1.  On 8 September the English break camp and cross the Till to march north, skirting Doddington Moor to encamp at Barmoor in the shadow of Watch Law.
2.  The Lord Admiral ascends Watch Law to view the Scots position, to be greeted by a loud if ineffective Scottish cannonade.
3.  On the morning of 9 September the English begin their approach to Branxton by marching westward, past Duddo, to reach Twizell Bridge and the Heaton Fords.
4.  The English cross the Pallinsburn on their approach to Flodden, the Lord Admiral leading the van and Surrey the main body.
5.  The Scots, perceiving the movement, begin to shift their army and their guns toward Branxton over the shallow dip between the two ridges; the camp followers set fire to the accumulated rubbish which provides a pall of greasy smoke.

Map 3  The Battle.

The great English war bow had dominated Anglo-Scottish warfare since Falkirk in 1298. It destroyed Scottish armies at Dupplin Moor (1332) and the next year at Halidon Hill. It facilitated the English triumph at Neville's Cross in 1346 and, virtually unaided, trounced a Douglas-led army at Homildon in 1402. In this, however, the last major battle in which it was to feature, it did not achieve its customary dominance. Weather undoubtedly, being both wet and windy as the fight began, was a contributory factor but the stout harness of the leading ranks augmented by the heavy wooden shields or pavises clearly performed well.

If the bow did not prove to be the decisive weapon at Flodden, it remained deadly. The Scots may have suffered less than their ancestors had at Halidon Hill or Homildon, this is not to say they did not suffer at all. These massed pikes were an archer's dream, and not all were as well harnessed as those at the front. Even if wet and wind inhibited the arrow storm to a degree, many shafts would still find their mark, most tellingly as the Scots crowded to cross the burn.

What the Scots had not anticipated was the dip, mire and rise beyond (*Plate 13*). To succeed, the pike phalanx needed to retain impetus, discipline and cohesion. If these were lost then so is the unstoppable steamroller effect and pikes become vulnerable. It was precisely this which now occurred. Stung by arrows, assailed by shot, Scots stumbled into the mire and began to lose their formation. As they struggled toward the English line, their cohesion vanished. This was the literal pitfall that Swiss officers would always strive so hard to avoid.

For the phalanx to remain invincible it must come swiftly to contact, its ranks and files intact, driving over its opponents like a juggernaut. The beast must keep its claws and fangs aligned and ready. To stumble was to fail. And the Scots had failed, before ever coming to contact, pounded by English guns, winnowed by arrows and now with all impetus lost. Keeping formation during the descent would not have posed a problem. Niall Barr quite rightly concludes[30] that even splashing through the burn would not, of itself, have proved so much of an obstacle, but cohesion and momentum would have been irretrievably lost.

The Swiss had remedies for this. Each phalanx had a body of halberdiers in the centre, akin to English bills, and these would step forward to literally hack a path into the enemy line, shearing left and right enabling the pikes to resume their relentless advance. Swordsmen, wielding their fearsome double-handers, would play a similar role. The Scots had neither halberds nor blades. It is possible to argue, at least in part, that Home and Huntly enjoyed such signal success because the Highlanders were equipped with their formidable *langswerds* and knew how to use them.

Archers, who would have stepped out from their companies to shoot, could retire behind their billmen comrades who immediately came into their own.

It was now to be a slogging match, a soldier's battle; pikes against bills. In the melee the latter was to prove far superior:

> Our bills quit them very well and did more good that day than bows, for they shortly disappointed the Scots of the long spears wherein was their greatest trust, and when they came to hand-strokes, though the Scots fought sore and valiantly with their swords, yet they could not resist the bills that lighted so thick and sore upon them.[31]

The admiral's division was drawn up on the forward slope of Piper's Hill, they may even have moved forward to meet shock with shock and the slope, hardly steep, nonetheless worked heavily in favour of the English.

The bill, with its 8ft (2.5m) ash stave, was 10ft (3m) shorter than the pike. It was thus handier and had the advantage of possessing both point and blade. The spike could be used to parry whilst the axe blade could lop heads off attacking pikes and reduce them to so much firewood. The English had long years of drill and experience behind them. Bills had complemented bows for the best part of the past two centuries.

A Venetian ambassador described the English bill in correspondence and though he was writing nearly three decades later, his observations could have applied in 1513: '[English bills] have a short thick shaft with an iron like a peasant's hedging bill, but much thicker and heavier than what is used in the Venetian territories, with this they strike so heavily as to unhorse cavalry and it is made short because they like close quarters.'[32] Sweeping strokes from English bills hacked the disordered pikes clear, allowing the defenders to close the gap and get at their foes. A tense moment for Thomas Howard and his officers for it was here this fight would be lost or won. The immediate precedent of his brother's division on their right was hardly encouraging and this earlier rout would have shaken even the steadiest and most resolute.

Howard's division, as well as having advantage of numbers or at least parity, also deployed his thousand crack marines, well versed in bill tactics. Thrusting, now hacking and slashing, the English billmen gained an early ascendancy. The pike is essentially a 'one shot' weapon; its effectiveness lies in an irresistible disciplined rush of the cohesive body. Once that momentum is lost and without fracturing the enemy line then the column is both vulnerable and exposed. Casting aside the now useless pikes, 'you saw so many weapons lowered that it seemed as if a wood were falling down',[33] the attackers drew swords and fought on.

But the sword, though effective against a single bill, is disadvantaged against a line of them, completely outreached by the longer weapon. That key advantage conferred by the rush of pikes was lost but the Scots were not of a mind to concede defeat, 'determined to win the field or die'.[34] The melee, with 'many onsets, muckle slaughter, sweating and travail',[35] was fought with ferocity and ruthlessness, neither side asking or giving quarter. Outmatched by slashing bills the Scots died hard, their gentry so well harnessed that 'they would not fall when four or five of our bills struck on one of them at once'.[36] Such fighting is terribly exhausting. A heavily armoured man could not maintain the fight at full stretch without respite for more than a few minutes.

Many must have toppled with exhaustion only to receive the dagger's thrust, through the eye slits of their visors, beneath the arm or to the groin. Heat of battle does not allow much time for mercy. As an Australian soldier from the Great War recalls; 'they will keep firing until you are two yards off them and then drop their rifles and ask for mercy. They get it too right where the chicken gets the axe ... I will fix a few more before I have finished. It's good sport ... when the bayonet goes in their eyes bulge out like prawns'.[37]

A French surgeon encountered three desperately burned enemies during a French campaign in Italy some twenty-odd years after Flodden:

> Beholding them with pity there came an old soldier who asked me if there was any means of curing them. I told him no. At once he approached them and cut their throats gently and, seeing this great cruelty, I shouted at him that he was a villain. He answered me that he prayed to God that should he be in such a state he might find someone who would do the same for him.

No doubt there were many on the field of Flodden who were likewise favoured.

The slaughter continued. St Cuthbert's fabled banner, floating serene above the press, was targeted by the three Scottish earls and their retinues but 'they got no advantage but great loss and damage of their folks; and yet few or none being under the same banner were slain, though many hurt'.[38] The redoubtable bills continued to do their work and all three magnates, with many of their affinities, fell. No less than eighty-seven Hays were killed (Errol being their clan chieftain).[39] No glory here just the hack and fury of terrible men. An account from the Great War offers some clue as to the horror:

> ... just berserk slaughter. A man sprang at the closest ... and thrust and sprang aside and thrust again and again ... the grunting breaths, the gritting teeth and the staring eyes ... the sobbing scream as the bayonet ripped home ... bayonet fighting is indescribable, a man's emotions race at feverish pace and afterwards words are incapable of describing feelings.

Howard's men were now bolstered by some organised survivors from their right. Rates of attrition, as the frenzied bills hacked down their opponents,

worked heavily in their favour. Hall asserts that the fighting here was particularly intense and that the English felled a great many Scots. *The Gazette* insists
that the Scots fled. These two accounts are not incompatible for whilst many
Scots did fight and die it seems very likely that others broke and ran at quite
an early stage. Pitscottie and other Scottish writers tell us little. (For detail of
the position of opposing forces at this juncture in the action refer to *Map 3*).

The French military writer Ardant du Picq, a noted military theorist, who
himself became a casualty of the Franco-Prussian war of 1870–71 wrote: 'the
contagion of fear changes the direction of the human wave; it bends back
upon itself and breaks to escape danger.'[40] The rot, therefore, never starts at
the front. Those embattled there are far too busily engaged in the business of
survival, besides the Scots had placed their best and bravest to the fore. Those
behind, less well harnessed, less beleaguered, had more thought for flight.
A trickle, swiftly expanding into a river, then becoming a torrent as survivors
broke and ran – 'shortly their backs were turned'.[41]

## King James' advance

Never in all the long, bloody years of the border wars had so great a press
of men advanced in a single commanded body, with Surrey's banners their
objective: 'toward whose standard, the King of Scots personally marched,
being accompanied by many bishops, earls, barons, knights and gentlemen of
the realm with a great number of commons, all chosen men with spears on
foot, which were the most assuredly best harnessed that had been seen.'[42]

None on the English side could have failed to have been impressed if not
overawed by the steady advance of King James' grand division. Unlike the
earls on his left, the king enjoyed superior numbers. This great forest of pikes
descending Branxton Hill in such impressive order, despite the constant winnowing of guns and bows, would have been an epic spectacle. Warriors inhuman beneath closed visors, silken banners waving proudly above dun coloured ground, the grand panoply of chivalry; for James, the very moment of
his triumph. Did the king, at this stage, feel his life vindicated, did he sense
the elixir of victory in his nostrils? Would this be the hour in which the caution of his lords would wither with the contempt of his brother-in-law? Was
he now to win his place in the great counsels of Europe; crowned by victor's
laurels. It must have been a sublime moment. It was not to endure.

Attacking to the right of the earls, the king's vast phalanx fared less badly in
the mire and still had sufficient impetus to push Surrey's men back or, perhaps
more likely, the English gave ground so as to draw the Scots into a narrow
salient. Deployed in linear as opposed to columnar formation the English

could afford to employ more flexible tactics. In part, this battle is an instance of line versus column, such as would characterise Wellington's much later battles in the Peninsula. Having lost momentum, the column becomes inefficient and unwieldy. Now the Scots were assailed on three sides as the admiral's victorious bill-men added their weight to that flank. James may have thrust Surrey's division back by as much as 200yds (180m),[43] the king's household; 'the most noble men of his realm'[44] acting as tip of the lance.

Hall is full of admiration for the elan exhibited by the King of Scots and his affinity, having exalted James' courage for fighting as a mere captain:

> But of what avail was his fine armour, the strength of his great champions with whom he descended the hill, in whom he so much trusted that with his strong company and great number of men, he was able, as he thought to have vanquished the greatest prince in the world, if he had been there as the Earl of Surrey was, or else he thought to achieve so high an enterprise himself that he should surmount the enterprises of all other princes; but it happened that God gave the stroke, and he was no more regarded than a poor solider for all went one way.[45]

Here the combat was particularly savage. Lords Maxwell and Herries were amongst the first Scottish peers to fall. On the English side were lost both Sir John Gower and Sir Richard Harbottle (the latter, it was said, in single combat against James). No prisoners were taken as the English 'intending to make all things sure took little regard of prisoners but rid all that came to hand both King, bishops, lords, knights, nobles and others'.[46] Of the king's household men only Sir William Scott and Sir John Forman the Sergeant Porter were taken captive.[47] The fight in the centre probably began around 4.30 p.m. and lasted for two long, bloody and exhausting hours.

At some point Bothwell committed the reserve but ineptly, so that his men crowded the rear of the king's division rather than attacking on the flank where they might have had an effect. Possibly, the rearward ranks of the king's division were already beginning to fold and Bothwell was trying to stem the rot. Niall Barr observes that in refusing quarter it was the English who were adhering to ruthless Swiss doctrine which ordained that victory was all and personal gain could wait: 'Many other Scottish prisoners could and might have been taken but they were so vengeable and cruel in their fighting that when the Englishmen had the better of them they would not save them, though it so were that diverse Scots offered great sums of money for their lives.'[48]

We have noted that a fit and trained man can fight in harness, with little restriction on movement, but he is prone to the effects of intense heat generated within his carapace. Sweat runs in streams. He is quickly dehydrated and needs water frequently. His helmet, whilst offering vital protection, closes down vision and hearing. He sees only what the narrow slit of his visor permits, more than half blind, dust and steam rises around like a cloying shroud, disorientated by the ferocious din, nostrils assailed by the stink of blood and ordure.

It is probable that the English archers, with no surviving Scots to trouble them, again stepped forward and massed on each flank of Surrey's division. The tightly packed ranks of the king's column were a perfect and now stationary target. Such had occurred at Dupplin Moor where many of the compressed ranks of Scottish spearmen died of suffocation. On that murderous field piles of dead were said to rise as high as spear's length! The English fought with the cold fury of men who began the day thinking themselves under sentence of death. Frenzied bills slashed and gored the lightly armoured and battered well-harnessed gentry. Immobile and surrounded, individual Scottish knights were picked off one by one. This was no chivalrous contest, one billman would block the Scotsman's weapon whilst another would seek to hook around and drag the victim to ground. Both or a third would punch their spikes through the vulnerable points in the stricken man's armour.

James had planned to employ modern weapons technology and contemporary tactical doctrines to overcome those traditional advantages of English armies and to avoid adding another disaster to a long list of failures. He, his knights and indeed the rank and file would be very aware the plan was somewhat awry. What they were now confronted with was an old-fashioned slogging match where the enemy enjoyed a distinct advantage. For the gentry there was no choice. They drew swords and fought manfully. Whatever might be said of the Scots at Flodden, they could never be accused of faintheartedness: 'it is not to be doubted but the Scots fought manfully, and were determined either to win the field or die.'[49] For the commons, particularly those at rear, the situation was somewhat different. That the tactics had failed was blindingly obvious even to the most optimistic but they did have a second option – flight.

Feudal obligation was the cement which bound these men to the field, to follow their betters as their fathers and forefathers had done. Relatively few might have seen military action, certainly not on this scale. Furthermore, as Niall Barr points out,[50] they did not possess the fierce professionalism of the mercenary Swiss whose example they were expected to follow. With magnates and knights tied into the melee, the roar and fury of battle swallowing them up; nothing in their experience could have prepared them for such a maelstrom. That some, perhaps many, elected to defect is scarcely to be wondered at. They would all know men who'd deserted the ranks during the continuance of the campaign and such commonplace conduct might suddenly exert a high level of appeal.

## Death of a king

The English shafts in volleys hailed,
In headlong charge their horse assailed; front, flank and rear, the squadrons sweep
To break the Scottish circle deep,
That fought around their king.
But yet, though thick the shafts as snow,
Though charging knights like whirlwinds go,
Though billmen ply the ghastly blow,
Unbroken was the ring.[51]

James, in the thick of the action, fought valiantly. He is reputed to have impaled five opponents but mere valour would never be enough. At some point, probably as the shadows lengthened, he must have come to the realisation that the day was as good as lost. His was not the temperament to withstand so disheartening a realisation. Flight was inconceivable there was only one remedy, [he] 'thought there was no other way for him but death to preserve himself from the reproach that was like to follow … and he rushed into the chiefest press of his enemies and there fighting in a most desperate manner was beaten down and slain'.[52] With Howard's men falling upon one flank and now Stanley's upon the other, the only hope was that his great division could still punch through Surrey's line.

Having rallied what remained of his Household, James had led a last-ditch assault against the earl's banner. If he could break through then this might yet tip the balance. But this surge was a stil-born thing. There was no momentum left in the Scots. In the dense carnage the king fell unnoticed, no more than a 'spear's length' from the earl's position. Around him lay the bodies of his natural son the Archbishop of St Andrews, together with the Earls of Bothwell, Cassillis and Morton.

When the corpse was identified (by Dacre the next day), it was found that the king's left hand had been virtually severed, his lower jaw shot through with an arrow and his throat slashed, presumably by the stroke of a bill. His was but one of many hundreds of bodies piled on bloodied turf. The entire hillside from the brook northward was a killing ground, the dead, maimed and horribly injured competing for space, severed limbs and steaming slime of entrails. The din would be terrific, hoarse shouts and the screams of dying men, the crash of spears, a crescendo rising and swelling like breakers against the shore.

For a while, the fact their king was down did not percolate through those depleted ranks of the Scottish remnant but, as rumour thickened, they were seized by 'such perplexity that they knew not what to do, but looked at one another without stirring to or fro as those that were in despair'.[53] As dusk approached, surviving Scots broke and fled this field of horror, leaving their comrades stacked in writhing, moaning piles, grass spiked with blood, water choked with dead and literally running red.

It is Holinshed who tells us that the fight here remained bitterly contested for some time and that James' final charge was not mere quixotic folly but a considered response to a growing tactical problem as both the Lord Admiral's and Stanley's men, victorious in their own prior contests, began to hem both flanks. To push forwards and break the English line in front was the only recourse when the stark alternative was a spiral of fatal attrition. He also suggests that Dacre completed the encirclement of the king's division by deploying his border lances against the exposed rear.

This would suggest that the perceived threat from Home and Huntly had gone which would only be the case had the two Scots divisional commanders withdrawn their forces to the top of Branxton Hill and the stalemate below had ended. We are not entirely persuaded. What we understand of the Scottish left is that these forces remained on the field, watched by and watching Dacre. From both armies' perspective this would seem sensible, Scottish left and English right were both secure. Pitscottie goes rather wild in his account, suggesting James defeated two English battles before Thomas Howard led his division 'to the number of twenty thousand fresh men into the fight, till that the streams of blood ran on either side so abundantly that all the fields and waters were made red with the confluence thereof'.[54] If the account is incorrect the dramatic flow of blood in such liberal quantities is probably far more accurate.

## Sir Edward Stanley now appearing on the English left

Only one reserve formation that might have come to the aid of the king's division was now available, Highlanders under Argyll and Lennox, with D'Aussi's company in support. Stanley's division, shorn of guides, had detoured through Crookham to finally reach the valley of the Pallinsburn and cross at Sandyford and only now gained the field. His men, though tired after eleven hours on the march, were full of fight. Sir Edward speedily spotted the possibility of mounting a flank attack against Argyll and Lennox from the north-east face of Pace Hill. This necessitated a tough scramble as the banks were very steep, 'his folks could scarcely fast their feet but forced on hands and knees to creep'.[55]

His approach was partially obscured in dead ground, the unsuspecting Scottish chiefs diverted by what was happening in the centre. They clearly had no orders to move and D'Aussi was, rightly, reluctant to engage fearing they themselves might be taken in flank and any advance meant abandoning the silent guns. Again opinion may differ as to whether James had, through failure of command, allowed these troops to stand idle or if indeed he intended them to hold fast where they were. Simply by maintaining their ground, they were providing some infantry protection to James' right flank.[56] Sir Edward sent a commanded party to feint toward the Highlanders' front whilst he formed the rest of his division into three battalions under Sir William Molyneux, Sir Thomas Gerrard and Sir Henry Kighley respectively.

The general assumption is that after their tricky ascent, the English achieved complete surprise. The actual lie of the ground, as Colonel Elliot points out,[57] suggests otherwise but the attack was put in so swiftly the Highlanders were given no time to alter their dispositions. Buchanan tells us that Lennox and Argyll attacked in a 'very disorderly manner',[58] despite efforts by the French to halt their impetuosity. Their rush led them directly onto Stanley's bows and bills and caused them to cede the advantage of higher ground. As they fell on, disordered, Stanley unleashed his commanded parties under Molyneux, Gerrard and Kighley upon their exposed flank.[59]

As Stanley's archers let fly, his arrow storm provoked the clansmen's mad rush, 'to avoid the sharp storm the Scots were constrained to break their array and fight one separate from another'.[60] This is echoed by Jones who claims the effect of Stanley's arrows was to force the Highlanders to break ranks and *attack* rather than flee. In a wild rush they initially pushed the billmen back but were eventually broken by Stanley's flank attack,[61] as Scott in *Marmion* more poetically describes:

> Far on the left, unseen the while,
> Stanley broke Lennox and Argyle;
> Though there the western mountaineer
> Rushed with bare bosom of the spear,
> And flung the feeble targe aside,
> And with bare hands the broadsword plied.

When the English bill-men laid on, a storm of hacking blades and wicked points, even the formidable *langswerds* of the Highland warriors could not break through and, after the sudden fury of desperate melee, the resulting rout was total. Both the Highland earls, Lord Darnley, the chiefs of Campbell of Glenorchy, MacLean and MacIan of Ardnamurchan were cut down 'doing all they could to stay their people from running away'.[62] With his own hand, Sir William Molyneux captured two standards and, with their fall, any last hope for the embattled Scottish centre vanished; fleeing Highlanders passed by the dead bodies of their sovereign and his household without so much as a backward glance. Stanley's men, who had 'marvellously acquitted themselves'[63] abandoned the hot work of pursuit to pillage the piles of dead, 'fell a spoiling, and despoiled the King of Scots and many that were slain in his battle but they knew him not'.[64]

What greater irony than this? The man whose ambition drew these great armies into the arena lay sprawled and nameless, hacked and bloodied as any of his meanest subjects piled around. He was just another dead Scotsman; one who presumably provided rather better pickings for English scavengers harvesting the spoils of their great victory. Edward Hall tells us of Stanley's brilliant feat but alleges the Earl of Huntly was with Argyll and Lennox and that 'he took a horse and saved himself';[65] this is most unlikely as Huntly appears to have remained on the left with Home throughout.

As victorious English pursued their defeated enemies they fell to despoiling the dead rather than mounting a concerted effort against the flank of the king's embattled division, James' corpse being amongst those littering the field. This confusion of detail is only to be expected and it is very possible that Stanley's men did arrive in time to complete the destruction of James' men and that the king fell at some point around this time, whether it was Surrey's or Stanley's bills that felled him cannot be answered.

At least one Scottish source, the ancient verse 'Flodden Field' – attributed to the Cornet of the Hawick men[66] – ascribes the failure of the king's division to the timely intervention of Stanley's men:

Bravely was the field defended,
Victory's palm was long suspended,
Till some English, like tornado,
Rushed from deepest ambuscade.

Now the struggle was unequal,
Dreadful carnage crowned the sequel;
Hardy Scots, borne down by numbers,
Strewed the field in death's cold slumbers.

## New Light

Colonel Leather asserts[67] that, having brushed aside Edmund Howard's thin line, Home simply pressed on, following orders to retreat into Scotland, in the assumption that the division of the three earls, following behind would guard their exposed flank against the Lord Admiral's forces. Colonel Leather absolves Home from any taint of faintheartedness, he simply continued on his way ignorant of the encounter battle now developing behind him, having thought that the forces he'd routed were just a commanded party. It would only be after he had crossed the border that fugitives from the wrack of the main Scots force caught up, causing him to march his forces back over the Tweed next day to see what, if anything could be salvaged. In Leather's account, Lord Dacre with his cavalry does inflict a check upon Home before returning to the main fight developing in the centre.

Errol, Crawford and Montrose, spotting the admiral's division veer to their right, descend the hill and prepare to engage. Once these have been dealt with, Howard is able to swing around and throw his weight onto the flank of his father's division whilst Dacre's horse, now returning, circle to the other flank. In Colonel Leather's version, the lateness of Stanley is explained by the fact his division was timed to march out of camp some time after Surrey's.[68] The Highlanders, bringing up the rear of the withdrawing Scottish army, spot an opportunity to take Stanley in flank by Crookham Dene.[69] Stanley has, however, already sent a detachment which has ascended past the ruin of Fishes Stead to investigate the Scottish camp.

Next the Highlanders sweep down in a wild charge from Pace Hill. Despite losses they were able to close to contact and a hard-fought action ensued. Only when Stanley's undetected reserve attacked the Highlanders from flank and rear did the clansmen rout. The English rearguard was thus able to join in the final decimation of King James' grand division in the centre.

## NOTES

1. Grossman, pp. 1–4.
2. MacDonald Fraser, p. 275.
3. Quoted in Holmes, R., *Acts of War* (London, 1985), p. 378.
4. Machiavelli, *the Art of War*, p. 97.
5. Hall, *King Henry VIII*, vol. 1, p. 108.
6. Laing, *the Trewe Encountre*, pp. 143–4.
7. Hall, *King Henry VIII*, vol. 1, p. 109.
8. James, *Articules of the bataille* in James, *National Manuscripts*, p. 2.
9. Baird, *Scottish Feilde and Flodden Feilde*, p. 13.
10. Grossman, p. 124.
11. Born in 1480 Tunstall was immortalised as the 'Stainless Knight' after his heroic death.
12. Pitscottie, *Historie and Cronicles of Scotland*, p. 270.
13. Born in 1473 from Emley Castle in Gloucestershire and married into the Stanleys.
14. Hall, *King Henry VIII*, vol. 1, p. 108.
15. Elliot, p. 75.
16. Pitscottie, *Historie and Cronicles of Scotland*, p. 270.
17. *Ibid.*
18. *Ibid.*
19. *Ibid.*
20. Barr, p. 100.
21. Sir Humphrey Lisle had a long and chequered career, latterly hero of a subsequent siege of Wark, finally renegade and outlaw.
22. Jones, p. 81.

23. A 'tack' is Scots for a lease; a 'tacksman' was a leaseholder, probably kin to the chief.
24. Hall, *King Henry VIII*, vol. 1, p. 108.
25. Pitscottie, *Historie and Cronicles of Scotland*, p. 271.
26. *Ibid*., pp. 271–2.
27. Machiavelli, *the Art of War*, p. 109.
28. Hall, *King Henry VIII*, vol. 1, p. 109.
29. *Ibid*.
30. Barr, p. 100.
31. James, *Facsimiles of National Manuscripts*, Part 2, pp. 4–8.
32. Dillon, H.A., 'Arms and Armour at Westminster, the Tower and Greenwich, 1547' in *Archaeologia*, vol. 51 (1888), p. 235.
33. Italian poem *La Rotta de Scocesi*, Mackenzie, *Secret of Flodden*, p. 34.
34. Laing, *Trewe Encountre*, p. 150.
35. Kightly, p. 45.
36. *La Rotta de Scocesi*.
37. *Grossman*, p. 124.
38. James, *Facsimiles of National Manuscripts*, Part 2, pp. 4–8.
39. Reese, p. 156.
40. Du Picq, *Battle Studies*, p. 81.
41. James, *Articules of the bataille*, in James, *National Manuscripts*, p. 2.
42. Hall, *King Henry VIII*, vol. 1, p. 109.
43. Barr, p. 107.
44. *Ibid*.
45. Hall, *King Henry VIII*, vol. 1, p. 109.
46. Laing, *Trewe Encountre*, p. 150.
47. Hall, *King Henry VIII*, vol. 1, p. 109.
48. Laing, *Trewe Encountre*, p. 150.
49. *Ibid*.
50. Barr, p. 110.
51. Jones, p. 41.
52. Leslie, *Historie of Scotland*, p. 95.
53. Kightly, p. 46.
54. Pitscottie, *Historie and Cronicles of Scotland*, p. 271.
55. Kightly, p. 46.
56. Barr, p. 112.
57. Elliot, pp. 95–7.
58. *Ibid*.
59. The Highlanders' right flank was the only one exposed, their left abutted the right of the king's division.
60. Kightly, p. 47.
61. For his services at Flodden, Stanley was, in the following year, elevated to Lord Monteagle. Having sworn to give thanks to God for his success beforehand he commenced construction of a fine chapel at Hornsby, though he died before it could be completed. In the chancel an eagle was cut into the stone, the Stanley bird of prey, see Jones pp. 73–4.
62. Knightly, p. 47.
63. *Ibid*.
64. Hall, *King Henry VIII*, vol. 1, p. 109.
65. *Ibid*.
66. Jones, p. 34.
67. Leather, pp. 49–51.
68. *Ibid*., p. 55.
69. *Ibid*.

# 9

# SUCH A NOISE ... WAS NEVER HEARD BEFORE:
## AFTERMATH

… Whilst the face of war may alter, some things have not changed since Joshua stood before Jericho and Xenophon marched to the sea.

George MacDonald Fraser, *Quartered Safe out Here*

On returning ... minus my right arm, I was accosted twice ... by individuals who inquired, 'Where did you lose your arm? Vietnam?'

I replied, 'Yes'.

The response was 'Good, serves you right.'

US veteran of the Vietnam era

Why did King James IV lose the Battle of Flodden? The failure has largely condemned his memory ever since and cast a dark shadow over the preceding quarter century of solid achievement. In part, he was plain unlucky. War is a business of chance and the old adage that no plan ever survives first contact with the enemy is doubly true of Flodden Field. We can say that the king was neither reckless nor foolish. He did not allow chivalric nonsense to lead him by the nose to his death and the destruction of his army. Consideration of the brief campaigns of 1496 and 1497 shows that James was not prepared to accept the hazard of battle purely for its own sake and, cannily, avoided a fight in both cases. In these raids he was led by policy alone and the early stages of the Flodden venture show a similar detailed caution.

He did not have to fight a battle. Undoubtedly, he was aware that his army looked rather stronger on paper than was the case. His infantry were conscripts with minimal training in their new arms. They lacked that solid discipline, cohesion and mercenary imperative of the Swiss elite. They were deprived of key supporting weapons, halberd and broadsword. From his first position astride Flodden Edge, the king was able to place reliance upon his great guns which so totally dominated the level plain below. Nor did he allow the taunting of the Howards to draw him down onto level ground. For all the public posturing about Surrey's army being second rate, James and his officers knew the full mettle and toughness of their opponents.

James had allowed himself to be humbugged by Surrey's flank march. With hindsight, the best course of action would have been to strike camp and withdraw on 8 September. Hindsight is, however, a luxury battlefield commanders invariably lack. At the time, staying put in a strongly posted position seemed logical – and it was. On the day, James still thought his guns could win the battle; that their dominance would drive the English into struggling uphill. It was plainly not his intention to initiate an attack.

It was in his fine grasp of tactics that James came unstuck; that and the nature of the ground, horribly deceptive from his vantage atop Branxton Edge. A more experienced captain would have seen the difficulties posed by the marshy brook, would also have realised that his guns were in fact disadvantaged by their elevated location and that the more rapid firing English pieces were far better suited to a gunnery duel. In fact the day was lost when first the Scottish guns were silenced. This check removed all other options for James. He was committed to advance regardless.

As for his decision to lead in person, this has been heavily censured and with reason. It was necessary for him to distinguish the difference between the roles of commander-in-chief in the field and head of state – a 'rose nobill' indeed. His reasons for leading in person were sound in part – the need to share the hazard of his subjects, the imperative of setting his personal stamp upon hoped for victory, thus securing his place in the forefront of Renaissance princes. But it was still rank folly. It is likely the case that, had he stayed put, he still could not have influenced the outcome though he might have succeeded in deploying his reserve more effectively and perhaps in budging Home. Appointing a field commander need not have detracted from his victory and defeat whilst costly, need not have been as utterly disastrous.

Much of the emphasis in subsequent writings about Flodden focuses on the magnitude of the Scots' defeat. This is understandable but fails fully to take into account the fact that a prime cause of the disaster lay in the fact the English fought so well. With the exception of much of Edmund Howard's wing, the rest performed magnificently; tired, cold, wet and very hungry, after exhausting marches, outnumbered and seemingly at a grave disadvantage of ground. At the onset, the Scots still held a dominating position. Had the English been obliged to ascend Branxton ridge under fire, the outcome could have been very different. Surrey's plan had worked only insofar as he had outflanked his opponent, but he had failed to gain the advantage of level terrain.

Surrey's gunners all but won the battle with their opening salvoes. This swift success in the artillery duel virtually decided the outcome. James had quite plainly not envisaged having to attack. His hitherto cautious strategy in maintaining so strong a defensive position astride Flodden Edge is ample evidence of intent. He was clearly conscious that his foot were far from ready and perhaps as far from fully willing. Unity within the Scottish polity was largely a creation of James' reign and he was equally aware his magnates were not inclined to battle. As bellicose as the Scots' lords may have sounded in council, what they'd envisaged was a repeat of previous years on a rather grander scale. Those earlier raids of 1496 and 1497 had been as near risk free as warfare is likely to be. The Scots had used overwhelming force and the quality of their guns to hammer any purely local opposition. Fighting a major battle was another matter altogether.

James had placed heavy reliance on, as he perceived, superior technology and weight of shot. Both eminently sound, the difficulty being his men were not sufficiently trained in the use of pikes and his guns were deployed at a marked disadvantage. Ironically, it was those outmoded English tactics that won the day. Training and easy familiarity with their arms were all with them.

Their officers, if ageing, were brimming with experience and the hardness of dour northern English.


## Pursuit

> After the field was fought and the Scots fled, many Englishmen followed them into Scotland, and were so far that they didn't know which way to return home and so were taken prisoner by the Scots that were in the two battles that fled first and never fought: also several were taken by the Lord Chamberlain of Scotland [Home] which fought with Sir Edmund Howard's wing to the number of sixty.[1]

Estimates of the number of Scottish camp followers, the unseen and unheard of medieval armies vary; thousands certainly and this vast horde must have fled like a great torrent of refugees, passing by their forces still struggling or locked in death's embrace. Along with these, survivors from the Scottish divisions also routed, together, as we may presume, with any spectators who'd crossed the line to watch the show 'some passed over the water of Tweed at Coldstream Ford, and others by dry marches, during the time of the fight and the night after – many men lost their horses and such stuff as they left in their tents and pavilions by the robbers of Tynedale and Teviotdale'.[2] For the borderers it was business as usual and one man's catastrophe is another's opportunity. The English and Scottish marchers were very probably acting in concert, criminal affinities ranking rather higher than national pride.

Casualties in rout were in no small part dictated by the ground over which the vanquished were obliged to flee. So many fights are now marked by such chilling reminders as 'Bloody Meadow', 'Red Gutter', 'Dead Man's Bottom' or, most poetic 'the Bridge of Bodies'. Flodden, despite the severity of the Scots' defeat, does not have any such poignant commemoration. This may argue that the pursuit was perhaps not as ruthless or as murderous as in other defeats.

Seven o'clock in the late summer evening, light fading and the bloody work done, the English masters of a stricken field. Few of those Scots who sought mercy survived as the victors judged they 'had been so vengeable and cruel in their fighting so that when the English had the better of them they would not save them'.[3] Once dispatched the dead 'were no sooner slain, but forthwith despoiled out of their armour and array and left lying naked on the field'.[4] Here and there an English gentleman, with an eye to ransom, might intervene to spare a prisoner of rank; some of the dead king's household were 'with difficulty saved' by one English knight.

Dazed survivors straggled over the fords at Coldstream, by Wark, or Lennel near Cornhill. Some headed west to the Middle marches and vanished into the hills. Not all were cowed. A party of English, hungry for ransom, were surprised as the Scots turned to fight and found themselves taken captive. Polydore Vergil paints a depressing picture of the disgraced survivors 'bewildered and forgetful of their duty they had not attempted either to avenge the death of the king or to help their comrades in their extremity and so had branded their country with everlasting shame'.[5] Pitscottie tells us that the fatal brook and other streams literally ran red and fields were saturated with pooling blood. This sounds apocryphal but may well have been true for the slaughter in certain areas had been prodigious and without quarter.

Those English busy looting the Scots camp were impressed by the rich store of plunder and, of more immediate sustenance, foodstuffs. They marvelled at how well fed these naked and stiffening corpses of their enemies appeared. The author of the *Trewe Encountre* suggests at least some feared this bounty might have been poisoned! Surrey, as was customary, dubbed forty new knights on the field including his wounded son Edmund (see Appendix Two): no man could have done more to earn his spurs:

Lord Dacre with all his company stood still all day not having fought [this was untrue as Dacre had ably checked Home's assault]. When the field was done and the scouts brought word, that there were no more Scots appearing, but all had returned [to Scotland] the Earl thanked God with a humble heart and called to him certain lords and other gentlemen and them made knights, as Sir Edmund Howard his son, and the Lord Scrope, Sir William Percy and many others.[6]

When the earl returned to the camp late that September evening, he found the English borderers, with fine impartiality, had also robbed their own countrymen bare! The Lord Admiral sat down to write a dispatch to Queen Katherine. He had much to disclose, the finest triumph of English arms in several decades, the highlight of an otherwise desultory and very costly campaign. To secure the field and captured ordnance Surrey detailed:

Sir Philip Tilney,[7] knight with the Lord Admiral's company and the company of Lord Scrope of Bolton, Lord Latimer, old Sir Marmaduke Constable, Sir William Percy, Sir Nicholas Appleyard [master gunner] and their companies, and a few others to keep the field to secure the English ordnance and the ordnance taken from the Scots.[8]

Guarding the captured guns that night must have been a grim chore. Men utterly exhausted, numbed by the ebbing of that great adrenaline rush which had kept them alive that afternoon. Around them, the stricken remnants of a proud army; no silence but the continual moaning and calling of the hundreds of wounded who suffered, unaided in the sharp night air.

Philip de Commines offers us a telling vignette of aftermath when recounting events on the field of Montl'hery, nearly half a century before:

> In the meantime, the Count of Charolais ate and drank a little, and all the rest of the army did the same; after which the wound in his neck was carefully dressed. To make room for him, before he could sit down to eat, four or five dead bodies had to be removed, and two trusses of straw were brought for him to sit on. As we were removing the dead men, one of the poor stark naked creatures called out for some drink, and on putting a little ptisan [a medicinal infusion, perhaps in this case, sweetened barley water] (of which the Count had drunk) into his mouth, he came to himself.[9]

By dawn, many would have died. Some quietly slipping away from shock and exsanguination; others more speedily dispatched by feral packs of human predators skulking in the darkness; camp followers and locals who had crept out in search of loot, ferreting amongst the dead and dying, human jackals, the carrion crows of war. As for those thousands of dead: 'Besides Branxton breathless in a brook they lien, Gaping against the moon their spirits were away.'[10]

It is probably fair to say that few in the world today, even those who have fought in those innumerable wars of recent times, have seen sights such as Branxton offered on the grey, damp dawn of 10 September. Then the familiar pattern of dun coloured moor and richer summer grass was loaded with a grim carpet of undiluted horror. Men in battle die neither quietly or easily, their passage marked by agony and terror; stiffening corpses, sack-like in the indifference of death, blood garnished, entrails slewed like a giant snail's wake. Many would be unrecognisable, skulls shattered, features swollen like overripe melons, limbless, blinded, pallor of naked flesh, amidst dark rich rivulets of blood still flowing liberally, puddling on damp grass, soaking a rich earth and draining in steady streams. Veterans will tell you that the shock and horror of war is not so much felt on the day of battle when red mist clouds but next dawn when victors must confront the price of their preservation.

For the English, their grand haul of captured guns was well worth watching over:

> ... five great curtals, two great culverins, four sakers and six serpentines; as fair ordnance as has been besides other small pieces.[11] It was as well the watch was so strongly posted for that very next morning as a grey dawn arose over the charnel valley ... the Lord Admiral came to the field and there some Scots

appeared on a hill: but William Blakenall which was the chief officer of the ordnance shot such a volley, that the Scots fled or else the Lord Admiral had been in great jeopardy.[12]

As the chronicler records, Sir Philip Tilney, commanding the reserve guard and aiming to secure both Scottish and English guns was, in the morning, confronted by a body of border horse, most probably commanded by Lord Home who sought to recover the Scottish ordnance, a hugely valuable prize. Hall tells us he'd been joined by Thomas Howard and a short, sharp contest followed till the Scots were panicked by a salvo from the English artillery and scattered, leaving Surrey and his forces with their hard won spoils.

## The butcher's bill

My Lord Howard hath sent me a letter to open to your Grace, within which is one of mine, by the which you shall see at length the great victory that our Lord hath sent your subjects in your absence; and for this cause there is no need herein to trouble your Grace with long writing but, to my thinking, this battle hath been to your Grace and all your realm the greatest honour that could be and more than should you win all the crown of France; thanked be to God of it.[13]

Queen Katherine was quite right in her estimation of the magnitude of Surrey's triumph; though pointing this out to her husband in such graphic terms was perhaps impolitic. The king himself wrote to the Duke of Milan on the same day (16 September), describing the campaign in rather more pragmatic terms:

England has been attacked by the King of Scots, who took part with France unmindful of ties of blood and of a formal treaty. He sent 10,000 Scots into England, all of whom were killed or captured by a force not exceeding 1,000 [he refers here to Home's 'ill-rode']. Thereupon, the King of Scots in person, with an immense army, invaded England and at the outset took a little old town that was almost tumbling down of itself, unfortified and practically deserted, belonging to the Bishop of Durham. The King then advanced some four miles within the English borders, where on the 8th August, he was met by the Earl of Surrey, who had been deputed to coerce the Scots. The fight was long and sharply contested on both sides, but at length the Almighty, avenging the broken treaty gave victory to the English[14]

Doubtless the Prince Bishop would not have been best pleased to read of his grand fortress being so disparagingly described and Henry was careful to suggest the God had intervened to punish the oath breaker rather than admit Surrey fought a better fight. When writing to Wolsey on 18 September, the bishop gave a clearly heartfelt description of the loss of Norham: 'which news touched me so near with inward sorrow that I had lever to have been out of the world than in it.'[15]

He reiterated his sorrow in subsequent correspondence, a mere two days after the last but which provides a much fuller listing of the ordnance recovered from the field and confirms the enemy had not lacked supplies: 'their abundance of victuals, wines of all sorts, bread, beer and ale tents and pavilions, far above our estimation, and not lightly credible, unless it had been seen, tasted and viewed by our folks to their great refreshing.'[16] He contrasts this with the poor state of the English commissariat 'destitute of victuals and having nothing to drink but only water for the space of three days', perhaps not surprisingly the bishop attributed the English victory to the intercession of St Cuthbert! He did, however, suggest that Surrey's efforts merited a dukedom; perhaps he felt the king might be grudging on this!

Meanwhile, Branxton Church (*Plate 18*) was commandeered as a temporary resting place for the English dead, including Sir Bryan Tunstall and those others who had fallen so bravely on Edmund Howard's wing. Sir Thomas admitted to 400 casualties though this is probably far too low. Disproportionate as the losses were, fighting had been far too savage and prolonged for the victors to have escaped so lightly. Of the 500 men in his father's retinue only 293 survived, attesting to the fury of the fight around the earl's banner.[17] Edward Hall, who apparently had access to the muster rolls and paymaster's accounts, puts the English loss at nearer 1,500,[18] a far more likely figure 'as it appeared by the book of wages when the soldiers were paid'.[19] It would seem the majority of the commons who had fallen were laid in mass graves south and west of the fighting in the right centre.

For all the lords of their land were left them behind,
Beside Brymstone [Branxton] in a brook breathless they lie
Gaping against the moon, their ghosts were away.[20]

On the Scottish side the butcher's bill was vastly greater. Estimates at the time were between 10,000–12,000 dead. Hall inclines towards the higher figure[21] though again, there may have been some exaggeration and the true loss may be somewhere from 5,000–8,000.[22] Amongst these lay the flower of Scottish chivalry including not just representatives of magnatial families but many from the higher ranks of the clergy. Alexander Stewart, Archbishop of St Andrews, primate and chancellor, George Hepburn, the Bishop of the Isles, two abbots and the dean of Glasgow. They were joined in death by nine of the country's twenty-one earls, fourteen out of twenty-nine lords of Parliament and at least 300 lesser gentry.[23] Niall Barr makes the highly apposite observation that such high loses from the magnatial elite and gentry would not be seen again till the Great War 1914–18 and then the blow fell mainly on the young, rather than more mature and established figures.[24]

Of those nobles on the field only Home, Huntly and Lord Lindsay escaped. Of the gentry, Sir Andrew Ker of Ferniehirst, Ian Mackenzie, Bishop Forman, Sir William Scott of Blawearie, Sir John Colquhoun and James Logan were taken prisoner. Astonishingly, none of the gentry' families was completely extinguished. Fathers and sons perished together including David Pringle of Smailholm whose four eldest sons died with him, leaving only one, an infant, to succeed to the lairdship of Galashiels.[25] The provost of Edinburgh was dead, lying with a slew of the burgesses who, in turn, were joined by many of their contemporaries from Glasgow, Perth and Aberdeen. It is a doleful testament to the lethal intent of the English soldiery that so few men of note were taken.

## Fate of the late King of Scots

Pedro de Ayala, admittedly an unabashed admirer of James IV and one whose description was written some years before the campaign of 1513, commented on the king's appearance that '[He] is of noble stature, neither tall nor short, and as handsome in complexion and shape as man can be ... He never cuts his hair or beard. It becomes him very well'.[26] This rather macho look did not survive his wedding to Margaret Tudor and the king is shown as clean-shaven in all of his subsequent portraits. He is also generally represented as being dark haired though his colouring was probably more reddish. The antiquary John Stow,[27] who saw the embalmed remains years later, describes James' hair and beard as being red. It is possible that James for convenience allowed his beard to grow on campaign.

De Ayala had observed that the king 'loves war so much'.[28] The Spaniard also describes how much the Scots in general were addicted to war. For all his considerable achievement and *realpolitik* there was a middling dash of the crusader in James, a quixotic tendency that lurked only just beneath the surface. His reign was characterised by a love of tournaments, befitting a proud and martial prince and very much in keeping with the contemporary myth of chivalric tradition.[29] He found death upon the field considerably less than glorious; shot, slashed, hacked and despoiled like any common footsoldier.

It was Lord Dacre who identified the half nude, mangled corpse of the Scottish king:

> Well known it was by those who fought and also reported by Scottish prison-
> ers, that their king was taken or slain but his body was not found till the next
> day, because all the mean people both Scots and England were stripped of their
> apparel as they lay on the field, yet at the end he was found by Lord Dacre, who
> knew him well by his private tokens in that same place, where the earl of Sur-
> rey's battle and his first joined together … the king had several deadly wounds,
> and especially one with an arrow, and another with a bill as showed when he
> was naked.[30]

Formal identification was carried out at Barmoor when Sir William Scott and the ever-faithful Forman confirmed, sorrowfully, that these were the mortal remains of their sovereign. This was Forman's last service to James IV.[31]

At Barmoor, in the English encampment, the body was eviscerated and then embalmed before being sent down to Newcastle en route to London, sealed in a lead casket.[32] Queen Katherine dispatched the dead monarch's bloody surcoat as a handy souvenir to her husband in France. On receiving the news of his general's victory on 25 September Henry ordered a celebra-tory cannonade and a Te Deum to be sung in the Cathedral of Tournai, the city having just recently surrendered:

> Then he thanked God and highly praised the Earl and the Lord Admiral and
> his son and all the gentlemen and commoners that were at that valiant enter-
> prise: howbeit the king had a secret letter that the Cheshire men fled from Sir
> Edmund Howard, which letter caused great heartache and many words but the
> king thankfully accepted all things, and wished no man to by dis-praised.[33]

Henry must have sat through these celebrations with grated teeth; his forgot-ten army had scooped all the headlines.

The corpse was taken to the Carthusian monastery at Sheen by Richmond whilst King Henry considered what to do next. James IV was a head of state and thus entitled to a bit of a show but he had died excommunicate. The new pope was minded to show some clemency and suggested a state funeral in St Paul's Cathedral with the dire sentence being lifted during the rites. Henry, in his mercurial way, had forgotten his dead brother-in-law by the time this communication arrived and the remains lay untended for decades after the dissolution, stacked with other forgotten trifles.

John Stow tells us of the eventual outcome:

workmen there for their foolish pleasure, hewed off his head; and Lancelot Young, master glazier to Queen Elizabeth, feeling a sweet savour to come from thence, and seeing the same dried from all moisture, and yet the form remaining, with the hair of the head and beard red, brought it to London, to his house in Wood Street, where for a time he kept it for its sweetness, but in the end caused the sexton of that Church to bury it amongst other bones taken out of their charnel.[34]

A final ignominy, the man who would sit at the high table of Europe disappears unremembered into a mass grave. Interestingly, what are said to be James' sword and dagger, recovered from the field, are now in the College of Arms in London, although they cannot be positively confirmed as those of the king. Some excellent facsimiles, crafted by the rather colourful Charles Dawson[35] at the turn of the twentieth century may be seen in Ford castle along with other memorabilia.[36]

As Norman Macdougall notes, disasters need explaining.[37] Ideally, someone is to blame and James IV was ideally suited to the scapegoat role. It was he rather than any other who brought his countrymen to Branxton Edge. He it was who ignored the counsels of caution and elected to fight. As commander-in-chief he bears the full burden of responsibility. Within ten years of the battle writers were adding to the dead man's burden by blaming the defeat on his reckless rejection of good advice. The chronicler Hector Boece, who wrote up the life of his patron Bishop Elphinstone, shows his subject as the wise and diligent counsellor which he undoubtedly was, cruelly dismissed when he advised against war 'a tumult of opposition'.[38] A later translation of Boece omits the episode in council and shifts the blame onto the French in whose cause the king and his nobles perished!

Perhaps the most influential writer in the aftermath of the disaster was Sir David Lindsay of the Mount who, within two decades, wrote a long verse essay directed at the youthful James V, distilling much perceived political wisdom. Lindsay dedicates a section of his work to the king's dead father. He lists James IV's numerous qualities and achievements, particularly the imposition of law and order in hitherto lawless regions.[39] He praises the king's addiction to tournaments, a necessary show amongst princes. Nonetheless, Lindsay also blames James' fall on his failure to take advice. He suggests his campaign against England was motivated by 'ardent love' of France and that he was undone 'not by the virtue of English ordnance/ But by his own wilful misgovernance'. The poet suggests that if James had listened he would have survived.[40] Lindsay's view carries specific weight because the writer actually knew James though, as a guardian of the infant prince, he was not present on the field.

Some of course, took the view that James IV did not die at Flodden but somehow survived. Adam Abell, an Observantine friar, writing at Jedburgh only a few years after Lindsay, blames poor Andrew Forman as the pernicious Svengali figure who offers evil counsel whilst also pruriently commenting on the king's sexual appetites.[41] He does however suggest, rather ambiguously, that James was or might not have been killed in the battle. This rather hesitant offering is soon picked up by subsequent chroniclers who create a survival mythology. Bishop Lesley claims the corpse Dacre identified was that of the laird of Bonjedward, who certainly died in the fight. Lesley, writing five-and-a-half decades later, claimed James not only lived but went on a pilgrimage to Jerusalem and spent the rest of his life in seclusion as penance.[42]

George Buchanan goes even further, claiming that Dacre found the body of Alexander, Lord Elphinstone,[43] who had been liveried as a double for the king, being of similar age and build. It was not uncommon for kings to provide look-alikes on the field, 'bullet catchers' as they might now be described. He also suggests numerous un-named witnesses saw James re-crossing the Tweed in safety only, and bizarrely, to be done to death by Home's men anxious to preserve their lord from censure.[44] There are some echoes of this in other accounts but the notion has to be entirely apocryphal. Dacre knew James well enough and we can almost certainly accept his identification as accurate.

## Aftermath

> We shall say nothing of those who often come home crippled from foreign wars ... They use their limbs in the service of the commonwealth or the king and their disability prevents them from exercising their own craft, and their age from learning a new one.
>
> More, *Utopia*

Meanwhile, the pragmatic business of profitable salvage went on. Not only had the magnificent Scottish guns fallen into the bag but so had a vast haul of arms and armour. That fine harness which had rendered the Scottish knights so annoyingly difficult to kill was recovered and sold off in job lots. One William Gur was selling off kit on the field and some 350 harness, which failed to find buyers, were sent down to Harry Coste, Sheriff of Nottingham. Gur disposed of a further score of lots with a careful tally of monies due to the king.[45] Surrey's wage bill, at least in part, was being recovered.

Further correspondence from Brian Tuke, Clerk of the Signet, writing on 22 September to Wolsey's secretary Richard Pace, makes mention of a captured document. This had been extracted from the purse of a fallen Scottish gentleman and refers to the considerable quantity of aid received from France, imported through Dunbar. Louis had disbursed 25,000 gold crowns, 40 cartloads of gunpowder, two cannon, culverins, some 400 arquebuses and 600 hand culverins, with shot for all.

This is the first mention of handguns. We have no mention of their appearance on the field (which may not, of course, be conclusive). A significant quantity of pikes accompanied the ordnance together with the Sieur d'Aussi, forty officers and fifty harnessed foot.[46] Tuke concluded 'and this is the end of James, late king of Scots, of all mankind the falsest'.[47] This item of correspondence offers a most interesting insight. As Professor Macdougall notes, the writer confused Dunbar with Dumbarton but it does clearly imply the French sent substantial aid which arrived late. It would seem likely this reinforcement left France after 12 August.[48] It may be that the noble corpse was that of Lennox,[49] if for no other reason than he was a leading adviser to the king who might well have had conduct of these matters beforehand.[50]

In 1522, less than a decade later Alexander Myln, abbot of Cambuskenneth, wrote up a history of the bishops of Dunkeld. He follows Boece in criticising the king for ignoring the sage advices of his clergy. He alone, however, alleges James tarried in England after taking Norham 'for fifteen days awaiting the warriors of France, but all in vain'.[51] No other chronicler suggests this. Was James anticipating major French military intervention and was his base on Flodden Edge merely a balcony from which to wage an altogether more concerted campaign? This is tempting but too tantalisingly vague and unsupported. If a joint endeavour was on the cards we would expect to have heard more and the season was already well advanced, rather too far in fact.

On 14 September Surrey deemed it safe, and expedient, to pay off the bulk of his army. Some 18,689 men were discharged, including most of the many wounded.[52] The earl felt satisfied he'd saved the exchequer a fortnight's wages but undoubtedly many of the rank and file would feel cheated of their pay. The rewards would certainly not match the scale of the English effort or the magnitude of their victory. Surrey did finally regain his family's ducal title, forfeit since Bosworth, and the Lord Admiral succeeded to the earldom. Sir Edward Stanley was elevated as Lord Monteagle.

It is easy to conclude that Henry, whilst he might appreciate the scale of the deliverance, remained jealous. His own triumphs in France included the capture of Therouanne and Tournai, together with that most modest of successes, advertised as the Battle of the Spurs. When he later sailed for home, Henry crossed the Channel without in any way being inconvenienced by the attentions of the Franco-Scottish fleet. This had suffered from adverse weather and *Michael*, James' great flagship, then ran aground. The Scots had no more luck at sea than on land! The ship was later sold to Louis XII for £12,000 Scots, banal end to so great a dream. The dead king's additional pride, his great guns had, of course, all fallen into English hands along with numerous lighter pieces, all of which were moved firstly to the shell of Etal castle and from there to Berwick.

Polydore Vergil recorded that the Scottish survivors from the field ravaged their own country for sustenance, all supplies now lost to the hungry English, as they withdrew.[53] Such of the French cadre as had escaped the slaughter provided ready scapegoats and were swiftly hacked to death, 'of the Frenchmen who served in the Scotch army, some fell in the engagement, others were cut to pieces by the Scots, who reproached the French with being the cause of their destruction'.[54] The defeat was not of their making but they suffered in its wake and their deaths, in reality, mark the passing of the Auld Alliance.

Scots might remain allied to France for some time but few would be willing to cross the border on their account. Any seat in the councils of Europe was too dearly bought at this price. The survivors' only reward would be the lasting opprobrium of contemporaries. No man who flees such a sorely stricken field is likely to receive thanks especially as most at home now feared the English would invade. In Edinburgh the surviving burgesses hastily threw an improvised rampart around the capital and expected the worst but the worst had in fact already occurred.[55]

Those who remember the conflict in Vietnam in the 1960s and 1970s will recall how, as anti-war feeling in the USA escalated, many survivors, as they came home, traumatised and confused, were treated as mere pariahs. The effects on these young draftees, who had been under the apparent illusion they were serving the cause of civilisation, and who found themselves branded as murderers and oppressors were considerable. For them, the consequences were often a lifetime's bitterness and disillusionment. To taste defeat after so much blood and toil is devastating. To be hated for it by your own countrymen, far worse.

Perhaps an illuminating comment on the reign of James IV is how well his government continued to function despite the loss of the reigning monarch and so many of his magnates. It has to be a tribute to the king's administrative reforms that, within three days of his defeat and death, the lords of council met in session at Stirling to consider those steps now necessary to secure the realm and to plan a coronation of the infant James V. The council also prepared to see to the nation's defences. Queen Margaret was confirmed as tutrix to her son, as the king's last will had specified. On 21 September, the dead king's infant heir was crowned James V in the Chapel Royal of Stirling, perhaps the greatest of all Scottish bastions.[56]

The scale of loss and magnitude of this disaster notwithstanding, Scots were thirsting for revenge and had every intention of renewing the conflict.

Before the year was out, Lord Fleming had been dispatched as an emissary to Louis XII to discuss future joint operations. At home, garrisons were provisioned and regular musters or 'wappinschaws' held. Hopes of revenge were to be short lived. Factionalism, scourge of Scottish royal minorities, swiftly reared its head in the council. The queen marginalised herself by, to universal dismay, marrying the Douglas Earl of Angus, grandson of Archibald 'Bell the Cat' who had supervised the mass cull of James III's favourites at Lauder in 1482. No strangers to internecine strife, the Douglas affinity were to provoke bitter hostilities during the young king's early years, particularly with Angus inclined to seek support from England.

Henry had magnanimously declared that he would not deign to conduct further military operations against his widowed sister and her infant sons. Queen Margaret 'wrote to the king to have compassion on her and his two nephews, her sons, for she was in fear lest he would invade her realm. The king, moved with brotherly compassion, sent her word that if the Scots kept the peace; he would keep the peace'.[57] Such apparently chivalrous declarations would not prevent the king from continuing to intermeddle in Scottish affairs for the remainder of his reign. The cost of his continental adventures had already crippled the treasury and consumed that careful legacy amassed by his parsimonious father.

Scotland was spared as Henry had fresh plans for France. These were frustrated when the Holy League dissolved in March 1514. An Anglo-French truce was brokered in the same month and, through intense diplomatic effort on Wolsey's part, a permanent peace signed on 7 August. As part of the overall package, Henry's youngest sister Mary was offered in marriage to the ageing Louis XII. Even the old king's death in the following year did not bring severance of this new accord. Francis I had no immediate wish to revert to enmity.

An inevitable casualty in this rush of cross-Channel diplomacy was the Scottish interest which their French allies now, as so often in the past, were apt to overlook as expediency dictated. The Scots were to find that, without their knowledge or consent, they had been included in the treaty to the extent that they were obliged to refrain from the customary border raids that so characterised life on the marches. No such restriction was imposed on the English. It is hardly surprising that enthusiasm for their fickle allies waned. Even the Francophile Albany struggled to raise an army in 1522 to support Francis I, now at odds with England. Even when mustered, the Scots balked at crossing the Tweed. It looked as though the Auld Alliance had very nearly run its final course.

## The raids of 1513

Home's division had marched off the field with only modest casualties and their formation intact. Indeed, their morale was clearly not devastated by their comrades' decimation for they reappeared next morning in an effort to salvage the Scottish guns. These were not the actions of beaten men. From the outset Home had been weighing the odds. Even if the tale of his refusing to come to the king's relief is apocryphal, he did not stir once he'd secured stalemate on the Scottish left. As early as the first week in October, he was meeting with Dacre.[58] The English warden found his Scottish counterpart remarkably bullish for a man whose national army had been so mauled. Dacre may have had instructions to launch a warden raid in that month but bad weather had frustrated any plans. Besides Dacre, an old hand in these affairs, was aware of how risky an enterprise these could be. The warden's observations suggest that the overall state of the Scottish marches had not been materially affected by losses at Flodden.

King Henry would, nonetheless, have his raids, one blow to fall on the west another in the middle. Dacre, as a tactician, seemed generally opposed to the larger warden raids or 'rodes' – he preferred the sustained application of minor force, successive lightning descents.[59] Consequently, the warden dispatched four contingents into Teviotdale and a further three against Annandale; these incursions occurred between 10 and 15 October.[60] It cannot be argued these were an immediate riposte following hot on the heels of victory, too long had elapsed. Next month, he mounted a far more serious affair which he subsequently reported in full to the king in his dispatch of 13 November. Col. Elliot, having cast a soldierly eye over the correspondence concludes, quite rightly, and frustratingly, that it in fact tells us very little.

As was usual in such instances, Dacre assembled his marchers, rather more than 4,000 of them,[61] for a pincer movement coming in from both east and west. Jedburgh may have been an objective. The town was regularly beaten up in the course of cross-border forays. We do know Dacre found some of his marchers, particularly the Northumbrian gentry, as evidencing little enthusiasm. A number, including Lord Ogle, Constable of Alnwick, simply did not appear at the muster point.[62] The warden himself would lead the eastern contingent whilst his brother, Sir Christopher, commanded in the west. In the course of the earlier, smaller raids, the Tynedale men had ravaged Teviotdale and burnt Ancrum. As the eastern prong turned into such a damp squib, Dacre had to send a column to warn off his brother whose force, being now isolated, might have had cause to fear. None of this suggests a beaten or cowed enemy.

After careful analysis, Colonel Elliot[63] concludes that Dacre completed his muster on 10 November, crossing the line that same date, pushed on beyond

Jedburgh then withdrew to Harbottle,[64] all in the course of the following day. Christopher Dacre had also pulled back his own forces which camped at Otterburn before returning westwards via Tynedale.[65] The younger Dacre's force, unlike the warden's, comprised a mix of horse and foot, thus only capable of moving at a slower pace (though the 'foot loons' of the era could cover ground at a highly respectable speed). From analysis of his own account, once he'd crossed the border on the second day of his raid Lord Dacre split his column into two raiding parties, one under another sibling, Philip and the other led by Sir Roger Fenwick. A couple of minor holds were torched but the warden kept well clear of Ferniehirst, where he could be assured of a warm welcome from the Kers.[66]

With the minor 'touns'[67] of Lanton and Ruecastle in flames and some towers slighted, the warden was confronted by Scottish riders intent on punishing his aggression. It was, at this point, that a hasty withdrawal became attractive, especially as Sir Christopher's forces had failed the rendezvous. A running fight to the border ensued, a lively affair 'right sore to the Sclater ford [on the Fodderlee Burn] on the water of Bowset where the Scots bickered with us and gave us handstrokes'.[68] Dacre tells us that, as the fight for the ford warmed up, his adversaries were reinforced by Ker of Ferniehirst, the laird of Bonjedward[69] with Douglas of Cavers, Sheriff of Teviotdale. The warden judged the Scots reinforcement to be some 700 strong, now outnumbering him. He refers to inflicting some minor damage but was clearly relieved when younger brother Christopher with his mixed brigade finally came up.[70]

Christopher Dacre had not been idle. His force was far superior in numbers to the warden's and, having crossed the line, had sent out two raiding parties each 500 strong. These had taken up a number of touns, netting a haul of captives and some handy 'insight' gear.[71] As the marauders went about their task Sir Christopher followed up with the reserve, still with 2,000 horse and 400 foot in hand. This was a tried-and-tested tactic. The Dacres knew their trade; the reserve was there to provide both rapid reinforcement and a muster point if either or both flying columns were attacked. Even after both English contingents were reunited they were by no means safe for Home with a further 2,000 riders appeared to swell the ranks of Scots marchers.[72]

No battle was fought. The two sides eyed each other warily but both wardens were canny enough not to push their luck. Dacre had carried out his instructions and Home had done his bit to see the English off: 'We put in array and came homeward, and rode no faster than nolt [cattle], sheep and swine than we had won would drive, which was of no great substance, for the country was warned of our coming and the beacons burnt from midnight forward. And when the Scots had given us over we returned home and came in at the Redeswire.'[73] It is worth noting that the English warden had no great enthusiasm for this raid, he favoured a more tactical approach and clearly the marchers were no keener. Colonel Elliot defines the raid as a defeat; we are more inclined to suggest stalemate or stand off. What, is however, abundantly clear is that the Scots were not depleted and certainly not cowed. On the borders it was business as usual.

NOTES

1. Hall, *King Henry VIII*, vol. 1, p. 111.
2. *Ibid.*, p. 112.
3. Laing, *Trewe Encountre*, p. 150.
4. *Ibid.*
5. Vergil, *Anglica Historia*, pp. 219–20.
6. Hall, *King Henry VIII*, vol. 1, p. 112.
7. Sir Philip Tilney (Tylney) was Surrey's brother-in-law from his second marriage and the earl's first wife had been Tilney's cousin, effectively the paymaster of Surrey's army, fought in Surrey's division.
8. *Ibid.*
9. Boardman, p. 182.
10. Baird, *Scotish Feilde and Flodden Feilde*, p. 16.
11. Hall, *King Henry VIII*, vol. 1, p. 112.
12. *Ibid.*, pp. 112–13.
13. Ferguson, J.A., *The Battle of Flodden, Contemporary Letters & Documents* (Northumberland, 2011), p. 16.
14. *Ibid.*, p. 17.
15. *Ibid.*, p. 21.
16. *Ibid.*, p. 22.
17. Mackie, J.D., 'The English Army at Flodden' in *Miscellany of the Scottish History Society* vol. VIII (Edinburgh, 1951), p. 82.
18. Hall, *King Henry VIII*, vol. 1, p. 111.
19. *Ibid.*
20. Baird, *Scotish Feilde and Flodden Feilde*, p. 16.
21. Hall, *King Henry VIII*, p. 111.
22. Barr, p. 118.
23. Hall, *King Henry VIII*, p. 110–11, lists the Scottish casualties (see Appendix Two).
24. Barr, p. 119.
25. *Ibid.*
26. Macdougall, p. 283.
27. John Stow (1525–1605), noted Elizabethan antiquary.
28. Macdougall, p. 286.
29. *Ibid.*, p. 294.
30. Hall, *King Henry VIII*, p. 112.
31. *Ibid.*
32. *Ibid.*
33. *Ibid.*, p. 113.
34. Barr, p. 121.
35. Charles Dawson (1864–1916), eccentric amateur archaeologist most famous or notorious for his creation of Piltdown man, a clever hoax which, embarrassingly, fooled the experts for some time.
36. Ford Castle is not presently open to the public.

37. Macdougall, p. 289.
38. *Ibid.*, p. 290.
39. *Ibid.*, p. 292.
40. *Ibid.*
41. *Ibid.*, pp. 296–7.
42. *Ibid.*, p. 299.
43. He'd been elevated to his lordship in 1510, his son the 2nd Lord was subsequently killed at Pinkie in 1547.
44. Macdougall, p. 299.
45. Ferguson, p. 26.
46. *Ibid.*, p. 37.
47. *Ibid.*
48. Macdougall, p. 292.
49. *Ibid.*
50. *Ibid.*
51. *Ibid.*
52. Surrey believed that by paying off the bulk of the army at this point he'd saved the costs of 18,689 men for a full two weeks. As the train and his personal affinity were excluded, we could assume the total force after the battle amounted to some 19,500 men. If we accept losses of 1,500 this would give the earl a force on the day of 20,000–22,000 (Barr, p. 55). Niall Barr contends that if the army was 26,000 strong before the fight then losses were much higher. However, we feel this assertion needs to be tempered in that the Scots were unlikely to be the only side suffering from desertion which will very likely account for the discrepancy.
53. Vergil, *Anglica Historia*, pp. 219–20.
54. Sir Thomas Spinelly, ambassador to Spanish Netherlands writing to Cardinal Bainbridge, Ferguson, pp. 24–5.
55. This was a rather hastily erected *enciente*, enclosing that area of the city hitherto unprotected, see Barr, p. 123.
56. *Ibid.*, p. 124.
57. Hall, *King Henry VIII*, vol. 1, p. 119.
58. Elliot, p. 140.
59. *Ibid.*, p. 142.
60. *Ibid.*
61. *Ibid.*, p. 145.
62. *Ibid.*
63. *Ibid.*, pp. 148–52.
64. Harbottle castle in Coquetdale was a major border garrison in this era.
65. Elliot, p. 152.
66. *Ibid.*, p. 156.
67. 'Toun' or 'ferm toun' was an expression implying a Scottish hamlet or settlement.
68. Elliot, p. 158 and n. p. 160.
69. This laird was presumably the successor to he who had fallen at Flodden; this indicates just how smoothly the successors had become established.
70. Elliot, p. 158.
71. 'Insight' gear implied domestic goods and chattels, the borderers tended to be very thorough as looters.
72. Elliot, p. 160.
73. *Ibid.*, p. 162.

# 10

# FLOWERS OF THE FOREST:
## LEGACY

… those opposed eyes
Which, like the meteors of a troubled heaven,
All of one nature, of one substance bred,
Did lately meet in the intestine shock
And furious close of civil butchery,
Shall now in mutual well-beseeming ranks,
March all one way, and be no more opposed.

Shakespeare, *King Henry IV*

Scotland had learnt regency councils presiding over royal minorities were fraught with risk. All four James had succeeded as children or, in James IV's case, as a young man. The indefatigable Bishop Elphinstone, earlier decried for his steadfast opposition to war, together with the Archbishop of Glasgow and others worked hard to keep the wheels of government turning smoothly. Inevitably, this proved most difficult and 1514 saw tensions rise within the council, fuelled disputes over succession to vacant sees and the mettlesome young widow whose relationships with councillors were frequently difficult.

That August, she injudiciously married the new Earl of Angus, thus nailing her colours firmly to the mast of the contentious Douglas faction. For this, she was stripped of her tutelage rights. An open rift yawned. In that same year, Henry VIII restored Surrey's dukedom of Norfolk, one has to feel rather grudgingly. The plain fact was that his continental adventures had soaked up a £1 million, a staggering sum, depleting the reserves left by his father's frugality. Moreover, he had nothing of substance to show for it; a skirmish won and little else. Small chance there was of a French Crown, the new Pope was careful to take a step back from his predecessor's ostensible largesse.

Some have seen the defeat at Flodden as the canker underlying Scotland's ills during the remainder of the sixteenth century. This is probably over simplification. The nation suffered further dismal defeats at the hands of the English. James V, though he lost fewer men and none of magnatial status, suffered a dire humiliation in the rout of Solway Moss in 1542 where his army, under pressure from a vastly inferior marcher force, simply fell apart. James himself was not present, already suffering from an undiagnosed malady. The shock and shame of the affair were said to have hastened his early death thereafter. At Pinkie, the Scots again lost heavily but never did they cede sovereignty and at no point was there any real likelihood of an English conquest. Nor was the tide of battle entirely one way. Scottish arms scored notable successes at Hadden Rigg in 1542 and three years later upon Ancrum Moor.

James IV was a strong and successful monarch. More than any of his predecessors he had managed to establish centralised and efficient governance. The mere fact the Scottish polity functioned as well as it did in the wake of Flodden indicates just how embedded these processes had become. With James dead, minority rule and factionalism weakened the nation. Neither James V nor his daughter Mary was anywhere near as accomplished as their father and grandfather. James VI it was who secured the final, great prize of union.

In no small part the kernel of James IV's tragedy is personal. He was a successful king who had ruled long and wisely. Chroniclers agree he worked tirelessly. The trappings of monarchy, tournaments, building projects, his artillery, even the navy were the expected tools of a Renaissance prince. James' attested ability to impose law and order on the disparate regions of his realm was a signal triumph. His weaknesses; a measure of vanity, a love for the trappings and ideal of war, a desire to punch above his weight in the counsels of Europe, were shared in equal measure by his brother-in-law. Henry VIII is generally fondly remembered by Englishmen though he was capricious, mercurial, bombastic and cruel, a man whose idea of sentiment was hiring an expert swordsman to spare his wife the added agony of the axe!

If it had not been for the afternoon of 9 September 1513, James would have enjoyed a better press than Henry VIII. His early expeditions over the border in 1496 and 1497 had achieved their purposes, albeit limited ones. James' reign had seen the end of English naval hegemony and the creation of a strong, modern fleet able to meet anything his brother-in-law could float. He had studied war, invested heavily in state-of-the-art ordnance and attempted to instil the tactics of the day. It is this very care which renders his final failure all the more telling. By rights he ought to have won or at least fought Surrey to a standstill but fate is as capricious as kings. The nature of Flodden as a battle, fought over the ground it was, exposed the king's most telling weaknesses, his lack of experience and a misplaced level of aggression. Previously, he had retreated rather than fight. To have done the same again would have stood him rather better in the posterity stakes.

As his biographer observes,[1] when James led his proud army down the fatal slope he did so as the popular monarch of a united realm, supported by his magnates, in so many cases to the death. None of his successors would enjoy such a strong fellowship. None would lead a great army over the border. After Flodden the Scots had no taste for aggressive warfare on the grand scale. The campaign of Homildon in 1402 had been their only real attempt in the fifteenth century. With Flodden, the sixteenth century witnessed an even more dire defeat. Solway Moss was a fiasco and though Pinkie was a significant disaster, it was a defensive rather than an offensive debacle.

Professor Macdougall comments that Lindsay of the Mount 'grieved over a lost golden age of Scottish government. For Lindsay, a courtier who lived through the trauma of 1513 and its aftermath at close quarters, James IV was the 'glore of princelie governyng', who had brought justice and peace to his country and European fame to his house'.[2] As this assessment is from a contemporary, it must carry considerable weight and serves as a worthy epitaph. And perhaps, for James, there was a form of rehabilitation in the nineteenth century and later as the nationalist debate intensified. His achievement and fall are seen as being elements in a tragedy of oppression, that he fell, as did Wallace, in a greater struggle to secure his nation's independence. This is untrue of course and yet can be persuasive. To be judged the gallant underdog has its attractions. Wallace, like James, failed in the final analysis, yet his legend is undimmed, bolstered by the heroism of the struggle itself.

That Scotland should be a free and independent nation state, with a seat in the councils of Europe goes to the heart of the devolution debate. At no time in its history did the country come nearer to this than during the reign of James IV. He came to the throne as a minor after a disastrous reign, marred by civil war. He inherited a land divided with lawlessness and fissiparous magnates scrimmaging in the Highlands, fighting over the corpse of the lordship and the borders in customary disarray. Most of these difficulties were overcome, at least in part, and a strong central kingship established. Few during his father's reign or those of his predecessors would have seen Scotland as an emerging naval power or a player on the European scene. In quarter of a century of hard work James accomplished a great deal.

Perhaps we should leave the last word to Edward Hall, who was after all from the 'enemy' side. He writes admiringly of King James' valour:

> Oh what a noble and triumphant courage was this for a king to fight in a battle as a mean [mere] soldier but what availed his strong harness, the strength of his mighty champions with whom he descended the hill, in whom he so much trusted that with his strong people and great number of men, he was able as he thought to have vanquished that day the greatest prince in the world.[3]

Had James succeeded he would have been hailed as the very epitome of the Renaissance prince and Henry's feeble achievement in France would have counted for little against a catastrophe on the borders. He failed, however. Both he and Scotland paid the price.

As a final anecdotal observation on the impact of the disaster upon the capacity of the Scottish borderers to resist renewed aggression, Elliott records a tradition that, in 1514, a body of English riders struck at Teviotdale. The citizens of the town refused to yield or withdraw and prepared to offer the raiders a warm reception. Some 200 foot were mustered and the company moved out towards Trows, around 2 miles distant. The Scots advanced cautiously, using ground to best advantage and surprised their enemies who were distinctly off guard and, after a sharp fight, saw them off with considerable loss. In their urgent haste to be elsewhere the survivors abandoned their colours which were jubilantly taken up by the victors, a fracas commemorated on the anniversary ever since.[4]

## Lost voices

Flodden is generally portrayed as a purely male enterprise with women as supporters or mourners of the fallen; pious nuns retrieving corpses of the slain;
*femmes fatales* like Lady Heron and her daughter. Or we may be offered the spectacle of the great ladies: the royal figurehead (Katherine of Aragon), beneficiaries
of chivalric endeavour (Anne de Bretagne) or even the jealous wife (Margaret
Tudor). One might not think these women active 'players' on the stage of nation
building, people who made history in their own right. These flowers of the forest
bear a few thorns, the brambles part of their DNA, never mind their upbringing.
Many other women whose names go largely unrecorded were there at Flodden,
as they usually were at every other conflict fought on English soil.

Most armies of the period had large numbers of camp followers – usually
families but also a fair smattering of prostitutes, chancers and general hangers-
on. They offered a range of services: sexual and practical. Cooking, cleaning,
sewing – morale boosters, sutlers and carers:

> For personal hygiene, women groomed both other women and the men and
> children. Searching for lice and fleas was an essential task because of the diseases
> carried by these parasites. The only effective method for removing lice was a close
> personal search by hand with a comb … Women, slaves and prisoners performed
> practically all field sanitation. In camps without women, disease was rife.[5]

For most wounded men, the only real source of medical care was that provided
by the wives and children who accompanied them, a mix of accumulated
knowledge, traditional remedies, some quackery and a lot of basic nursing.
Women were the logisticians, responsible for getting men onto the battlefield,
foraging for the supplies necessary to keep them there and getting them away
afterwards; often undocumented, except by inference. Much later, in 1792, the
French government passed legislation regulating cantinières (*The Law to Rid
the Armies of Useless Women*). In this case, they banned women from the battlefield with the exception of two *vivandières*, responsible for selling food and
drink. This legislation specifically refers to the essential nature of the services
provided in maintaining morale and dealing with practical arrangements not
otherwise officially provided for.

Two of those anonymous women from the sixteenth century are mentioned
on what has been called the first war memorial in England – the stained-glass
window dedicated to sixteen archers from Middleton in Lancashire. The text
in St Leonards Church tells us 'In memorie of certayec menne of ye auncient
parrishe of Myddilton and theyre Lorde Ricardus Assheton howe didd ansere
ye calle to armmes of Thomas Howarde Earle of Surrey and playede theyre

part in defeete of a gryte armie of scotishe invayders'.[6] Thomas Cheetham
and Edward Wylde were two of Sir Edward Howard's command. The memorial tells us that Cheetham and Wylde's wives accompanied their husbands to
Flodden but does not give us their names. Just two who were there amongst,
we'd suspect, a host of others. We should bear in mind that there is now a
question about the age of the window itself: recent research dates it to 1505,
long before the battle took place. However, the text is quite explicit.

## Isabella Hopringle

It takes local knowledge and a bit of luck to happen across Isabella Hopringle,
Prioress of Coldstream. Although, of course, once identified, you find a host of
intriguing references start to crop up. Thomas Grey, 2nd Marquess of Dorset,
records Margaret Tudor's description of her and his own assessment, 'her grace
reported that the Prioress had been very goode and kind to her … another
cause which moved us to assure the sayd house was by cause the prioresse there
is one of the best and assured spyes that we have in Scotland'.[7] Margaret might
have been less positive had she known of Isabella's opinion of her, 'she is very
fickle: therefore counsel the man ye know not to take on hand overmuch of
her credence'. Thus reports Sir William Bulmer to Earl Surrey on 7 October
1523, a report Surrey forwards on to Wolsey.[8] Surrey mentions another prioress
(that of Eccles) who is also providing information; perhaps another tantalisingly, under-reported female occupation of the sixteenth century!

Isabella was a member of a well-known reiver family, firmly Scots by this
time but with affiliations and affinities on both sides of the border. Their grand,
impossibly romantic tower at Smailholm is now administered by Historic
Scotland. This Pringle hold (the family name was shortened from Hopringle
sometime in the course of the century), is also famous as the boyhood inspira-
tion of Sir Walter Scott who spent much time there with his grandparents.
Isabella was but one of a series of Hopringle Prioress's at Coldstream, an insti-
tution whose proximity to the border crossing made it of interest to both
countries. Letters of protection were issued by Henry VII, advising the English
Wardens that servants of the Priory were to be allowed into England to buy
lead (not untypical of cross-border commerce). Isabella had been prioress for
four years when James IV issued a licence to 'intercommon with Englishmen
in the buying of vitallis, sheep, horses … and other lawful goods'.[9]

Fiscal records suggest Coldstream had rights at Plesset Mill and Shipley in
Northumberland as well as extensive holdings in the immediate area. A 1589
plan reveals church, chapterhouse and cloister nestled next to what was, presumably, accommodation for the prioress. It also reveals a range of ancillary

buildings including a guesthouse and service facilities (most likely, kitchen, brew house, bakery and malt kiln), in addition to burial grounds, orchard and farm buildings. All of it substantial enough to be of interest to raiders from both sides as well as armies on the march.

We know that the Scots sacked the priory in 1310 (maybe following the example of Edward I in 1296 although the damage he left behind is perhaps better expressed as the consequence of too lively a set of house guests). English armies certainly dispersed the nuns in 1543 and 1545. Isabella was concerned enough about potential raids in 1515 (when the Priory was sheltering Margaret Tudor) to seek assurance from Lord Dacre that he would do no harm. Margaret wrote on their behalf and was guaranteed safety as long as the house were not supporting any who would harm the king, 'nor keeping nor receiving into hir hous any Scottishemen of war'.[10]

Local difficulties are underlined by a comment in a note to Bulmer in 1523, in which Isabella asserts she dare not come out of doors for fear of her neighbours at Wark. Isabella seems to have been even handed in her distribution of information leaving this author with the clear impression that what really mattered to her was the protection of her house. Nor is it hard to understand the necessity.

We hear her voice quite vividly in 1523 talking about life on the borders:

Lately heard from her that the Queen is gone to Stirling, and has taken with her all the Frenchmen that were about her son. Monday after Palm Sunday the lord Lieutenant was with Dacre at Morpeth. The latter has undertaken that the Riddisdale men shall make redress for all the robberies committed by them since lord Rosse's departure, by the 1st of May. Ralph Fenwick has done the same for the Tynedale men, and brought in half a score of them as sureties. My lord Lieutenant and himself have made proclamations for injured persons to bring in their bills to them. Since his coming hither, strange to say, there have been no offences on either side. Seldom has there been peace so long.[11]

It is said that on the morning after the battle, wagons were sent from the Priory to gather up the noble dead and provide a burial for them. Sadly, no record remains to confirm or deny this story. However, we do have a tantalising glimpse from Robert Chamber's, *Picture of Scotland* (1827) which refers to 'many bones' unearthed on the priory site. Even more interesting is a report by a Captain McLaren in the 1834 issue of *Gentleman's Magazine* which is quoted in *Second to None*: 'On a spot said to have been the burying ground of the Priory of Cistercian nuns, immediately below the surface discovered a great number of human skeletons, which seemed to have been buried in the greatest confusion.'[12] It is impossible to tell, of course, without access to the burial, what period these bones belonged to. But it does set the imagination working.

## The Queen of France

There is no shortage of active imaginations when it comes to the women associated with the events of September 1513. Stories of Lady Heron of Ford Castle and her daughter are much informed by salacious speculation. Just as much myth is associated with Anne de Bretagne, Queen of France. Anne, we are told, persuaded James to launch his assault on England for love of her. The turquoise ring she sent him became as inseparable as the penitential chain round his waist and is numbered amongst the belongings supposedly found after the battle and lodged with the College of Arms in London. Despite the fact that myths over the identification of James' body persisted in the aftermath, the story of the ring still has a modern twist. There is currently an online petition demanding that the college lodge these items with a Scots museum, the ring being cited as proof that these items must be those of the fallen king.

Attempts to argue that the sword and dagger associated with the ring appear to be of the wrong date (which they assuredly are) are not seen as credible by the petitioners. The romance of the story is compelling, especially when one compares the aspirations and expression of Breton nationalism with that of Scotland. Anne of Brittany is as much a symbol of Breton independence as William Wallace is for Scotland. Hardly surprising: the richest woman in Europe was married to two kings (one of them twice) and an emperor, inherited despite Salic Law and has become both a cultural and political icon. Three operas have been produced about her life (one of them a recent rock version). The reliquary which contained her heart (removed from its casing and destroyed in 1792) is still on display in the Musèe Dubrèe in Nantes.

She inherited the duchy at the age of 12. Her father, in an attempt to preserve regional semi-autonomy, had persuaded the Breton Estates to recognise her right of succession. A peace treaty with France had stipulated that neither she nor her sister could marry without French consent. Nonetheless, she swiftly entered into an alliance with Henry VII, Ferdinand of Aragon and Maximilian of Austria. A proxy marriage to Maximilian took place in 1490; a ceremony which was regarded as legally binding at the time.

France then laid siege to Rennes. In the absence of any support from wily Maximilian, Anne was forced to surrender and a betrothal ceremony (equivalent in most eyes to a marriage) to Charles VIII was organised immediately. A second ceremony took place (face to face this time) in 1491. It was an unhappy alliance marked by ongoing disputes about Anne's right to use her title as duchess and her insistence on continuing to exercise governance.

The marriage contract stipulated that whichever of the two parties survived the other would retain rights to the duchy and committed Anne to marriage with Charles' male heir if he died without a son. In 1498, aged 21 and childless despite seven pregnancies, Anne was required to fulfil her contract. Louis XII was already married to her sister-in-law: speedy annulment was sought and within a year a new and very different relationship had begun. Widowhood had brought a new independence and control over her affairs, an experience well known to many women of the time. The Dowager Queen of France was no longer an inexperienced 15-year-old girl. Not that Anne had ever been a fragile character: all the accounts of the period suggest someone of considerable intelligence and capacity, with a formidable disposition and imperial bearing.

Brantome, writing a generation later, describes her relationship with her sister-in-law, Anne de Bourbon.

> She (Anne de Bourbon) wished to make use of some prerogative and authority on her side, but she met with her match for the Queen was a shrewd Bretonne, very proud and haughty with regard to her equals, therefore, Madame de Bourbon had to yield and give place to the Queen.[13]

How then, did a woman of such dignity and position come to be writing letters like this:

> La Motte, the French ambassador, arrived in the Firth of Forth with four ships laden with flour and wine, besides some English prizes he had taken in his voyage. But the most valuable portion of his cargo consisted of a French golden coinage called crowns of the sun, which he profusely distributed to the Scottish King and his nobility. At the same time letters were delivered to James from Anne of Bretagne, the Queen of the French monarch, written in an amorous strain, as if from a high born lady in distress, appealing to his chivalrous feelings, terming him her knight, assuring him that she had suffered much blame in the defence of his honour, and beseeching him to advance only three steps into England with his army for the sake of her who considered him her knight and defender. James also received from this princess a present of fourteen thousand crowns and a valuable ring.[14]

In fact, these are not unusual terms for diplomatic exchanges of the time. Indeed, it appears that Anne addressed Ferdinand of Aragon equally directly earlier in the same year – a message carried by the Provincial of the Observant Friars of Aragon, captured en route to England and who was returned to Spain with a despatch suggesting a truce involving both England and the emperor. Anne was a highly cultured woman, responsible for the production of a book of hours. She employed the flowery language and idiom of her period.

And it is reciprocated:

> He (De Borne) is to return to the Queen of France and to speak to her as fol-
> lows, in answer to what the Queen has proposed to him (King Ferdinand). He
> is glad to hear that the King and the Queen of France enjoy such good health.
> Thanks the Queen of France for her good offices concerning the Spanish
> merchant vessel which was captured off Brittany … Since he saw the King of
> France at Savona he loves him so much that he is ready to do all in his power to
> reconcile him with all the princes of Christendom. Begs the Queen of France
> to ask the King her husband to state very clearly on what conditions he thinks
> that a general peace of Christendom and a war with the Infidels can be made.[15]

We have further confirmation that Anne was an active in the Auld Alliance:
her gift and the correspondence carried by De la Motte are confirmed in
the Treasurer's Accounts.[16] The record of correspondence contained in the
'Flodden Papers'[17] provides further and vivid evidence of this ancient amity
between France and Scotland. Translation and description of diplomatic correspondence between these two Crowns is often fascinating, especially in so
far as it offers an insight into James IV's thinking (as expressed in his letters to
his allies). In particular, it highlights the importance of the Breton connection.

Ironically, one of the causes of debate between James IV and Louis XII was
a pension being paid by the latter to the English Crown. In fact, payment was
disbursed to buy the English off. Henry had laid siege to Boulougne in 1492
in response to that enforced marriage between Charles VIII and Anne. The
matter was resolved by the Treaty of Etaples which pledged Brittany as guar-
antor for the compensation package. Louis' correspondence makes it clear
why James wants the money:

> As for the help asked by the King of Scots for that war in money, provision,
> artillery, gunners, cavalry, infantry and engineers, the King represents his great
> expenses both in France and in Italy, where he maintains 25,000 infantry besides
> cavalry and artillery, and must continue to do so since his enemies are being
> reinforced against him. He begs the King of Scots to remember these things and
> to rest assured that he will send help when he can, and, for all that, to declare
> war against England by land, whilst the King wages war by sea.

> As to the King of Scots' request that the King should inform the King of
> Denmark that he is willing to give the English pension to the King of Scots, it
> is answered that the money is not given as a pension but to repay the sum for
> which the Duchy of Brittany was pledged to the English, in return for help
> to the Queen, but that the King will spare neither his goods nor his soldiers,

ships nor navy to help the King of Scots in any enterprise and will never abandon him in prosperity or adversity. He begs the King of Scots to impart these matters to his uncle, the King of Denmark, and to the King of Norway, the latter's son so that they four may be united for the good of their kingdoms and increase of their lands, the peace of Christendom and the exaltation of the Catholic faith.[18]

James had been occupied for most of 1511 in matters of shipbuilding and had sent to his uncle, the King of Norway and Denmark, for timber for masts. He clearly recognises Anne as a political force in her own right, corresponding directly with her in 1513 regarding a proposed marriage for his cousin, Christian of Denmark. Brittany was valued not just for its resources. At this point it was one of the richest economies in Europe but the skills and experience of its sailors were also prized, as this instruction issued by Louis XII to his ambassador at the Scots court demonstrates:

He is to thank the King of Scots for his willingness to observe the close alliance between the kings, kingdoms and subjects of Scotland and France recently renewed, which the most Christian King will keep in all the heads and articles agreed on … He has chosen some of the best fighters for his ships among those of Brittany, Normandy, Guienne and Picardy and in great numbers.

Because the English are making the greatest navy they can, the King begs for some of the ships of the King of Scotland, principally the largest of which he understands that there is none like it in Christendom and of which de la Mothe has spoken. These should be sent so soon as possible that the navy may make sail against the English. De la Mothe is charged to remind the King of Scots that he has had what he wished from France for his ships and other affairs.

As to the army which the King of Scots intends to lead into England at midsummer, because then grass may be found, the King finds the idea good … As to the help by the King to the King of Scots, de la Mothe will explain that it will be ready so soon as the Scots navy is joined to that of France, in money, artillery, ammunition and other things, but it cannot be sent safely till the navy are together.[19]

## The Queen of England

Sent safely? That would not prove to be the case, regardless of the long-term preparations which had gone into the matter. They had failed to take into account another formidable woman, Katherine of England. It seems odd to be writing that; we are all so used to referring to her as Katherine of Aragon. The queen showed all the signs of being a devoted daughter – her correspondence with both parents is regular, dutiful and affectionate. But she clearly held the view that her responsibilities as Queen of England and wife of Henry took precedence. Indeed, Antonia Fraser quotes the Spanish ambassador in 1514 complaining that she is not paying enough attention to the needs of Aragon, 'the Queen has the best intentions but there is no one to show her how she may become serviceable to her father'.[20]

Katherine's mother, the redoubtable Isabella of Castille had been unusual for her time; queen regnant as well as spouse to Ferdinand of Aragon. Isabella managed to pull off that rare double act of maintaining the firm conviction her husband was the authoritative figure in marriage whilst at the same time exercising control on her own behalf. Isabella declared herself '*la reina proprietaria*' (queen in her own right) of Castile. Despite the very real affection and respect she had for Ferdinand, sovereignty was vested in her rather than jointly held with her husband; she cannily rejected all requests to alter Castilian succession law. By insisting that her eldest daughter should succeed if she died without male issue, she was barring inheritance to Ferdinand. For, as her second cousin, as well as husband, he was her male heir.

Katherine was raised with that same consciousness of status and the confidence in exercising authority that accompanied it. Indeed, she viewed such an exercise as her duty. Isabella's view of marriage and a woman's role within it was passed on to her daughter. Katherine placed Henry's interests first because she genuinely loved him and because it was *right*. From her mother, Katherine also acquired an intense piety and the useful capacity to maintain wifely devotion in the face of infidelity.

Intelligence and tenacity were characteristics of both parents, reinforced by the education provided to their daughters. The early death of their only son, Juan, was unanticipated. The Spanish princesses were groomed as consorts of princes; not rulers in their own right but supporters of their husbands. The hope was, of course, that these daughters would also be ambassadors for Spain. In Katherine's case, her awareness of her future country was quite singular, arrangements for her English marriage had begun when she was just 3 years of age.

Katherine showed herself disposed to adopt English ways within a very short time of arriving in her new home: just short of 16, she could have been forgiven for clinging to Spanish mores. Her chief attendant, Dona Elvira, had been placed in charge of the bride by Queen Isabella herself. Dona Elvira reacted with horror to a suggestion Katherine forgo the Castilian custom of veiling a bride from the eyes of her husband until their wedding day.

Nonetheless, Katherine did indeed honour Henry VII's request to carry out what was, effectively, an inspection.

The story of the next seven years is well known: early widowhood, the decision to affiance her to her dead husband's brother and the long term dispute over her dowry between father and notoriously avaricious father-in-law. Henry VII reacted to the failure to pay the balance due by denying financial support to Katherine and her household. This had unintended consequences. The king's reluctance to pay for the upkeep of Durham House threw her often into the company of the future Henry VIII as she spent time moving between royal palaces. We are assured Henry was a handsome youth, reminding contemporaries of his dazzling grandfather. Acts of kindness to a dispirited and isolated young woman would contribute to the growth of affection. Henry's less attractive qualities would become all too apparent in time.

By March 1509, Katherine was desperately writing to her father to explain that she could stand no more and was planning to return to Spain: 'She could no longer combat the petty persecutions of Henry VII. Only recently, he had told her that he was under no obligation to feed either her or her attendants: he added spitefully that her food was being given to her as alms.'[21] By June, the old miser was dead and she was celebrating her marriage to Henry VIII, the very epitome of a Renaissance prince.

In talking of this marriage, attention tends to get fixed on the 'King's Great Matter'; the events leading to their divorce and Henry's remarriage to Ann Boleyn. This was, nonetheless, a marriage that lasted twenty-four years and by all accounts was a happy one despite the sorrow of losing so many children. The queen's biographer, Antonia Fraser, suggests that Henry and Katherine went on sharing both bed and board up to 1526 even though the king was, by then, pursuing Ann Boleyn.

There is broad agreement that Katherine was her husband's most trusted confidante until pushed aside by Wolsey. Katherine played no small part in foreign affairs. She engineered the recall of the Spanish ambassador Fuensalida in August 1509, and received a commission from Ferdinand to be his official channel of communication with Henry.[22] Her appointment as regent when Henry went off to France reflects his high level of confidence in her capacity and experience. Nor was this appointment regarded as mere formality: there had already been discussion of Scottish 'pranks' [i.e. raids]. She had full authority to raise troops and to make appointments having been provided with an advisory council, headed by Archbishop Warham, the Lord Chancellor.

Henry made his confidence abundantly clear when admonishing the Scots' herald at Therouanne, 'Ye have well done your message; nevertheless it becometh ill a Scot to summon a King of England. And tell your master that I mistrust not so the realm of England but he shall have enough to do whensoever he beginneth; and also I trusted not him so well but that I provided for him right well, and that shall he well know'.[23] Much of Katherine's correspondence is addressed to Wolsey rather than Henry and refers to domestic activities, making banners and badges, as well as overseeing the running of the council. This domestic activity recalls the style of her mother Queen Isabella, who also combined military campaigning with production of morale boosting emblems, standards imbued with more than domestic significance, vital rallying points on campaign and, above all, in battle's heat.

She continued to keep Henry and Wolsey informed throughout the Flodden campaign as well as dealing with other, more humdrum business of state. Having sent Surrey north, she applied herself to mustering a further reinforcement which she planned to accompany. She refers to all this in a letter to Wolsey of 2 September in which she also alludes to her other great concern – the well-being of her husband:

> Received his letter by post informing her of the coming hither of the Duke (Longueville), and that he is to be in her household. Has advised with the Council. There is none fit to attend upon him except Lord Mountjoy, who is now going over to Calais. Advises he should be sent to the Tower, 'specially the Scots being so busy as they now be, and I looking for my departing every hour.' Begs to have an answer from the King. Excuses herself, that being so bound to Wolsey, she had sent him no letter. Had written to him two days before by Copynger.
>
> Her greatest comfort now is to hear from Wolsey of the King's health and all the news. 'And so I pray you, Mr. Almoner, to continue as hitherto ye have done; for I promise you that from henceforth ye shall lack none of mine, and before this ye should have had many mor, but I think that your business scantly giveth you leisure to read my letters.' Pray God 'to send us as good luck against the Scots as the King hath there.' Richmond, 2 Sept. Signed: 'Katherine the Qwen'.[24]

Finally, on 16 September, she is able to write to Henry with the best of news:

> Sir, My Lord Howard hath sent me a letter open to your Grace, within one of mine, by the which you shall see at length the great Victory that our Lord hath sent your subjects in your absence; and for this cause there is no need herein to trouble your Grace with long writing, but, to my thinking, this battle hath been to your Grace and all your realm the greatest honour that could be, and more than you should win all the crown of France; thanked be God of it, and I am sure your Grace forgetteth not to do this, which shall be cause to send you many more such great victories, as I trust he shall do.[25]

It was perfectly natural that Katherine should have been rightly proud of her achievement; she had admirably discharged her role as defender of the realm. But her letter was not perhaps the wisest thing to send to someone like Henry, especially given his rather less significant attainment in France. Essentially, what she was saying was 'Hi Honey; you'll be pleased to know I sorted out that little problem for you while you were off playing with the boys. Beat that'. The Tudors could be charismatic and outgoing, generous even, witness the lenient treatment Henry VII meted out to the young pretender Lambert Simnel but Her Henry could as easily be capricious, mercurial, petty and vindictive. In the long term, this may have been the point at which her fate was sealed.

## The Queen of Scots

Mary Jean Stone, that most fiercely Catholic of historians, is harsh in her judgement of Henry and his sister, Margaret Tudor, Queen of Scotland. A viewpoint coloured by the events of the Reformation and Dissolution only partly explains her description of them:

> ... strikingly alike in character. Both proved themselves to be cruel, vindictive, unscrupulous, sensual, and vain. Both were extraordinarily clever, but Henry being far better educated than his sister, contrived to cut a much more imposing, if not a more dignified, figure. In the matter of intrigue, there was nothing to choose between them ... Given two such characters, the only parts that were possible to them were dominating ones. Henry was master of the situation all through the piece; Margaret was not ... Had she been differently constituted, had she been barely honest, true, constant, and pure, there is no limit to the love and loyalty she would certainly have inspired.[26]

This seems a trifle harsh, especially since Stone goes on to note that James IV had sufficient confidence in his English wife to leave the treasury in her hands and his will appointed her regent for their son so long as she remained unmarried. He had taken Henry's sister as his queen following the treaty of 1502 which ushered in a period of prosperity and by local standards, relative peace. It seemed not unlikely that James might well find himself inheriting the adjoining kingdom through his wife (Henry was still childless at this point), whilst his turbulent, fissiparous nobility were, increasingly, coming under control.

His cousin, the Duke of Albany, was in exile in France. Albany's father, Alexander Stewart, younger brother of James III, had been forced to flee the country when he was found to be in treasonable communication with England; he had been to James III what the gifted but unstable George, Duke of Clarence; had been to Edward IV. The duke, although well respected and supported at the French court was no threat: Louis XII was far too conscious of James' value as an ally to risk the relationship. Attempts were made to effect reconciliation and to persuade James to relinquish control of Albany's Scottish estates but these were somewhat half-hearted in comparison to the level of aid sought from the Scottish monarch.

James was quite explicit in his hopes for the marriage:

> … as to the first two articles in which the King of Scots declares that, as requested, by the King's ambassador, Cordier, and by the Bishop of Moray, he has kept peace with the King of England, and, if he break with him, he loses the reason of his marriage, the succession to the Crown of England to which he, by that marriage, is the nearest heir, apart from his ancient right.[27]

The 'ancient right' referred to is clarified in the same correspondence. James had a rather tenuous, ancient claim to the English throne through his ancestor St Margaret of Scotland (sister of Edgar Atheling) as well as through his wife, Margaret Tudor, 'The King knows also that the Kingdom of England belongs to the King of Scots as heir of St Margaret, Queen of Scotland, and also thorough his wife, elder daughter of the later King Henry. Thus he believes himself justified in helping him to obtain his rights.'[28]

We do not know if Margaret resented the thinking behind her marriage but it seems unlikely. She, like other royal daughters of the period, had been brought up to assume that a dynastic marriage was their duty, a means of bringing nations together and assuring the future of their children. Certainly, Margaret's brother seemed willing to countenance an offer:

> Being now informed that the King of Scots has declared war again the English, the King thanks him for a service he will never forget. Also he knows of the offers made by the ambassadors of England to the King of Scots, declaring him heir after the death of the king of England, if he dies childless, which he refused. And the King promises not to make peace without his consent.

The queen is often presented as a jealous woman, the expulsion of James IV's illegitimate children from Stirling Castle cited as an example. Any woman married to James might have had cause, as he was a notorious womaniser. Unusually for their time her own parents appear to have been monogamous. No evidence exists in her correspondence to confirm or deny the impression but we can point to Margaret's certainty of her role and rank. Regardless of her feelings, she was first and foremost the wife of a king. We do have evidence of complaints about the misbehaviour of her subsequent husbands which suggests that she was perfectly able to make her views known outside the offices of state.

Margaret at this point seems more concerned about money, very much a Tudor characteristic. She appears to be perennially short of funds (hardly surprising when we hear that, despite a generous marriage settlement, she was still forced to appeal to the exchequer for £60 for haberdashery). Disputes about finance, payment of income and misuse of her money by those about her were to be key themes throughout Margaret's life. This time, she and James were trying to recover legacies due to her from her father and grandmother being withheld by her brother. Henry had sent Nicholas West to Scotland to make it clear that payment of the legacy was dependent on James' good behaviour. The Queen of Scots made clear where her loyalties lay. She tells him that she cannot believe she is so strangely dealt with in the matter of their father's legacy and goes on (in what sounds to be phonetic Scots!): 'We ar eschamit thairwith: and wald God niver word had bene tharof … we lak na thing; our husband is evir the langer the better to ws, as knawis God.'[29]

West may have described Margaret as 'right heavy' at the news of Henry's departure for France and offering her good offices to foster peace. But, like her sister-in-law, she had put aside dominant loyalty to the country of her birth in favour of the rights of her husband. James would march to Flodden confident in his queen.

NOTES

1. Macdougall, p. 309.
2. *Ibid.*, p. 293.
3. Hall, *King Henry VIII*, vol. 1, p. 109.
4. Elliott, pp. 221–2.
5. *Medieval Logistics As Applied to the Classes of Quartermaster Supply* CPT John Woodard, CPT Taylor, CPT Danny Devereaux, CPT Kerry King. 'Quartermaster professional Bulletin' Winter 2000 www.au.af.mil/au/awc/awcgate/army/medieval_logistics.htm.
6. Ferguson, *Lords to Labourers: The Named English Participants in the 1513 Flodden Campaign*. For details of dating the widow see Hegbin-Barnes, P., The Medieval Stained Glass of Lancashire, *Journal of the Society Of Archer-Antiquaries*, 5; 2009, pp. 43–50.
7. 'Letters and Papers, Foreign and Domestic, of Henry VIII, 1519–23', *Second to None: A History of Coldstream* (Coldstream and District Local History Society, 2010), p. 38.
8. Brewis, J.S. (ed.), *Letters and Papers, Foreign and Domestic, Henry VIII, vol. 3: 1519–23* (1867), pp. 1421–22. Accessed at www.british-history.ac.uk.
9. Cited in *Second to None: A History of Coldstream*, Coldstream and District Local History Society, 2010, p. 36.
10. *Ibid.*, p. 38.
11. *Ibid.*, p. 39.

12. Brewis, J.S. (ed.), *Letters and Papers, Foreign and Domestic, Henry VIII, vol. 3: 1519–23* (1867). Accessed at www.british-history.ac.uk.

13. De Bourdeille Brantôme, Pierre, 'Dames Illustres', in *A Twice Crowned Queen: Anne of Brittany* (Constance, Countess de la Warr, Eveleigh Nash, 1906), p. 41. Accessed at www.archive.org/details/twicecrownedqueeoodelauoft.

14. *Historical Tales of the Wars of Scotland And of the Border Raids, Forays and Conflicts* (John Parker Lawson, 1839), p. 367. Accessed at www.electricscotland.com/history/wars/28BattleOfFlodden1513.pdf.

15. Bergenroth, G.A. (ed.), *Calendar of State Papers, Spain, Volume 2: 1509–1525* (1866), pp. 161–5. Accessed at www.british-history.ac.uk/report.aspx?compid=93622.

16. 'Accounts of the Treasurer of Scotland 1473–1580' (Edinburgh, 13 vols., 1877–1978), pp. XXIV, 411–12, in Morgan, Hiram, *Scotland in Renaissance Diplomacy, 1473–1603* (University College Cork, March 2008). Accessed at www.ucc.ie/chronicon/scottishdiplomats.

17. Wood, Marguerite (ed.), *Flodden Papers, Diplomatic Correspondence between the Courts of France and Scotland, 1507–17* (Scottish Historical Society, Edinburgh, 1933; printed at the University Press by T. and A. Constable Ltd).

18. *Ibid.*, Louis XII's answer to the secret credential – undated April 1512.

19. *Ibid.*, Blois, Instruction by Louis XII to the Seigneur de la Motte – 5 March 1513.

20. Fraser, A., *The Six Wives of Henry VIII* (Phoenix, 2002).

21. *Ibid.*, p. 19.

22. Davies. C.S.L., and Edwards, John, *Katherine of Aragon*, Oxford Dictionary of National Biography (Oxford University Press, 2004–11) accessed at www.oxforddnb.com/view/article/4891?docPos=1.

23. Brewer, J.S. (ed.), *Letters and Papers, Foreign and Domestic, Henry VIII, vol. 1: 1509–14* (1920), p. 972.

24. *Ibid.*, p. 908.

25. Ellis, Henry, 'Original Letters Illustrative of English History; Including Numerous Royal Letters', in *Autographs in the British Museum and One or Two Other Collections*, 1st ser., I (2nd ed., Harding, Triphook and Lepard, 1825), p. 88. Accessed at www.archive.org/stream/originallettersioielliuoft#page/n7/mode/2up.

26. Stone, J.M., *Studies from Court and Cloister: being essays, historical and literary dealing mainly with subjects relating to the XVIth and XVIIth centuries* (1905). Project Gutenberg, accessed at http://infomotions.com/etexts/gutenberg/dirs/etext03/stdsf10.htm.

27. Louis XII's answer to the secret credential – undated April 1512; Wood, Marguerite (ed.), *Flodden Papers, Diplomatic Correspondence between the Courts of France and Scotland, 1507–17* (Scottish Historical Society, Edinburgh, 1933; University Press by T. and A. Constable Ltd).

28. *Instructions to Master James Ogilvy by Louis XII – Blois 8th May 1513, Ibid.*

29. Ellis, Henry, 'Original Letters Illustrative of English History; Including Numerous Royal Letters', in *Autographs in the British Museum and One or Two Other Collections*, 1st ser., I (2nd ed., Harding, Triphook and Lepard, 1825), p. 65. Accessed at www.archive.org/stream/originallettersioielliuoft#page/n7/mode/2up.

# II

# THE BATTLE IN HISTORY AND MYTH

The Scots' view of Flodden seems odd to somebody raised in the traditions of Irish nationalism. Where are the glorious failures, the heroic last stands? For the Scots, Flodden seems to be a final flowering of an aspiring realm about to take its place on the European stage; the last chance in generations for an independent nation to act on its own behalf free from the shadow of domination. Flodden is a lost opportunity and a lost generation, or so it is portrayed. It is the death toll which seems to have made the greatest impact, yet Scots would go on to sacrifice thousands in the Great War. Not until 1914–18 do we once again find carnage that strikes at the Scottish psyche in this way.

Such high losses must have an inevitably greater impact on a small population (estimates put the total at around 500,000 in 1513). Everyone would
likely know somebody who was there. Wood claims there was trouble and
considerable rivalry over the filling of benefices left vacant by the death of
their holders at Flodden.[1] Some of the fiction written about the event (of
which there is a significant amount) seems almost driven by that consciousness. Take Elizabeth McNeill, for example, who, in the afterword to her novel,
*Flodden Field*, questions whether the 1707 Act of Union could have taken
place if men of power had not died on the battlefield: 'In 1513 … the country
was powerful, rich and on the crest of a wave but everything crashed to disaster in only two hours.' She contends the disaster was worse than Culloden,
'because by that time Scotland was already subdued and had been sold out'.[2]
It's an interesting approach.

## Flodden by the pen

Literary interest in the events of September 1513 started early. The earliest
printed poem appears in 1664. The author, Joseph Benson, a declared philomath ('lover of learning'), was an adherent of the Stanley family and is very
clearly writing from an English perspective. His nineteenth-century editor
asserts he had access to an earlier source held within that family but omits any
details. Benson's poem seems odd now since it misses out two elements which
rapidly became part of the Flodden story: the chivalrous nature of Scotland's
king and the duplicitous nature of Lady Elizabeth Heron of Ford. Instead he
launches into a paean in praise of Henry VIII:

> Thou God of War! Do me admit
> For to discourse with founding praise
> This bloody field, this founding fight
> Fought in our old forefathers days

It is remarkable how the tale of Lady Heron and her daughter has developed over the years, despite no contemporary corroboration of the allegations. Which could reasonably have been expected – Dacre, Dorset et al were
in regular correspondence with the court and quite routinely passed on the
most intimate details of the people round them. Dacre had no love for the
Heron family and would surely have made the most of this gift. The story has,
nonetheless, been gleefully seized on and developed further until we now
hear routinely that lady Heron was not only sleeping with the king but also
with her brother-in-law. Clearly, the Flodden story needs a bad girl as well

as a tragic heroine. The latter is usually the role assigned to Margaret Tudor who is often depicted as the lovelorn wife who knows (as a result of a prescient dream) that her darling will not return. Pitscottie, writing in the 1570s, appears to be the original source of the Lady Heron tale:

> Some say the Lady of Ford was a beautiful woman, and that the King meddled with her; and also his son Alexander Stuart, Bishop of St Andrews, with her daughter; which was against God's commandments, and against the Order of all good Captains of War, to being at Whoredom and Harlotry before any good Success of Battle or Victory had fallen unto them; and Fornication had a great Part of the Wyte (reason) of their evil Success.

> Notwithstanding, the King continued still there the Space of Twenty days without Battle till at the last all the Victuals and Vivers of the commons were spent: and many of the far North-land and Iles men were spent and wasted in the Famine; in this same manner; that it was force to them to pass home …

> But this wicked Lady of Ford seeing the Kings host so dispersed for Lack of Victuals, and knowing all the secrets that were among the Kings men and army, both of the King himself and of his secret council …

> … subdued and enticed by the Allurement and false Deceit of this wicked woman, gave her over hastily Credence in this Behalf and believed surely all that had been true that she promised … but this lady, thinking nothing that she had promised to the King, that, on no Ways, that she would keep it, for the Love she bore her native country; but hastily passed, with a deceitful mind, to the Earl of Surrey.[3]

This presumably explains why the chivalrous James, having given his word to safeguard her property, burnt Ford as he left.

Pitscottie is a useful resource but notorious as a credulous collector of information. For example, in the matter of what became of James' body, he records that a convict offered to show Albany the king's grave ten years after the battle, but the duke refused. From an early date, caveats have been expressed: noting that he is liable to recount as fact stories which do not appear anywhere else in the historical record. Bethan,[4] in 1804, makes this point as does Chatton[5] in 1835. Chambers, also writing in 1835, is even firmer:

> The earnest and honest simplicity of the good old chronicler, however, is exceedingly amusing. He aims at nothing beyond a mere record of what he conceived to be facts, and these he goes on detailing, with a great deal of incoherence, and

all the un-intellectual precision, of an artificial process, neither feeling, passion, nor mind ever appearing to mingle in the slightest degree with his labours. These characteristics of the chronicles of Lindsay have greatly impaired their credibility, and have almost destroyed all confidence in them as authorities.[6]

Sir Walter Scott was to set the alleged liaison firmly in the public mind by his reference to it in *Marmion* (1808). This epic poem culminating in the hero's return to prosperity (and the girl) because of his valour at Flodden was panned when first published. Nonetheless, it was an enormous hit with the public who happily paid 1½ guineas for the first edition at a time when a skilled engineer or surveyor could hope for a salary of £290 per year. It remained popular for over a century. This is the moment when Flodden can be said to take its place as one of the symbols of Scots identity. Scott was not a promoter of independence – in his view the union was a positive step, one which accommodated a romantic ideal of Scotland as one of the British nations (North Britain as some have called it).

His particular contribution to nascent nationalism was the creation of 'tartanry': that sense of identity expressed in an idealised, utterly romanticised Highland legacy. Even the bourgeoisie of the Lowlands, enthusiastic partners in a burgeoning empire and arch despisers of real Highlanders, had taken to the cult of Ossian and now went wholesale for tartanry. Ossian was reputed to be an ancient Gaelic bard who had recorded heroic tales of an earlier age, larger than life figures of myth on a par with those of the classics. Three books by James McPherson, published 1760–73, purported to be collections, most probably drawn from the oral traditions that still survived in the far north and much embroidered.

Flodden finds its place as part of Scots cultural legacy from the mid-eighteenth century onwards. Its other famous expression, *Flowers of the Forest*, seems to have been written around 1758 by Jean Elliot (although the tune is a much older one):

Dool and wae for the order sent oor lads tae the Border!
The English for ance, by guile wan the day,
The Flooers o' the Forest, that fought aye the foremost,
The pride o' oor land lie cauld in the clay.

A lament of the living for the dead which has found a very particular and specific niche in the years since it was written. These are now words of official commemoration and loss, a ritual akin to the reciting of *They shall not grow old* on Remembrance Sunday. Preserved almost exclusively for use on such occasions, it is known by many as *The Lament*. A recent search on YouTube produced a range of comments and reactions which confirmed this. This one strikes us particularly:

> As a piper I love playing this tune – I know it sounds odd but you feel as if you're playing that final musical salute to whomsoever you are paying tribute to. I find the tune itself either makes people well up in emotion of the death, or smile at the life, with no middle ground. Respects to those we can only remember.[7]

## A new Scotland?

The nineteenth century was a period of both change and division within Scotland. The Disruption of 1843 had profound civic as well as religious impact as the Church of Scotland split over issues of governance. Swelling urbanisation and changes in land tenure produced new communities more aware of status than ever before and the social changes of the period produced a more highly educated population. Pressure for home rule grew, culminating in the creation of the Scottish Office in 1885. It is surely no coincidence that this is also the period when references to Flodden as an icon of a unified Scots identity start to emerge once more, this time in that most populist form: the broadsheet, or broadsides as they were known in Scotland.

Among the many gems in the holdings of the National Library of Scotland are a collection of these broadsides, popular collections of news, fiction, songs and comment, passed round or pasted up on walls of inns and houses for all to read, debate and recite. And here we find Flodden once more in the public consciousness as a symbol of courage, loss and the capacity for hope. References may be to personal bravery, 'Tragedy of Sir James the Rose' (1869) a poetic tribute to a vocalist who could 'make us sigh for Scotia's wrongs'. 'An' Floddens day o' dool' (1849). Some come from the 'Poets Box' where, we are told, a list of popular readings and recitations is always to be had – including both *Edinburgh after Flodden* and a new method of promoting the rapid growth of whiskers! One of them holds out hope for the future, a nation and a people resurgent: 'Yet Scotland shall outlive thy stain, Dark Flodden Field; And distant lands shall sing their fame, Who die, but never yield. Here Scottish plumes and tartans wave, The foe will find thy sons as brave, As sires who filled the heroes' grave, on dark Flodden Field!'[8]

Modern novels on the subject are often found on the romance shelves, picking up on the twin themes: James IV as the chivalric (if flawed) hero and the devastating casualty rate. Elizabeth Byrd's 1969 book[9] focuses upon Margaret Tudor while Elizabeth McNeil's more recent volume follows the fortunes of a number of people, including, unusually, Isabella Hopringle.[10] McNeil again gives us the generalised view of the Stewart kings. In her epilogue she refers to an illegitimate son of Alexander Stewart, Archbishop of St Andrews who was born of his liaison with Judith Heron (daughter of Elizabeth). She tells us that, like all his Stewart ancestors, he too did not die in his bed. Rather more unusual is a more recent novel, *Tom Fleck*,[11] written from the view of an English archer present on the field.

## National perspectives

The most immediate impact of Flodden reflects matters still relevant today: the degree to which centralisation driven by a forceful monarch created a distinct nation state. Many have argued that Edward I was crucial to this process in English terms, fixing limitations on powerful magnates and enforcing royal authority at their expense. The creation of an administrative formula which was consolidated over succeeding reigns was a key component in the development of the English polity. By and large, it may be fair to say that most people living in this country now identify themselves as British first with their regional and personal affiliations taking a secondary (though still important) place. The evidence suggests things are rather different from a Scots perspective.

James IV had been engaged in a process of establishing control over his own magnates. This may seem rather late in the day in comparison to his neighbours but one needs to bear in mind that it was only in the reign of his father that the last geographical part of Scotland to remain outside Crown control was finally assimilated. The Orkney and Shetland Islands finally came to the Scots' Crown as part of the dowry of Margaret of Denmark in 1468.

The king had demonstrated his capacity to deal with potential troublemakers even when these were members of his own family. Despite the high regard shown by the French Crown for his cousin, the exiled Duke of Albany, James had made it clear that the latter was not welcome in Scotland. Nor was he willing to tolerate the longstanding quasi autonomy of the Lords of the Isles. By 1493 the title was forfeit, but his efforts to exercise hegemony through nominees were not successful and the dismantling of the Lordship caused far more problems than it solved.

James' death at Flodden unleashed a long term period of internal instability which, some writers assert, frustrated any hope of united opposition to the Act of Union, even if Scotland's aristocracy of the day had wished to do so. Tyler describes it vividly:

The dignified clergy, undoubtedly the ablest and best educated class in Scotland, from whose ranks the state had been accustomed to look for its wisest councillors, were divided into feuds amongst themselves, occasioned by the vacant benefices. The Archbishop of St Andrews, the Prelates of Caithness and the Isles, with other ecclesiastical dignitaries, had fallen in the field of Flodden, and the intrigues of the various claimants distracted the church and the council.[12]

The Dowager Queen did not help matters. A letter from Thomas Spinelly, Henry's representative in the Low Countries tells us that:

By the news brought to Zeland by the two ships from Scotland, it appears the Lords there are not pleased that the Queen should have the rule, as they fear she will comply too much with England. They are in constant intercourse with France, and their ships pass by the back of Ireland ... Angulem said 'they had won nothing by the death of the King of Scots, nor greatly lost, considering that the Duke of Albany should shortly go into Scotland, and there receive ... King, who, with his experience and the entire affection that he hath for France, will acquit himself better than did his predecessor.'[13]

Tyler suggests that the letter of instruction issued by Louis XII on 4 October 1513 was in effect a response to a secret embassy asking for the return of Albany and sent by those who feared English influence on Margaret. At this point, Louis notes a degree of uncertainty about the actual fate of James IV. Margaret's second marriage brought matters to a head. She would have been hard put to find a partner more likely to create dissension than one drawn from the Douglas family and in allying herself with Archibald Douglas, Earl of Angus, she had made a serious error. His own uncle described him as a 'witless fool' and it would not be long before he was at odds with her. Ironically, Douglas would later do good service at both Haddon Rigg and Ancrum Moor.

The immediate result was that she forfeited her regency (since she had remarried) allowing the Francophiles on the council to recall Albany. She managed to stage a coup in 1524, only to have control of her son seized by by her then estranged husband. By the time James V finally managed to escape the savage clutches of Douglas regents, both Highlands and Western Isles had lapsed into near anarchy and many other Scots nobles were at best offering lip service to the Crown.

## Consequences

These may have been long term. Even today, Scotland is notably different to most of the surrounding nations. Is this simply because the Scots are a particularly independent and proud nation? Of course, that is the case but there is more. Historiographer Royal Christopher Smout summed it up rather nicely in a 1994 paper for *Scottish Affairs*. Think of identity as a set of concentric rings – family, kinship or clan connections, locality (I belong to Glasgow), nationality, state (in this case, Britain), Empire (while it existed) and finally, to a more amorphous cross-border affiliation (be it the United Nations or the EEC).

Even beyond arguments about devolution or independence, Scotland has clearly been a nation wherein most would define themselves strongly as both Scots and Britons. This was something missing until recently in English consciousness – witness the air of embarrassment about recent attempts to enshrine St George's Day as a national holiday in reaction to the debate about what constitutes a United Kingdom. Almost as though somebody with a stiff upper lip were announcing, 'We don't talk about that sort of thing.'

Smout points to history as a driver of identity, as in the case of Bavaria within Germany, Catalonia within Spain or Scotland within Great Britain. He notes six key 'mythic' moments in Scots history, of which Flodden is one and which have come, collectively, to define both past and future, 'All the key myths involve a clash with England or "English" values; all but one are tragedies and defeats from the Scottish side; Scotland is, however, always Scotland the Brave. It is a tale operating to infuse a sense of Scottish pride with a concomitant sense of the inevitability of Scottish political failure'.[14] He ends with an interesting observation – that 300 years has taught the Scots not to fear absorption into a wider political entity; that it is possible to retain what is unique about a nation even whilst participating in a wider alliance. The modern example he cites is the European Union.

Not that the Scots need any lessons in being European as well as themselves: the Auld Alliance is an icon of nationhood and one which owes much to the events culminating in Flodden. The Franco-Scottish alliance was not a new one, nor was the use of that alliance against the English, or Scots support of French opposition to the English. What did change in the early sixteenth century was the way Scotland was caught up in France's European ambitions. She found herself standing with France against the combined forces of the Papacy, Spain, Venice and the Swiss. Some might say that change was disastrous. It has to be admitted the alliance from the outset was manipulated by the French in a wholly cynical matter and Franco-Scottish collaboration on the border, as in 1385, was generally a chastening experience.

In 1512, under a treaty extending the Auld Alliance, the peoples of Scotland and France effectively became nationals of each other's countries. It emphasised the importance of the relationship between the two. The Auld Alliance (actually a renewable treaty) had been in existence since before 1295 and was essentially a mutual-protection pact aimed at England. It had been renewed regularly since then, each party agreeing to invade English territory if the other were at war with the enemy over the border. The 1512 codicil was not simply a gesture on the part of Louis XII. Correspondence contained in *The Flodden Papers* makes it clear that France needed more than Scotland's willingness to act as a diversion whilst the real fight went on.

In a letter to Robert Cockburn, the King of France notes an offer by the King of Scots to supply soldiers. 'Yes please' is Louis's response, 4,000 of your experienced men would be of considerable use in Italy.[15] Scots had served under the French kings during the Hundred Years War and, as this correspondence notes, formed a bodyguard to the Kings of France since the reign of Charles VII. These served as volunteers rather than members of any expeditionary force. Manrent, that system of near-feudal relationships which allowed Scots to serve for an agreed period, was still very much in operation. It was notoriously difficult to persuade men contracted in this way to stay on once their term was finished.

Why was James so keen to venture abroad? Two reasons, or rather two ambitions, of the Scots' Crown reflect its growing confidence in Scotland's place in Europe. James had long maintained the ideal of leading a crusade against the infidel. Correspondence relayed through the French ambassador, Charles de Tocque, Seigneur de la Mothe, in April 1510, contains detailed discussion of James' proposals to act as Captain General of a new crusade to free the Holy Sepulchre and contain the incursions of the Moors into Europe.[16] The second target was closer to home: the English throne, a real possibility as Henry VIII was, at this stage without a male heir. Scotland may not have been a nation on the scale of France but it was, to a limited extent, a relationship of true partners, not a weak state overly reliant upon a powerful one.

Flodden changed that. Scotland would never really again be in a position to invade. Albany could raise little enthusiasm and James V's abortive attempts which culminated in near farce at Solway Moss, underlined the difficulties. Even if she were to make a fierce and finally successful defence of her own territory during the period of the 'Rough Wooing' this was essentially reactive and defensive in character. James V's daughter, Mary, might become Queen of France but as consort rather than co-ruler. From 1513, Scotland was more involved with her neighbour than with Europe. The Reformation, firstly in England, then more gradually in Scotland, changed the dynamic more effectively than any military action before or after.

Nonetheless, that sense of looking outward, driven by the Scots Diaspora and the totemic, if largely mythic, symbolism of the Auld Alliance would retain potency. Recall 1990, when Glasgow won the title of European City of Culture. This award ushered in a period when commentators would routinely refer to the cosmopolitan and European nature of the Scots polity as if it were a commonplace that had, somehow, been overlooked for a while.

Scotland has a longer memory. In 1995, celebrations were held in both France and Scotland to mark the 700th anniversary of the alliance. Much was made of the impact of French culture on architecture, law, the Scots language and cuisine. Many a wine merchant was quick to note that claret had long been the local wine of choice. Even after the Union of Parliaments with England in 1707, it continued to be smuggled into Scotland. 'It appears that Scots through the ages have sought to demonstrate their affinity with their French friends by toasting "the King over the water" with a fine drop of claret'.[17] And, of course, it was noted with glee that the promise of dual citizenship in both countries was only revoked by the French government in 1903.

What though, of the physical legacy of Flodden – those monuments and museum displays that you would expect to mark an event of such matter for two nations? There has long been a curious gap there, too often filled with myth and speculation rather than hard fact or evidence. Take note of an online debate conducted in 2005 between a Scottish/American and the College of Arms.

A petition was raised on the site and sent to the college stating:

> The College of Arms located in London England is in possession of the personal effects of James IV, King of Scots which were removed from his body after his death at the Battle of Flodden Field in 1513, whereas the English in years following the battle abused, disrespected and eventually lost the corpse of the Scottish King, it is only fitting that the personal effects taken from the body be returned to Scotland where they belong. We the undersigned hereby request that the The College of Arms located at Queen Victoria Street London EC4V 4BT England do their part to undo a great wrong of history and return the above mentioned items to the Scottish people at once.

The reply highlights a degree of speculation about Flodden artefacts that is still relevant:

> As an initial point I must state that it is by no means certain that the items that we hold really were the possessions of James IV, the King of Scots slain at Flodden; historians of weaponry are very doubtful that they really date back that far, and they may have very little historical value. The Scottish people would have

probably little reason to be grateful if we were to offload this cache of dubious material on them.[18]

Regardless of where you stand on this particular discussion, it does highlight the value of the work being done by the Flodden 500 project in seeking a historical and archaeological context for the battle.

NOTES

1. Wood, Marguerite (ed.), *Flodden Papers, Diplomatic Correspondence between the Courts of France and Scotland, 1507–17* (Scottish Historical Society, Edinburgh, 1933; University Press by T. and A Constable Ltd).
2. McNeil, E., *Flodden Field: A Novel* (Severn House Publishers Ltd., 2007).
3. Robert Lindsay of Pitscottie, *The history of Scotland: from 21 February, 1436 to March, 1565. In which are contained accounts of many remarkable passages altogether differing from our other historians; and many facts are related, either concealed by some, or omitted by others* (Baskett and Company, 1728), p. 113. Accessed at http://books.google.co.uk.
4. Rev. Bethan, William, Miller, *The Baronetage of England, or the History of the English Baronets, and such Baronets of Scotland, as are of English families; with genealogical tables, and engravings of their armorial bearings*, vol. 4 (1804). Accessed at http://books.google.co.uk.
5. Andrew, William, *Rambles in Northumberland and on the Scottish border; interspersed with brief notices of interesting events in border history* (Chatton, Chapman and Hall, 1835), pp. 234–6. Accessed at http://books.google.co.uk.
6. Chambers, R. (ed.), *A Biographical Dictionary of Eminent Scotsmen in Four Volumes, vol. III* (1835; Revised by T. Thomson, Blackie & Son, 1855). Accessed at www.archive.org/stream/biographicaldict04chamiala#page/n7/mode/2up.
7. YouTube – Isla St Clair; *Flowers of the Forest*, www.youtube.com/watch?v=hqY79y-SCbA.
8. *The Word on the Street: How Ordinary Scots in Bygone Days found out what was Happening.* Broadsides in the collection of the National Library of Scotland, accessed at http://digital.nls.uk/broadsides/index.html.
9. Byrd, E., *Flowers of the Forest* (MacMillan, 1969).
10. McNeil, *Op. Cit.*
11. Nicholson, H., *Tom Fleck* (YouWriteon.com, 2011).
12. Tyler, Patrick Fraser, *The History of Scotland* (William Tait, 1834), p. 90. Accessed on www.archive.org/stream/historyscotland18tytlgoog#page/n115/mode/2up.
13. Brewer, J.S. (ed.), *Letters and Papers, Foreign and Domestic, Henry VIII, vol. 1: 1509–14* (1920), p. 2445. Accessed at www.british-history.ac.uk/source.aspx?pubid=1120.
14. Smout, T.C., 'Perspectives on the Scottish Identity', *Scottish Affairs*, no. 6, winter 1994 (The Institute of Governance, University of Edinburgh). Accessed at www.scottishaffairs.org/backiss/1994.html.
15. Wood, Marguerite (ed.), *Flodden Papers, Diplomatic Correspondence between the Courts of France and Scotland, 1507–17* (Scottish Historical Society, Edinburgh, 1933; University Press by T. and A Constable Ltd); Louis XII instructions to Master Robert Cockburn, Postulate of Ross (sent from Briançon, 10 July 1507).
16. *Ibid.*, Charles de Tocque, Seigneur de la Motte in April 1510.
17. Historic-UL.com accessed at www.historic-uk.com/HistoryUK/Scotland-History/TheAuldAlliance.htm.
18. Our Scotland – Scottish Politics Discussion Forum; http://ourscotland.myfreeforum.org/archive/king-james-iv-personal-effects-helprequested__o_t__t_361.html.

# BY THE SPADE PROVIDED:
## ARCHAEOLOGY OF A BATTLEFIELD

Readers who wish to peruse a fuller account of the outstanding work being undertaking by the *Flodden 500* Project[1] and *Remembering Flodden*[2] should refer to the relevant websites. The former is the coordinating project which seeks to draw together the divergent strands from both sides of the border, working towards the 500th anniversary in 2013. What we offer here is an overview of the work undertaken to date. Any opinions expressed are those of the authors and should not be taken as representing the views of the archaeologists themselves.

Battlefield archaeology is a relative newcomer. The first full conflict excavation seems to be that undertaken by Dr Douglas Hunter in North Dakota on the site of the Custer battlefield. This was a fairly small-scale affair conducted by a blundering martinet but one which has fascinated movie-goers ever since. Battlefield archaeology is distinguished from 'recceology', a study of surface finds. The objectives may be said to represent an endeavour to set the field in its wider human context. Archaeology, as in the case of Culloden battlefield (1746), may often show us that the overall area covered by the conflict is much wider than the historical accounts may infer.[3]

From a historian's perspective, the beauty of archaeology lies in its cold, clear objectivity. Finds can tell us a great deal; they provide that compelling physical connection between 'us' today and 'them', those who were actually on the ground at the time. I defy anyone who has an ounce of historical sensibility not to be thrilled when he or she handles an actual artefact. And archaeology is coldly factual in its very muteness. We know, with Flodden, that the contemporary, primary sources are meagre and that much secondary material needs careful sifting. Writers are frequently partisan. We run off on tangents of our own; we misunderstand the evidence; we fail to study the ground. The spade suffers no such limitations; it literally lifts the lid on the past.

Of course, the science is only as good as the evidence. Battlefield traces are notoriously elusive and we can all fall prey to misinterpretation. Whilst the archaeologist, as scientist, must remain strictly objective and wisely cautious, the historian is allowed a measure of licence. We are free, for example, to use Colonel Burne's theory of military probability. Some will shudder but we maintain that the soldier's view can lend valuable insight provided we refrain from letting our imaginations run wild.

There is general agreement on the location of the field. Defoe in *A Tour of the Whole Island of Great Britain* observed:

> … that there was such a battle, and that this was the plane [field], is out of all doubt; and the field seems to be well chosen for it, for it is a large plain, flanked on the north side, which must be the Scots' right, and the English left by Flodden Hills, and on the other side by some distant woods. The river Tull [Till] being on the Scots' rear, and the Tweed itself not far off.[4]

Much of the solid archaeological work to date has focused on the area of the Scots' camp on Flodden Hill. Early maps by Armstrong clearly show a feature which very much resembles a small fort or sconce, having pointed bastions at each corner and covering roughly 2½ acres (1 hectare) of ground. Nineteenth-century authors defined this as a possible Roman structure and the site is now much obscured by subsequent planting.

Excavations, begun in the 2009 season,[5] revealed a substantial edifice, raised with dressed-stone inner and outer facings and having a complex fore-work at the entrance. This did not appear to be an earlier, Iron-Age survivor but possibly something dating from the Flodden era. Frustratingly, a lack of date-able finds defeated any attempt to fix the building in the early sixteenth century. Nonetheless, an abundance of discarded sharpening stones suggests the presence of significant forces equipped with edged weapons. A year before the battle, English secret agents had commented on a diamond-shaped bastion; the classic *trace italienne*[6] being added at Edinburgh Castle. Small forts or redoubts of the type identified at Flodden were not thought to have been a feature of field defences in Britain for another generation or so but we must always bear in mind the number of continental advisers in James' train.

The structure would appear to conform to the basic tenets of *trace italienne* design as laid down by Leon Battista Alberti in the mid- to late fifteenth century.[7] The structure would comprise low walls, wide in plan, with artillery towers projected at angles from the walls, complete with firing platform, the whole protected by a series of trenches and outworks. The parapet above the fighting platform could be built up of gabions; enfilade fire could be laid down from the bastions. Whilst it cannot be proven, the find does suggest that the Flodden redoubt is an early example of the *trace italienne*, possibly the earliest in Britain. It was previously thought that, in the case of Scotland, fifteenth-century developments in the gunner's art had not significantly affected defensive architecture save for the addition of gun-loops in existing fortifications. Threave Castle, the mighty insular Douglas hold which, for a while, defied James II, a consistent enthusiast in the science of gunnery,[8] boasted a gun-looped outwork and circular artillery bastions.[9]

As early as the year of Flodden, a 'blockhouse' was being raised to shield the vital harbour at Aberdeen. The indomitable Dacre was reporting, some ten years after the battle, on a similar construction now seen at Dunbar, commissioned by the Regent Albany. Here, the masonry rampart was up to 21ft (6.5m) in thickness[10] and the overall style, with its distinctive wide-mouthed gun loops, showed a clear French influence. Dacre was clearly impressed by the strength of the new redoubt 'and if the said bulwark could be won I think there is no doubt but the castle be won'.[11]

That feature known as the King's Chair stands some 3,000ft (1,000m) west of the redoubt and aerial photography has revealed the potential presence of further defensive enclosures which encircle the high ground, possibly linked by a system of trenches. Alberti would no doubt have approved. The whole of the enclosed area could very probably contain an army of say 25,000–30,000 plus a large number of rear–echelon personnel, wives and camp followers. Thus far, archaeology has not been able to provide any clues in relation to that vexed question of a Scottish smokescreen, masking their deployment on the morning of 9 September. No evidence of burning has surfaced – yet.

In addition to sharpening stones, the encampment area has yielded cement-stone fragments, almost certainly gunners' or engineers' chalks. Widening the initial search area has produced an array of small finds, horse nails, harness, buttons and coins. These artefacts were distributed rather too widely to focus our thinking on the overall location and of course the fight. We have referred earlier to nineteenth-century antiquarian's comments on to the amount of cannon shot lying over the field at that time. Cultivation and collecting have, of course, scooped these up long since, though some fascinating finds have surfaced more recently. The OS Map of 1866 does point to the location of two ordnance finds, just north-west of Branxton village.

Mr T. Rankin from Sunnilaws Farm built up an impressive pyramid of shot in the late nineteenth and early twentieth century, somewhere between forty–fifty items in total. This collection was subsequently broken up and scattered. One survivor is of 6in (or 152mm) diameter with a most distinct casting seam and prominent sprew left by the moulding. A pair of stone shot 2–3in (50–70mm) were discovered near Barmoor. These, and another iron ball which was unearthed during construction work in Crookham, could very possibly be from the lighter English field guns. The Crookham shot shows evidence of flattening on impact and, most interestingly, has been drilled to hold what must have been a lead core. Such practice was not uncommon for this technique added weight to shot whilst not increasing the bore, thus a heavier round could be thrown by a light gun. Furthermore, the round might shatter on impact, creating a shrapnel effect.

Some smaller stone and lead shot from the Scots side might be evidence that their gunners were preparing an early form of grape or lantern shot. Balls packed with flints and perhaps sawdust were crammed into a timber sphere and then fired when the enemy was coming to contact, point blank virtually. The effect was that of a large shotgun cartridge, devastating against massed ranks at close quarters. This might simply be the normal usage of war or could imply the gunners were aware of the limitations of their heavier pieces when deployed in the field, an attempt to add killing power at short range.

One question, an answer to which the ground stubbornly refuses to yield up, is whether either side employed handguns. None are mentioned by the contemporary accounts though this does not necessarily imply that none were deployed. The use of handguns had been evident a century beforehand. Whilst both England and Scotland had perhaps been rather slower to pick up on these new weapons, we are aware they were used in England during the Wars of the Roses, a generation and more beforehand. The Earl of Salisbury, one of the more talented English commanders during the later phases of the

Hundred Years War, was killed by a shot at the Siege of Orleans in 1428; 'a ball struck the earl a fatal blow'.[12] We know the Earl of Warwick employed a company of handgunners as mercenaries in the 1460s.

These early weapons were smooth-bored, single shot muzzle-loaders, generally with a short iron barrel lashed to a wooden stock. Early shooters fired from the hip or with their stock balanced on the shoulder. Ignition was a major source of difficulty. These weapons were discharged by means of a length of heated wire or match-cord being applied to a touch hole. By the time of Flodden, however, a major step forward had been achieved with the introduction of the 'serpentine'. This is a Z- or S-shaped lever, attached to the side of the wooden stock and able to pivot, a lighted match clamped in the pair of jaws at the business end.

When the long lever was depressed, like a primitive trigger, those jaws were lowered onto the touch hole and the weapon would (hopefully) fire.[13] Though a distinct improvement on its predecessors, these early matchlocks were still unreliable and wildly inaccurate. The psychological effects of early black-powder weapons partially compensated for their manifest inefficiencies. Though those stout yeomen who marched beneath St Cuthbert's banner might stand by their trusty war bows, the days of the men of the grey goose-feather were numbered.

Of pressing interest to historians and archaeologists alike is the question of burials. If say, 10,000 men fell at Flodden, where were they buried? Logic and precedent would suggest that interment usually occurred where the fighting had been thickest. The dead generally have no currency and getting them off the ground and into it was a necessary if unwelcome chore. In 1910, possible burial pits were unearthed just south-east of the monument on Piper's Hill and nineteenth-century records suggest further evidence of mass burials was uncovered during work in the churchyard. Grave pits represent one of the holy grails of battlefield detectives. It is hoped that, in due course, further archaeology will produce more evidence of these.

Hydrology has also come to the aid of historians. Dr Paul Younger in his fascinating and groundbreaking research into the impact of hydrology on the outcome of the battle, has looked at the geology of the vicinity and concluded that there are three 'convergence' zones. These are areas where the water table first clears ground then re-appears. The most notable is that at the foot of Branxton Hill which so materially affected the course of the fighting. Furthermore, the Scots atop Branxton Hill were likely to be standing on saturated ground whilst their enemies on Piper's Hill opposite remained dry. The effects of these factors on both morale and mobility should not be underestimated. Another convergence zone is located at the northern foot of Flodden Hill and would have constituted an obstacle the Scottish forces would have had to negotiate prior to their deployment.

Now this was far likely less of a surprise than the more northerly feature which did them so much damage and could have been crossed in a more considered or leisurely manner. Nonetheless, they almost certainly marched with wet and muddied footwear. We are reminded of the dire effects of clogging mud whenever we examine photographs and accounts from the Western Front in the Great War. The very name Passchendaele conjures up a nightmare, stricken landscape of omnipresent mud.

One ancient survivor, a prehistoric monolith standing some 8ft 2in (2.5m) in height and located just north-west of Crookham Westfield, is referred to and marked as 'the King's Stone'. This is said to mark the spot where James fell. A highly unlikely tale, unless of course we are prepared to accept that James survived the immediate wrack of his army and was done to death as he quitted the field.

Now, there is a good display board by the monument on Piper's Hill which explains the action quite clearly and this vantage provides an Englishman's view of the Scottish line along the crest in front. Imagine ground heaving with the great weight of Scottish pikes, points glinting in a pallid sun, the crash and roar of the great guns. The prospect is daunting.

In essence the field is unchanged. Step down into the line of the dip, look toward the English line and you can appreciate how so seemingly mundane a feature could lead to so total a disaster. Imagine now the burn, spread with marshes, swelled by the rains and churned by tramping feet, muddy waters turned red by the effusion of so much blood. A Scottish king who, if he failed as a general, did not fail as a knight. He did not desert those who followed him and they, true to their oath, fell around him.

## NOTES

1. www.iflodden.info.
2. www.flodden.net.
3. In the case of Culloden, battlefield archaeology has quite significantly altered our perceptions of both the area involved and of the action itself.
4. London, 1725.
5. The site was investigated in 2001 as part of the BBC series *Two Men in a Trench*.
6. Phillips, pp. 33–4.
7. *Ibid.*
8. James II died at the Siege of Roxburgh when one of his own guns exploded.
9. Phillips, p. 4.
10. *Ibid.*
11. *Ibid.*, p. 95.
12. Pegler, M., *Powder and Ball Small Arms* (Wilts, 1998), pp. 18–19.
13. *Ibid.*

# APPENDIX ONE

# ORDERS OF BATTLE

## The English

*The Vanguard; Thomas Howard, the Lord Admiral*
Left-hand brigade, Sir Marmaduke Constable, mainly family retainers and including 1,000 Lancashire men, officers drawn from family (brother, three sons, two cousins and a son-in-law, Sir William Percy with his Northumbrian affinity). A total of 2,000 men.

The centre, under Howard's direct control, included 1,000 of the total complement of 20 marines drawn from the fleet, each under their normal captains, 2,000 men under the Bishop of Durham's banners, drawn from the Palatinate and led by Lord Lumley and Sir William Bulmer. Most of the rest drawn from the Ridings – dalesmen under Lord Clifford and the North Riding men under Lord Conyers – 9,000 men in total.

The right-hand brigade led by Howard's younger brother Edmund, with him 1,000 of the Cheshire men (unhappy at not being brigaded with the Stanleys, their affinity) and including the Macclesfield company and 300 tenants of the Abbey of the Vale Royal, 500 from Lancashire, others from east Yorkshire including levies from Hull and Doncaster. Lastly, a stiffening of the remaining 200 marines under Maurice Berkeley, master of the *Mary George* – some 3,000 in all.

Total strength of the Vanguard = 14,000.

*The Main Battle; Thomas Howard, Earl of Surrey*
The left-hand brigade, commanded by Sir Edward Stanley, drawn almost entirely from his family tenantry and affinity, Lancashire and Cheshire men with Stanley retainers appointed as captains – 3,500 strong.

The centre under Surrey himself, 500 personal retainers and HQ staff, the South Riding men led by George Darcy, with Scrope of Bolton in charge of the Swaledale and Wensleydale contingents, in all some 5,000 men.

The right, Dacre's border riders, 'prickers' and light horse, including a troop from Northumberland under 'Bastard' Heron, the remainder of the horse from the West march with some East marchers from Bamboroughshire and Tynemouth; total of mounted arm, perhaps 1,800–2,000, the foot more Lancastrians, tenants and affinity of James Stanley, Bishop of Ely, and commanded in the field by his natural son, John – altogether perhaps, 3,500.

Total strength of Main Battle = 12,000.

Total strength of the English army = 26,000

## The Scots

*The Left;* Alexander Lord Home and Alexander Gordon, Earl of Huntly, mainly comprising Home's borderers from the Merse and Teviotdale brigaded with Huntly's Gordons from Aberdeenshire and Inverness, officered by Gordon tacksmen – 10,000 strong in total.

*Left Centre;* William Hay, Earl of Errol, John Lindsay, Earl of Crawford and William Graham, Earl of Montrose, the levies of Perthshire, Angus, Forfar, Fife and the N.E. Lowlands, many of the officers drawn from Graham's affinity – altogether, perhaps 7,000.

*T   he Centre,* personally commanded and led by King James IV, supported by the members of his household and the combined retainers and affinities of the Earls of Cassillis, Morton and Rothes, Lords Herries, Maxwell, Innerwick, Borthwick and Sempill, together with the town levy from Edinburgh, Ayr, Haddington, county levies from the south-west and Galloway – in total perhaps as many as 15,000.

*The Right;* Highlanders under Archibald Campbell, Earl of Argyll and Matthew Stuart, Earl of Lennox, under their banners, led by chiefs and tacksmen contingents of Mackenzies, Grants, MacDonalds under MacLean of Ardnamurchan, MacLeans of Duart, Campbells from Glenorchy and Loudoun, levies from the far north, Caithness, Sutherland and the Orkneys led by William Sinclair, lastly a stiffening of 50 French men at arms under D'Aussi – possibly 5,000 in all.

*The Reserve;* Adam Hepburn, Earl of Bothwell, the steady Lowland conscripts from the Lothians, Forest of Ettrick, the border burghs of Galashiels and Selkirk – 5,000 strong.

Total strength of the Scottish army = 42,000

# APPENDIX TWO

# CASUALTIES AND HONOURS

## English dead and prisoners

Sir Bryan Tunstall; Sir William Fitzwilliam; Sir Richard Harbottle; Sir Ralph Warcop; Sir Christopher Savage; Sir William Handforth; Sir John Booth; Sir John Gower; Robert Foulshurst; Maurice Berkeley; John Sankey; John Bostock and Thomas Venables. Thomas Whethill of Great Sankey in Lancashire succumbed to his wounds soon after the battle at Newcastle★. In addition Sir Humphrey Lisle and Henry Gray were captured.

★Source: John Ferguson

## Scottish dead and prisoners

King James IV of Scotland; Alexander Stewart Archbishop of St Andrews, Chancellor (the king's bastard son), George Hepburn, Bishop of the Isles, Lawrence Oliphant, Abbot of Inchaffray, William Bunch, Abbot of Kilwinning; the Earls of Argyll, Caithness, Crawford, Lennox, Montrose, Bothwell, Cassillis, Errol and Rothes; Lords Avondale, Elphinstone, Hay of Yester, Keith, Maxwell (and, by Halls' account, four brothers), Ross, Seton, Darnley, Crichton, Erskine, Herries, Lorne, Oliphant, Sempill and Sinclair; of gentlemen – Ninian Adair of Kinhilt; Abercrombie of Ley; Master of Angus; Andrew Anstruther; Arnot of Woodmill; Sir Gilbert Baird of Posso; John Balfour of Denmill; Andrew, Master of Blackadder; Sir Alexander Boswell of Balmuto; Sir Duncan Campbell; Sir Duncan Caufield; John Carnegie of Kinnaird; William Carr; Alan, Master of Cathcart; Robert Cathcart of Killochan; John Cathcart; Master Cawell, clerk of the Chancery; Alexander Clelland; Alexander Cockburn; Sir William Cockburn of Langton; Sir Robert Colville of Ochiltree, Director of Chancery; Cornwal of Bonhard; Crawford of Achnames; Crawford of Ardagh; Sir John Douglas; Sir William Douglas;

Sir John Dunbar; Robert Elliot of Redheugh; Fleming of Barochen; Alexander Forsyth of Nydie; Sir Alexander Gordon; Master John Grant; Graham of Callander; Graham Grierson of Garvock; Sir Alexander Guthrie; William Haig of Bemersyde; Sir John Haldane; Adam Hall, Henderson of Fordil; Sir Adam Hepburn; Cuthbert ('Cuddy') Home of Fast Castle; Sir David ('Davy') Home of Wedderburn; George Home; Sir John Home; Sir Patrick Houston; John Hunter; William Keith; Walter Lindsay; Sir Robert Livingstone; William Livingstone of Kilsyth; Sir Alexander Lauder; Sir George Lauder; Master of Lovat (Fraser); Lundie of Cushie (chief of clan MacFarlane); Sir Robert Lundy of Balgonie; Mackenzie of Kintail; Sir William McClellan; William Maitland; Sir Thomas Maule; William Melville of Rait; Sir John Moncrieffe, Pitcairn of Pitcairn; Sir Alexander Napier of Merchiston; David Pringle of Smailholm;* Sir Alexander Ramsay of Dalhousie; William Rollo of Duncrub; William, Master of Ruthven; Sir Alexander Scott of Hassendean; John Scrymgeour of Glassary;** Sir Alexander Seton; Sir William Sinclair; Alexander Skene of Skene; Sir John Somerville; Sir Alexander Stewart of Garlies; Sir John Stewart of Minto; Sir John Stuart; Spotiswood of Spotiswood; William Wallace of Craigie; Sir David Wemyss. Sir John Forman, Sir William Scott of Balwearie, Alexander Barrett, High Sheriff of Aberdeen; John Skirving of Plewlandhill*** and James Logan were the only men of rank taken prisoner.

*Smailholm Tower remains one of the most dramatic on the border whose gaunt spire inspired the youthful Scott.
**The Scrymgeours were the hereditary standard bearers of Scotland; an earlier laird had fallen at the Battle of Harlaw, the 'Reid' Harlaw a century before in 1411, bearing the royal colours.
***He who saved the Earl Marischal's gore spattered pennon.

## Knighted at Barmoor

Sir William Percy; Sir Edmund Howard; Sir George Darcy; Sir William Gascoigne the younger; Sir William Middleton; Sir William Mallory; Sir Thomas Bartley; Sir Marmaduke Constable the younger; Sir Christopher Dacre; Sir John Hotham; Sir Nicholas Appleyard; Sir Edward George; Sir Ralph Ellercar the younger; Sir John Willoughby; Sir Edward Etchingham; Sir Edward Musgrave; Sir John Stanley.

Source: *Trewe Encountre*

# APPENDIX THREE

# THE BATTLEFIELD TODAY

Apart from increased levels of cultivation and the effects of improved land drainage in the eighteenth and nineteenth centuries, the field remains remarkably unchanged. All of the principal features may clearly be identified. For the visitor, refer to OS Landranger Map 75 and OS Explore Map 339 which show the field [NT895371 (389596, 637112)], its immediate environs and elements of the English flank march. The present line of the B6352 runs westward from its junction with the A697 and skirts the base of Flodden Edge. The great strength of this first Scottish position is at once apparent. The rise completely dominates Millfield Plain below and the task facing any attacker would be an unenviable one, particularly with the great guns securely dug in and thus largely protected against counter battery fire.

At West Flodden, a right-hand turn leads past the flank of this position and continues over the saddle beyond that leads toward Branxton Edge. This, the lowest point, is traversed by a very minor road running east to west through Branxton-moor and Blinkbonny, a pretty farmhouse in restrained estate Gothic style. The road then breasts the lip of Branxton Edge and the field opens out before you. This apparently formidable Scottish second position lay astride the ridge. At this point you stand where those massed pikes of Errol, Crawford and Montrose division were deployed on 9 September 1513. For many, this was to be both their first and last battle. As a brisk wind plays over the brow of the hill, it is not at all difficult to envisage that great phalanx of serried staves, men shuffling nervous and uncertain. Skeins and eddies of smoke from burning rubbish, a rush of stinging, cold rain driven by an east wind, then a tentative sun, men turning to empty bladders, throats dry, odours of stale sweat, human waste, wet wool.

Captains, perspiring and purple, as they shouted commands then the crash of the guns, ear-splitting, terrifying, the loudest noise by far that most had ever heard. English round shot now finding its range; balls shearing limbs, splattering brains and intestines, punching over whole files like bloodied mannequins. Then those dreaded arrows; if magnates and gentry had improved protection, commoners for the most part did not. To the east would have stood the bulk of the king's great division with Bothwell in reserve (located to your right rear in the depression). Beneath the ridge, English brigades, spreading out beyond the rise of Piper's Hill, the admiral's men deploying just below the present monument, Edmund Howard's brigade lining up to the west facing Home and Huntly.

As one descends this modest hill, the line of that fatal burn is clearly visible. Now much tamed by ploughman and drain-layer, the nature of this obstacle is still apparent, a marked dip with an uphill struggle to the English line beyond. Westwards and the dip evens out, merges into the smoother contours that fronted Home and Huntly. Here topography creates a far more level descent and one can see how, on this wing, ground so favoured the Scots. At the base of the ridge, ground swells left toward the monument on Piper's Hill beyond that, Windy Law and a drop into the shallow valley of the Pallinsburn, again much drier now than then. Beyond, north and east, toward Twizel Bridge, stretches the line of the English approach march.

To follow the line of the English flank march, take the B6525 which branches eastwards from the main A697 at Wooler. Follow this road through Doddington with the links and Iron-Age settlements on high ground to your right. Barmoor Castle (much later and now a shell) is on the left, as is Watch Law as you pass over the crossroads just west of Lowick. Bear left at Bowsden toward Duddo, remains of the sixteenth-century tower, a lone defiant gable, make a good landmark. From Duddo, head due westward to the Till, the delightful bridge at Twizel and the Heaton Fords.

At Etal Castle where the shells of both gatehouse and keep survive, English Heritage has mounted a splendid series of tableaux depicting the events of the battle. Ford Castle also still stands though much modified and is not generally open to the public (*Plates 19–22*). 'The Queen of Border Fortresses', great Norham Castle remains, also in the care of English Heritage. The massive, square stone keep is formidable, if denuded, as is the circuit of the walls. Mons Meg, which predates the battle, remains impressively housed in Edinburgh Castle. Royal Armouries in Leeds contains an array of arms and armour from the period as does the Wallace Collection in London.

In terms of further reading, an essential start for any detailed study of the 1513 campaign is Norman Macdougall's excellent biography of James IV. Scarisbrick's seminal biography of Henry VIII does not offer us as many insights into 1513, Scotland for Henry was always very much a sideshow and this is inevitably reflected in any account of his life. For the military background, Gervase Phillips' definitive study of the Anglo-Scottish wars of the first half of the sixteenth century is comprehensive and insightful, meticulously researched and offering a most useful commentary upon developments in the art of war in Europe.

Students may always fall back upon Sir Charles Oman's classic account in *The Art of War in the Sixteenth Century*, now somewhat elderly but always extremely readable. His account of the battle and that of Colonel Burne, as ever with these writers, is both lucid and accessible. Burne, when the sources fail, was wont to fall back upon his theory of inherent military probability (IMP). This has been somewhat derided by recent writers but an old soldier's eyes have a value. Those who have actually fought wars are often better equipped than those who only write about them.

For the battle itself, some of the earlier works, Lieutenant Colonel Elliot's account of 1911 is well worth reading as is G.F.T. Leather's *New Light on Flodden* published in 1937. Perhaps the best modern account is that by Niall Barr (2001), closely followed by that of Peter Reese (2003). Shorter accounts include the co-author's own in the Osprey *Campaign* Series of 2006 and Charles Kightly's succinct but excellent work from 1975. For those who wish to pursue the local aspect and the involvement of the riding names could refer to Ralph Robson's *The Rise and Fall of the English Highland Clans* (1989) or to Macdonald Fraser or indeed John's earlier work, *Border Fury* (2004). An excellent and meticulously researched series of booklets written by John and Ann Ferguson, who have devoted years of patient and painstaking study to the field, are available locally and highly commended.

# APPENDIX FOUR

# THE GUNS SPEAK OUT

Part of the particular fascination of Flodden lies in the nature of that opening gun duel and the subsequent debate as to why the English fire proved so much superior. That armies of the day employed a whole range of artillery pieces is beyond doubt. An inventory compiled by Sir John Paston after the seizure of Caistor Castle, listing the defenders' ordnance specifies:

> Two guns with eight chambers shooting a stone seven inches thick, twenty inches compass. Two lesser guns with eight chambers shooting a stone five inches thick, fifteen inches compass. Three fowlers shooting a stone twelve inches in compass; two short guns for ships with six chambers. Two small serpentines to shoot lead pellets; four guns lying in stocks to shoot lead pellets; seven handguns with other equipment belonging to said guns.[1]

In the year before Flodden, on 11 April, was fought the great Battle of Ravenna where French guns inflicted a crushing defeat on their Spanish foes. Gaston de Foix, Duke of Nemours, deployed thirty of his own and two-dozen pieces supplied by an Italian ally. His frontal assault against a prepared position was preceded by two hour's constant barrage and featured the use of enfilade fire. The age of the field gun had fully arrived. Sixteenth-century writers, such as Grose, in *Military Antiquities* observes that the Scots were quicker in terms of developing their train and that Henry VIII did not begin casting his own guns till probably a decade or so after Flodden.[2]

The Lord Treasurer's list provides details of the Scottish guns taken in the wake of the disaster at Flodden. The heavier *courtaulds* or more tellingly named *murtherers* weighed in at 6,000lb (2,700kg) with a 6.5in (17cm) bore, throwing a 33.5–36lb (15–16kg) shot. A large cast culverin was of similar weight but longer barrelled and thus of smaller bore. The lighter *sakers* weighed some 2,850lb (1,300kg), throwing a 10lb (4.5kg) ball, cast bronze *culverin moyanes* were far lighter still, at some 1,500lb (680kg), of 2.5in (6cm) bore and throwing a 5lb (2kg) ball. A number of smaller *falcons* were recovered and these are described as breech loaders.[3]

It would seem likely that, whilst the handier pieces were mounted on wheeled carriages, bigger ordnance may still have been laid on fixed platforms. We know that two heavier guns were carried by cart from Threave to join the train and that cranage was employed to move the barrel from transport to firing platform.[4] Given the rapidity with which all were moved prior to action, it would nonetheless seem reasonable that all were then mounted on carriages. The heavier guns required teams of three-dozen oxen, medium sixteen oxen and a single horse, the lighter pieces eight oxen and a solitary horse. It seems most likely that these single horses were placed between the shafts of the carriage.[5]

In July 1513, a larger piece was transported from Glasgow, en route to service in Ireland. This necessitated six carts with thirty-six draught horses, accompanied by eight 'close' carts, each transporting a single barrel of powder and a further pair laden with gun-stones weighing 33.5lb (15kg). The train that accompanied James included thirteen transport wagons, each laden with four barrels of blackpowder and twenty-eight draught animals loaded with shot crammed into panniers or creels.[6] One Ottoman monster in the care of Royal Armouries in Leeds is a cast-bronze leviathan, manufactured in two halves then threaded together. Each section weights a full 8 tons (8,000kg) and the gun threw a stone ball weighing 670lb (304kg)! So effective was this massive ordnance it remained in service, guarding the Dardanelles for a full four centuries!

In recent years, Royal Armouries has experimented with Tudor guns of the post Flodden era, inspired by those found by the wreck of the *Mary Rose*. They aimed to construct a working replica of an older-style gun, constructed of wrought-iron staves and hoops. An expert blacksmith and team carried out this work which relied upon as many historic methods and tools as was practicable (evidence suggests Tudor smiths did use water-driven trip hammers). The staves, nine in all, were heated and carefully beaten into shape around a solid timber core and held in place by temporary clamps. A series of wrought-iron hoops and rings were then fashioned and hammer welded, laid on heated so as to contract to a snug fit. Placed alternatively the rings would take up the entire length of the barrel and were fitted with the staves and core in a vertical position.[7]

The finished barrel, with simple sighting ring foremost, was fitted and lashed to a timber-wheeled carriage and moved onto a range for test firing. Loading was from the breech and not muzzle, as was indeed commonplace. The wrought-iron 'beer-jug' breechblock was part filled with powder, topped with sawdust and straw, wadded and then sealed with a timber bung. The beauty of this arrangement was that several chambers could be kept loaded to permit rapid fire and loading at the breech was far safer.[8] Once the first projectile, lantern shot in this case, was loaded then the block was lifted into position (a substantial effort and four crewmen were required), the block was furnished with lifting rings and timber staves used to facilitate lifting. The first blast, effectively of grape, shredded a timber target and the death-dealing potential of lantern shot at close range was amply evidenced.

Next, solid shot. A stone ball from *Mary Rose* was fired. The weapon was aimed using the simple sight and elevated by means of a timber post and cross pin. To effect a tight seal at the breech the jug is buttressed with a timber forelock and then squeezed tight by an additional iron wedge. The ball easily punched through oak planking intended to match that of a man-o'-war.[9] A vast cloud of smoke accompanied each discharge and we can easily envisage how the field would very quickly become shrouded in a dense blanket.

We are offered a valuable contemporary glimpse into guns, gun making and the Scottish train in the campaign by the Accounts of the Lord High Treasurer. These record that, in the July, James had received a dozen cartloads of 'harnes(s)' from Denmark.[10] John Barton had brought the king a handgun as early as 1507[11] and James was clearly fascinated, echoing the example of his unfortunate grandfather. At the outset it appears that most of the experts employed were continental immigrants, such as the 'French gunner' who was paid a handsome £3 10s per month, rather more than his Scottish comrades though rather less than those Flemings also in the king's service.[12]

From 1508 onwards the Scots were casting guns at Stirling and, latterly, Edinburgh. One Alexander Bow, an Edinburgh potter, was placed in funds to the amount of £5 to buy metals for casting. Within a very short time, this sum had swollen to £65.[13] Whilst Stirling was the first manufacturing centre to get underway, Edinburgh swiftly became the more important. The king's obsession with firepower continued and we are told, in the accounts, of his setting up targets in the Abbey Close (doubtless to the great alarm of the Abbot). We also know that powder was being milled at the same time.[14] We can further deduce from subsequent entries that the king had sourced canvas, six ells [45in or 137.2cm] of the fabric, to fashion into suitable targets 'quhilk the king schot gunnies at'.[15] James also experimented by using guns for stalking 'ane deir'.[16] These handguns clearly proved a favourite for we have record of the king commissioning several more at prices varying from £4–10.

From 1511, the serious business of gun founding got underway in Edinburgh Castle. Continental specialists such as Hans, Henryk and Wolf Urneburg were training up a generation of Scottish students; Seton, Nicolson, Baillie and Ormiston. Specialist craftsmen from Europe; one Gervase, John Garnere, Stephen Davennois and M. Jacat seem mostly to have been recruited from James' ally France. Large sums were disbursed in buying in powder and shot – a mill was then established in Dundee where Urneburg was remunerated in the monthly amount of £4 4s,[17] a substantial emolument by the standards of his day.

It was the Scot, Robert Borthwick, appointed 'Master Meltar' (i.e. in charge of casting guns) who, in turn, engaged a team of highly skilled Dutch and French artisans.[18] By August 1512, the output from Borthwick's foundry had been sufficient to equip the Scottish fleet with first-rate ordnance (each piece required six carts for transport to the docks).[19] By spring of the next, fateful year he was employing ten master craftsmen and a quartet of smiths; these in turn would have their journeymen, apprentices and labourers attached. Carpenters were busy building wagons and carts and Barcar the smith was fitting sets of iron tyres to their wheels.[20]

It is from the Treasurer's Accounts that our main listing of the Scottish ordnance derives: five large cannon, two 'gros [large] culverins', four 'culver-ins-pikmoyane', six 'culverins moyanne'.[21] This arsenal must have included Borthwick's collective masterpiece, the Seven Sisters. Each of these monsters for the long, hot march south required a team of oxen which, for the smaller pieces required eight beasts, one trace horse and half a dozen pioneers. The really big guns needed up to thirty-six oxen and a platoon of pioneers, twenty-strong, presumably under an NCO or vintenar. The slow, plodding oxen averaged one driver for every four beasts. Eighty oxen were kept as a mobile reserve to make good losses and assist over the steeper gradients. The guns were secured by ropes front and rear to facilitate the uphill and control the downhill. Men were paid at the rate of 12d for service north of the border upped by fourpence once the line had been crossed.[22] It seems likely that the train moved the 48 miles to Coldstream via Soutra (where those additional beasts would surely be urgently needed!

The ordnance was dragged from the castle by sweat and muscle till the pieces could be harnessed and got underway. Borthwick commanded twenty-six gunners plus ancillaries, the former being paid 2s a day, a single crane for loading/unloading was carried by the train and twenty-eight pack horses, loaded with heavy panniers, carried the shot. A tail of carts would transport powder, mobile forges and blacksmithing gear, additional stock of pioneer tools. At least one ox was lost at Dalkeith, run over by the huge weight of the piece it was hauling, perhaps a case where the restraining process failed? It was not all bad news however, for a replacement was sourced at 32s and the men ate well that day![23]

We also know that charges were incurred for the sewing and transport of quantities of tentage, both leather and canvas, with a team of forty labourers to pitch and strike the gear. Banners too, the panoply of war were not forgot, even if left to the last moment. Two great flags one for St Margaret, the other St Andrew were designed and made, heavily fringed and using four ells of blue taffety, trailing three ells in length. James' own standard, slightly smaller, was in red; all came in leather cases.

Whilst we have no specific note from chroniclers of the employment of handguns we do have one tantalising reference from immediately after:

> That I, John Cragges, laid out at Barwyk [Berwick] for carriage of the king's ordnance from the field [Flodden] to the town, viz; carriage of 16 pieces of guns of brass and two cartloads of hagbushes [Hagbut] and pellets in 18 wains from the field to Barwyk town, 21s. Prests to 11 German gunners at Newcastle, 41s. Storing the pellets and hagbushes in a house and shipping the ordnance 23s 4d. Attending at Barwyk and homewards, 40 days, 26s 8d. Boat hire from Barwyk to the Islands, to go aboard a crayer that carried the ordnance, 5s.

A hagbut was a particular type of early hand-held firearm, barrel hooked to project over fixed defences. This account would clearly suggest such weapons had been present in the Scots' arsenal, thought it cannot confirm the weapons were necessarily used on the field.[25]

## NOTES

1. Quoted in Boardman, p. 152.
2. Rogers, Colonel H.C.B., *Artillery through the Ages* (London, 1971), p. 28.
3. *Ibid.*, p. 29.
4. *Ibid.*, p. 30.
5. *Ibid.*
6. *Ibid.*
7. Hall, N., *Building and firing a Mary Rose port piece* (Royal Armouries Year Book, no. 3, 1998), pp. 57–66 and Hall, N., *Casting and firing a Mary Rose culverin* (Royal Armouries Year Book, no. 6, 2001), pp. 106–16.
8. *Ibid.*
9. *Ibid.*
10. Balfour, Sir J., *Accounts of the Lord High Treasurer of Scotland, vol. IV: 1507–13* (Edinburgh, 1902), preface, p. XXXVII.
11. *Ibid.*, p. LXIII.
12. *Ibid.*, p. LXIV.
13. *Ibid.*, p. LXV.
14. *Ibid.*, p. LXVIII.
15. *Ibid.*, p. LXX.
16. *Ibid.*
17. *Ibid.*, pp. LXXII–LXXIII.
18. *Ibid.*, p. LXXIII.
19. *Ibid.*, p. LXXIV.
20. *Ibid.*, p. LXXV.
21. *Ibid.*, p. LXXVI.
22. *Ibid.*, p. LXXVI.
23. *Ibid.*, p. LXXIX.
24. *Ibid.*, p. LXXXII.
25. Henry VIII; February 1514, *Letters and Papers, Foreign & Domestic, Henry VIII, vol. I: 1509–14* (1920), pp. 1153–63.

# GLOSSARY

'Almain' – a Central European mercenary – *Landsknecht*

'Almain rivet' – mass-produced harness, munition quality

'Backsword' – a form of weapon with one sharpened cutting edge and the other flattened and blunt, primarily a horseman's weapon designed for the cut

'Base' – small gun, throwing a ½lb ball

'Bastion' – projection from the curtain wall of a fort usually at intersections to provide a wider firing platform and to allow defenders to enfilade (flanking fire) a section of the curtain

'Bastle' – often confused with 'pele', a form of defensive dwelling, a squat stone blockhouse with thick walls, pitched stone-flagged roof and, typically barrel-vaulted basement, access to first floor by ladder only

'Batter' – outward slope at the base of a masonry wall to add strength and frustrate mining efforts

'Battery' – a section of guns, may be mobile field artillery or a fixed defensive position within a defensive circuit

'Battle' – a division on the field, armies comprised left or vaward, centre or main and rear or right-handed units, deployed in a linear formation

'Battlements' – the merlons and crenellations atop the parapet walk of a castle or fort, often reinforced by timber additions in time of war, castle builders required a 'licence to crenellate' before erecting castles

'Bill' – formidable military variant of a peasant's agricultural tool, combining axe blade with sharpened point

'Blinde(s)' – a bundle of brushwood or planks used to afford cover to trenches

'Border Horse' – irregular troops of lightly armed marcher cavalry, latterly the 'Steel Bonnets', the hobilars of the fourteenth and fifteen century

'Breast and back' – body armour comprising a front and rear plate section

'Breastwork' – defensive wall

'Brigandine' – lightweight padded body armour, similar to the 'jack' but reinforced by an inner layer of small metal plates

'Broadsword' – a double- edged blade intended for cut or thrust, becoming old-fashioned though many would do service, often with an enclosed or basket hilt

'Buckler' – small round shield used for parrying and blows

'Cannon' – heavy gun throwing a 47lb (21kg) ball; a demi-cannon fired 27lb (12kg) ball; cannon-royal shot a massive 63lb (29kg) ball

'Centenar' – company commander of a unit of foot 100 strong, essentially a senior NCO

'Chevaux-de-frise' – a large baulk of timber set with sharpened blades to form an improvised defence, often employed to seal or attempt to seal a breach in the defender's walls

'Claymore' or *cleadamh mor* 'great sword' – a Highland bastard sword with distinctive down-swept quillons finished with lobed rings

'Commission of Array' – this was the ancient royal summons issued through the lords lieutenants of the counties to raise militia forces, in the context of a civil war such an expedient was of dubious legality as clearly unsanctioned by Parliament

'Corselet' – this refers to a pikeman's typical harness of breast and back, with tassets for the thighs

'Culverin' – a gun throwing a 15lb (7kg) ball; mainly used in siege operations the guns weighed an average of 4,000lb (1,800kg). The lighter demi-culverin threw a 9lb (4kg) ball and weighed some 3,600lb (1,600kg)

'Curtain' – the section of fortress wall linking two towers

'Defilade' – where one party, probably a defender uses any natural or man-made obstacle to shield or conceal their position; see also 'enfilade' below

*Doppelnsolder* – swordsman deployed to guard the flanks of the pike phalanx

'Drake' or 'Saker' – gun firing a 5¼lb (2.5kg) ball

'Embrasure' – the more open and splayed form of battlements used to facilitate siting of guns

'Enceinte' – the circuit or whole of the defensive works

'Enfilade' – where one party is in a position to direct fire onto the longest exposed axis of the other's position, e.g. an attacker is able to shoot along a defender's trench from the flank

'Ensign' (or 'Ancient') – a junior commissioned officer of infantry who bears the flag from which the name derives

'Falcon' – light gun firing a 2¼lb (1kg) ball

'Falconet' – light gun throwing a 1¼lb (0.5kg) shot

'Field-works' – a system of improvised temporary defensive works employed by an army on the march or protecting an encampment

'Fleche' – a projecting V-shaped defensive outwork

'Foot' – infantry

'Foot-band' – a reinforced company of English infantry, usually the affinity of a knight or captain

'Foray' – essentially a raid intended to lift livestock and glean intelligence, fore-runner of the modern fighting patrol

'Gabion' – wicker baskets filled with earth, which formed handy building blocks for temporary works or sealing off a breach

'Glacis' – a sloped earthwork out from the covered way to provide for grazing fire from the curtain

'Guns' – artillery

'Halberd' – a polearm, outdated in war but carried as a staff of rank by NCOs

'Harness' – plate armour

'Herce' or deployment en herce (harrow) – positioning of the archers by English captains on the field, either in commanded bodies in the line or on the flanks, still employed in the early sixteenth century

'Kern' – a lightly armed Irish foot soldier, likely to be employed as a mercenary. The Scottish or Highland equivalent was the 'cateran'

'Lance' – this refers not just to the horseman's staff weapon but to a tactical unit, the immediate affinity and retinue of a knight, variable in size

'Matross' – a gunner's mate, doubled as a form of ad-hoc infantry to protect the guns whilst on the march

'Meutriere' – or 'murder-hole', space between the curtain and corbelled out battlements enabling defender to drop a variety of unpleasant things onto attackers at the base of the wall

'Minion' – gun shooting a 4lb (2kg) ball

'Munition armour' – mass-produced foot armour of questionable quality

'Ordnance' – artillery

'Pike' – a polearm with a shaft likely to be 12–18ft ª3.5–5m) in length, finished with a diamond-shaped head

'Pioneers' – labourers used as navvies to help level roads for the guns or to dig fortifications, less skilled than sappers or engineers

'Postern' ('Sally Port') – a small gateway set into the curtain allowing re-supply and deployment of defenders in localised attacks on besiegers

'Prickers' – light cavalry vedettes and scouts

'Rapier' – a slender, long bladed thrusting weapon, more likely to be owned by gentry; bespoke and more costly than a trooper's backsword, often used in conjunction with a left-handed or *main gauche* dagger

'Shot' – musketeers

'Redoubt' – a detached, square, polygonal or hexagonal earthwork or blockhouse

'Reiver' – similar to Border Horse as the riders frequently combined both functions, a breed of men to whom cattle raiding and the deadly feud were a way of life, as much a menace to their own side as the enemy

'Robinet' – light field gun firing a 1¼lb (0.5kg) shot

'Scarp' – inner wall of ditch or moat

'Sconce' – a small detached fort with projecting corner bastions

'Serpentine' – field gun throwing a 7lb (3kg) ball

'Small-Beer' – weak, watery ale drunk instead of water, the latter often being unsafe

'Snap' – cold rations carried in a 'snap-sack'

'Targe' – a laminated timber, leather-covered buckler used with a single-handed broadsword, associated with Scottish Highlanders but widely used on the borders

'Tasset' – a section of plate armour hinged from the breastplate intended to afford protection to the upper thigh

'Touch hole' – the small diameter hole drilled through the top section of a gun barrel through which the linstock ignites the charge, fine powder was poured in a quill inserted into the touch hole

'Train' – a column of guns on the move, the army marches accompanied or followed by the train

'Victualler' – responsible for logistics and supply of foodstuffs and small beer in the field

'Vintner' – NCO in charge of a small platoon of twenty (*vingt*) footmen

'Wappinschaw' – a regular muster of Scottish fighters which provided for the weapons and gear provided by each

# BIBLIOGRAPHY

## Primary Sources

Ascham, R., *Toxophilus* (London, 1902)

Balfour Paul, Sir James (ed.), *Accounts of the Treasurer of Scotland 1473–1580* (Edinburgh, 1901)

Bethan, Rev. William Bethan, *The Baronetage of England, or the History of the English Baronets, and such Baronets of Scotland, as are of English families: with genealogical tables, and engravings of their armorial bearings, Volume 4* (Miller, 1804)

Baird, I. (ed.), *Scotish Feilde and Flodden Feilde; Two Flodden Poems* (London, 1982)

Bergenroth, G.A. (ed.), *Calendar of Letters, Despatches and State Papers relating to the negotiations between England and Spain* (London, 1862)

Bower, Walter, *Scoticronicon* (ed. and transl. by D.E.R. Watt) (Aberdeen, 1991)

Brewer, J.S. (ed.), *Letters and Papers, Foreign and Domestic, Henry VIII, vol. 1: 1509–1514* (1920). Accessed at www.british-history.ac.uk/source.aspx?pubid=1120

Brewer, J.S. (ed.), *Letters and Papers, Foreign and Domestic, Henry VIII, vol. 3: 1519–23*. Accessed at www.british-history.ac.uk

Brie, F.W.D., *The Brut or Chronicles of England* (London, 1906)

*Calendar of State Papers and Manuscripts existing in the Archives and Collections of Milan* (ed. and transl. A.B. Hinds, 1912)

*Catalogue of the Cotton Manuscripts* www.hrionline.ac.uk/cotton/cotframe.htm

Dyboski, R. and Arend, Z.M. (eds), *Knyghthode and Bataille* (Early English Texts Society, 1935)

Federer, Charles A. (ed.), *The Battle of flodden-field.: Which was fought between the English under the Earl of Surrey (in the absence of King Henry VIII) and the Scots under their valiant King James IV who was slain on the field of battle, in the year, 1513: An heroic poem, in nine fits or parts, collected from antient manuscripts* (Joseph Benson, Philomath, London 1644; reprinted as 'The Ballad of Flodden Field, a Poem of the XVIth Century' (Henry Grey, Manchester, 1884)). Accessed at www.archive.org/stream/balladoffloddenfoofede#page/n1/mode/2up

*Guides to Scottish state papers* www.nas.gov.uk/guides/statePapers.asp

Hall, Edward, *The Triumphante Reign of Kyng Henry VIII*, vol. 1 (London, 1904)

Hall, N., 'Building and firing a Mary Rose port piece', *Royal Armouries Year Book*, no. 3 (1998), pp. 57–66

——, 'Casting and firing a Mary Rose culverin', *Royal Armouries Year Book*, no. 6 (2001), pp. 106–16

Hannay, R.K. (ed.), *The Letters of James IV, 1505–1513* (Scottish Hist. Society, 1953)

James, H. (ed.), 'Account of the Battle of Flodden Articules of the bataille bitwix the Kynge of Scottes and therle of Surrey in Brankstone felde the 9 day of Septembre', in *Facsimiles of National Manuscripts from William the Conqueror to Queen Anne* (Southampton, 1865)

Laing, D. (ed.), 'A Contemporary Account of the Battle of Flodden 9 September 1513: Hereafter ensue the Trewe Encountre or Batayle lately don between Englande and Scotlande: In Whiche Batayle the Scottsshe Kygne was slayne', *Proceedings of the Society of Antiquaries of Scotland*, vol. 7 (March, 1867)

Laing, D. (ed.), *The Poetical Works of Sir David Lindsay of the Mount* (Edinburgh, 1879)

Lindesay of Pitscottie (ed. A.J.G. Mackay), *The Historie and Chronicles of Scotland* (Edinburgh, 1899)

Mancini, Dominic, Armstrong, C.A.J. (eds), *The Usurpation of Richard III* (Oxford, 1969)

Morgan, Hiram, *Scotland in Renaissance Diplomacy, 1473–1603* (University College Cork, March 2008)

Pinkerton, 'History of Scotland', *Gazette of the Battle of Flodden* (Heralds' College, London), M.S., vol. II, p. 456

Polydore, Vergil (ed. and trans. by D. Hay), *The Anglica Historia AD 1485–1537* (Royal Historical Society, 1950), Camden Series, vol. 74

Skelton, J., *A Ballade of the Scottyshe Kinge* (London, 1882)

Talhoffer, Hans (ed. and trans. M. Rector), *Manual of Swordfighting* (facsimile edn, 2000)

White, J.T., *The Death of a King being Extracts from Contemporary Accounts of the Battle of Branxton Moor September 1513* (Edinburgh, 1970)

Wood, Marguerite (ed.), *Flodden Papers; Diplomatic Correspondence between the courts of France and Scotland 1507–1517* (Edinburgh, 1933)

Younger, P.L., *Crouching enemy, hidden ally; the decisive role of groundwater features in two major British battles, Flodden 1513 and Prestonpans 1745* (Newcastle Institute for Research on Sustainability; unpublished research paper)

# Secondary Sources

Archibald, E.H.H., *The Wooden Fighting Ship* (London, 1968)

Arthurson, I., *The Perkin Warbeck Conspiracy 1491–1499* (England, 1977)

Bain, J., *Calendar of Documents Relating to Scotland*, 4 vols (Edinburgh, 1881–88)

Barbour, R., *The Knight and Chivalry* (London, 1974)

Barr, N., *Flodden* (Gloucestershire, 2001)

Bartlett, C., *English Longbowman 1330–1515* (Osprey, 1995)

Bates, C.J., *History of Northumberland* (London 1895)

Bingham, C., *The Stewart Kings of Scotland 1371–1603* (London, 1974)

Blackmore, H.L., *The Armouries of the Tower of London I Ordnance* (London, 1976)

Blair, C., *European Armour* (London, 1958)

Boardman, A.V., *The Battle of Towton* (England, 1994)

———, *The Medieval Soldier in the Wars of the Roses* (London, 1998)

Brantôme, Pierre de Bourdeille, 'Dames Illustres', in *A Twice Crowned Queen, Anne of Britany* (Constance, Countess de la Warr, Eveleigh Nash, 1906), p. 41. Accessed at www.archive.org/details/twicecrownedqueeoodelauoft

Brenan, G., *The House of Percy*, 2 vols (England, 1898)

Brander, M., *Scottish Border Battles and Ballads* (London, 1975)

Burne, Col. A.H., *The Battlefields of England* (London, 1950)

———, *More Battlefields of England* (London, 1952)

Byrd, Elizabeth, *Flowers of the Forest* (MacMillan, 1969)

Caldwell, D.H., *The Scottish Armoury* (Edinburgh, 1976)

———, *Scottish Weapons and Fortifications 1100–1800* (Edinburgh, 1981)

Chambers, R. (ed.), *A Biographical Dictionary of Eminent Scotsmen in Four Volumes, vol. III: 1835* (Revised by T. Thomson, Blackie & Son, 1855). Accessed at www.archive.org/stream/biographicaldicto4chamiala#page/n7/mode/2up

Chatton, W.A., *Rambles in Northumberland and on the Scottish border; interspersed with brief notices of interesting events in border history* (Chapman and Hall, 1835), pp. 234–36. Accessed at http://books.google.co.uk/books?id=PO4-AAAAYAAJ&dq=lady+Elizabeth+heron+of+ford+norham&source=gbs_navlinks_s

Chrimes, S.B., *Henry VII* (London, 1952)

Coldstream and District Local History Society, *Second to None: A History of Coldstream* (Coldstream and District Local History Society, 2010)

Cook, Bernard A. (ed.), *Women and war: a historical encyclopedia from antiquity to the present* (Santa Barbara, ABC-CLIO, 2006)

Coward, B., *The Stanleys, Lord Stanley and Earls of Derby 1385–1672* (England 1983)

Craig-Brown, T., *The Flodden Traditions of Selkirk* (Edinburgh, 1913)

Cruickshank, C., *Henry VIII and the Invasion of France* (Stroud, 1994)

Cummins, M., *Shadow Over Flodden* (London, 1988)

Davies, C.S.L. and Edwards, John, *Katherine of Aragon*, Oxford Dictionary of National Biography (Oxford University Press, 2004–11). Accessed at www.oxforddnb.com/view/article/4891?docPos=1

Dodds, J.F., *Bastles and Belligerents* (Newcastle, 2001)

Ducklin, K. & Waller, J., *Sword Fighting* (London, 2001)

Durham, K., *The Border Reivers* (Osprey, 1995)

Elliot-Fitzwilliam, A., *The Battle of Flodden and the Scottish Raids of 1513* (Edinburgh, 1911)

Ellis, Henry, *Original Letters Illustrative of English History; Including Numerous Royal Letters: From Autographs in the British Museum and One or Two Other Collections,* 1st ser., I (2nd edn, Harding, Triphook and Lepard, 1825), p. 88. Accessed at www.archive.org/stream/originallettersi01elliuoft#page/n7/mode/2up

Featherstone, D., *Armies and Warfare in the Pike and Shot Era 1422–1700* (England, 1998)

Ferguson, J.A., *The Campaign in Northern England 1523 by Thomas Howard, 2nd Earl of Surrey* (Cold Harbour Press, 2011)

*The Battle of Flodden 1513 & Thomas Howard 1st Earl of Surrey*

*The Flodden Helm and Events Linked to the Death of Thomas Howard in 1524*

*The Encampment of the English Army at Barmoor, 8th September 1513 before the Battle of Flodden*

*Lords to Labourers – the Named English Participants in the 1513 Flodden Campaign*

Fidler, K., *Flodden Field September 9th 1513* (London, 1971)

Fiorato, V., Boylston, A. & Knussel C. (eds), *Blood and Roses: The Archaeology of a Mass Grave from the Battle of Towton AD 1461* (Oxford, 2000)

Fraser, G.M., *The Steel Bonnets* (London, 1971)

Gairdner, J., *Henry VIII* (London, 1889)

Glen Eaves, Richard, *Margaret Tudor*, Oxford Dictionary of National Biography (Oxford University Press, 2004–11). Accessed at www.oxforddnb.com/view/article/18052?docPos=2

Grant, A., 'Richard III in Scotland', in Pollard (ed.), *The North of England in the Reign of Richard III* (England, 1996)

Griffiths, R.A. (ed.), 'Patronage', in *The Crown and the Provinces in Later Medieval England* (England, 1981)

*King and Country: England and Wales in the Fifteenth Century* (England, 1991)

*The Making of the Tudor Dynasty* (England, 1985)

*Kings and Nobles in the Later Middle Ages* (England, 1986)

Fraser, Antonia, *The Six Wives of Henry VIII* (Phoenix, 2002)

Grossman, Lt. Col. G., *On Killing* (New York, 2009)

Gush, G., *Renaissance Armies 1480–1650* (Cambridge, 1979)

Hammer Anderson, C., Lars, C., Orbesen Troest, M. & Stig Nielsen, M., supervised by Robert Thomsen, *The Development of Scottish Nationalism* (Aalborg University, Denmark, 1997). Accessed at http://earth.subetha. dk/~eek/museum/auc/marvin/www/library/uni/projects/scotsnat.htm

Hardy, R., *Longbow* (London, 1976)

Hepple, L.W., *A History of Northumberland and Newcastle-upon-Tyne* (London, 1976)

Jones, R., *The Battle of Flodden Field Fought September 9th 1513* (Edinburgh, 1864)

Keegan, J., *The Face of Battle* (London, 1976)

Keen, M., *English Society in the Later Middle Ages 1348–1500* (England, 1990)

———— (ed.), *Medieval Warfare – a History* (Oxford, 1999)

Kightly, C., *Flodden: The Anglo-Scottish War of 1513* (London, 1975)

Lawson, John Parker, *Historical Tales of the Wars of Scotland And of the Border Raids, Forays and Conflicts* (1839), accessed at www.electricscotland.com/ history/wars

Leather, G.F.T., *New Light on Flodden* (Edinburgh, 1937)

Lomas, R., *Northumberland – County of Conflict* (East Lothian, 1996)

————, *North-East England in the Middle Ages* (Edinburgh, 1992)

Long, B., *The Castles of Northumberland* (Newcastle-upon-Tyne, 1967)

Lynch, M., *A New History of Scotland* (London, 1991)

Macdougall, N., *James III: A Political Study* (Edinburgh, 1982)

————, *James IV* (East Linton, 1997)

Mackie, J.D., *History of Scotland* (London, 1991)

————, 'The English Army at Flodden', in *Miscellany of the Scottish Historical Society*, vol. VIII (Edinburgh, 1951)

Mackie, R.L., *King James IV of Scotland* (Edinburgh, 1958)

Mackenzie, W.M., *The Secret of Flodden* (Edinburgh, 1931)

McNeil, E., *Flodden Field: A Novel* (Severn House Publishers Ltd, 2007)

Miller, D., *The Landsknechts* (London, 1976)

————, *The Swiss at War 1300–1500* (Osprey, 1979)

Nairn, Tom, *The Break Up of Britain* (London, NLB, 1977)

National Library of Scotland, *The Word on the Street: How Ordinary Scots in Bygone Days found out what was Happening* Broadsides in the collection of the National Library of Scotland, accessed at http://digital.nls.uk/broadsides/index.html

Neillands, R., *The Wars of the Roses* (London, 1992)

Nicolle, D., *Medieval Warfare Source Book* (London, 1999)

Nicholson, Harry, *Tom Fleck* (YouWriteon.com, 2011)

Nicholson, R., *Scotland, the later Middle Ages* (Edinburgh, 1989)

Norman, A.V.B. and D. Pottinger, *English Weapons and Warfare 449–1660* (London, 1966)

*Northumberland County History*

Oakeshott, R.E., *A Knight and his Weapons* (London, 1964)

Oman, Sir C., *A History of the Art of War in the Sixteenth Century* (London, 1937)

*Our Scotland* – Scottish Politics Discussion Forum: http://ourscotland. myfreeforum.org/archive/king-james-iv-personal-effects-help-requested __o_t__t_361.html

Paterson, R.C., *My Wound is Deep: A History of the Later Anglo-Scottish Wars 1380–1560* (Edinburgh, 1997)

Phillips, G., *The Anglo-Scottish Wars 1513–50* (Woodbridge, 1999)

Perry, Maria, *Sisters to the King* (Andre Deutsch, 2002)

Pevsner, N. & I. Richmond, 'Northumberland', in *The Buildings of England* Series (London, 1992)

Pollard, A.J., 'Percies, Nevilles and the Wars of the Roses', in *History Today* (September, 1992)

——, 'Characteristics of the Fifteenth Century North', in Appleby, C. and Dalton, P. (eds), *Government, Religion and Society in Northern England 1000–1700* (England, 1977)

——, *North-eastern England during the Wars of the Roses: War, Politics and Lay Society, 1450–1500* (Oxford, 1990)

Pollard, A.F., *Henry VIII* (London, 1905)

Prestwich, M., *Armies and Warfare in the Middle Ages* (London, 1996)

Reese, P., *Flodden: A Scottish Tragedy* (Edinburgh, 2003)

Ridpath, G., *The Border History of England and Scotland* (Berwick-upon-Tweed, 1776)

Rogers, H.C.B., *Artillery through the Ages* (London, 1971)

Rose, A., *Kings in the North* (London, 2002)

Sadler, D.J., *Battle for Northumbria* (Newcastle, 1988)

*Border Fury: England and Scotland at War 1296–1568* (London, 2004)

*Scottish Battles* (Edinburgh, 1996)

Saunders, A., *Norham Castle* (London, 1998)

Scarisbrick, J.J., *Henry VIII* (London, 1970)

Seymour, W., *Battles in Britain*, vol. 1 (London, 1975)

Smout, T.C., 'Perspectives on the Scottish Identity', in *Scottish Affairs*, no. 6, winter 1994 (The Institute of Governance, University of Edinburgh). Accessed at www.scottishaffairs.org/backiss/1994.html

Smurthwaite, D., *The Ordnance Survey Guide to the Battlefields of Britain* (London, 1984)

Stone, J.M., *Studies from Court and Cloister: being essays, historical and literary dealing mainly with subjects relating to the XVIth and XVIIth centuries* (1905). Project

Gutenberg, accessed at http://infomotions.com/etexts/gutenberg/dirs/
etext03/stdsf10.htm

Summerson, H., 'Carlisle and the English West March in the Late Middle
Ages' in *The North of England in the Reign of Richard III* (England, 1996)

Thrupp, S.L., *The problem of replacement Rates in Late Medieval English Population*
(ECHR 2nd Series, 1965–66)

Tomlinson, W.W., *A Comprehensive Guide to Northumberland* (Newcastle-
upon-Tyne, 1863)

Tough, D.L.W., *The Last Years of a Frontier* (Oxford, 1928)

Trevelyan, G.M., *A History of England* (London, 1926)

Tuck, A., *Crown and Nobility, 1272–1462* (England, 1985)

Tytler, Patrick Fraser, *The History of Scotland* (William Tait, 1834). Accessed at
www.archive.org/stream/historyscotland18tytlgoog#page/n115/mode/2up

Wagner, P. and S. Hand, *Medieval Sword and Shield* (California, 2003)

Warner, P., *Sieges of the Middle Ages* (London, 1968)

Warr, Constance, Countess de la Warr, *A Twice Crowned Queen, Anne of
Britanny* (Eveleigh Nash, 1906). Accessed at www.archive.org/details/
twicecrownedquee00delauoft

Watson, G., *The Border Reivers* (Newcastle-upon-Tyne, 1974)

Weiss, H., 'A Power in the North? The Percies in the Fifteenth Century', in
*The Historical Journal* (1965)

Wise, T., *Medieval Heraldry* (England, 1980)

———, *The Wars of the Roses* (London, 1983)

Woodard, CPT John, Taylor, CPT, Devereaux, CPT Danny King, CPT Kerry,
'Medieval Logistics As Applied to the Classes of Quartermaster Supply',
*Quartermaster Professional Bulletin* (winter 2000). Accessed at www.au.af.
mil/au/awc/awcgate/army/medieval_logistics.htm

Woolgar, C.M., *The Great Household in late Medieval England* (London, 1999)

Young, P., and Adair, J., *Hastings to Culloden* (London, 1964)

YouTube – Isla St Clair, Flowers of the Forest, www.youtube.com/
watch?v=hqY79y-SCbA

# INDEX

Visit our website and discover thousands of other History Press books.

**www.thehistorypress.co.uk**